COP 99/00
John Smith
£12·37

Copy ②

18567
ADAMS
658·1511

D0530991

Management Accounting for the Hospitality Industry

LIBRA
PERTH CO.

Books are

Also published by Cassell:

F. Buttle, *Hotel and Food Service Marketing: A Managerial Approach*

J. Heap, *Productivity Management: A Fresh Approach*

N. Johns (editor) *Productivity Management in Hospitality and Tourism*

P. Jones (editor) *Introduction to Hospitality Organizations*

P. Jones with P. Merricks, *Management of Foodservice Operations*

R. Lucas, *Managing Employee Relations in the Hotel and Catering Industry*

R. Teare (editor) with D. Adams and S. Messenger, *Managing Projects in Hospitality Organizations*

R. Teare and A. Boer (editors) *Strategic Hospitality Management*

R. Teare, S. Calver, J.A. Mazanec, S. Crawford-Welch, *Marketing in Hospitality and Tourism: A Consumer Focus*

R. Teare (editor) with L. Moutinho and Neil Morgan, *Managing and Marketing Services in the 1990s*

MANAGEMENT ACCOUNTING FOR THE HOSPITALITY INDUSTRY

A Strategic Approach

DEBRA ADAMS

CASSELL

LONDON AND WASHINGTON

Cassell
Wellington House
125 Strand
London WC2R 0BB

PO Box 605
Herndon
VA 20172

© Debra Adams 1997

All rights reserved. No part of this publication may be reproduced or transmitted in any form or by any means, electronic or mechanical including photocopying, recording or any information storage or retrieval system, without prior permission in writing from the publishers.

First published 1997

British Library Cataloguing-in-Publication Data
A catalogue record for this book is available from the British Library.

ISBN 0–304–32908–8 (hb)
    0–304–32906–1 (pb)

Typeset by York House Typographic Ltd, London

Printed and bound in Great Britain by Redwood Books, Trowbridge, Wiltshire

Contents

Preface

In today's world the business organization is operating in an environment which is in a continual state of change due to increasing advances in technology, fluctuating economic climates and changing manpower and customer expectations. In order to steer any business through these conditions successfully the modern manager needs to possess the skills to enable him or her to make effective use of powerful appraisal and control techniques.

This text book has been written with the purpose of providing the hospitality manager with a practical understanding of the key financial aspects of business in order to improve the level of effective decision-making in the strategic management process. The emphasis is on *how* financial management theories and techniques can be utilized in practice to support the decision-making process with examples drawn from the hospitality industry.

The process of strategic management is normally regarded as an integrated approach to the processes of planning, implementing and controlling business strategy in order to maximize the potential of the organization to meet its objectives. The first step in the process is to define clearly the long-term goals and objectives of the organization. Once this has been achieved there follows a comprehensive analysis of the environment in which the business operates to establish both where the business is at the moment and where it is likely to be operating in the future. This external analysis includes a review of competitors, suppliers, customers, the economy, governmental changes, as well as legal and other regulatory changes. This should be combined with a rigorous internal analysis of all resources and internal operations. Consequently, having established *'where the organization is'* and *'where it wants to go'* it is now possible to develop a practical business strategy.

If the accounting process is to support strategic management, then procedures must adapt and change to meet the needs of an evolving environment. Traditionally, the role of management accounting has been heavily biased towards the comparison of costs with revenues, focusing on the internal operations of the business. Accounts are, by definition, historical and inward-looking, and the process of accounting is governed by the underlying concept of prudence. However, there is a need in most organizations for accounting information to be produced with a strategic perspective in mind. This involves considering not just the internal operations but also the external environment and the role of the competition.

If used effectively, the process of strategic management accounting can provide the financial information required to monitor existing business strategies and provide support for the process of strategy formulation. Consequently, this book has been written to follow the chronology of the strategic decision-making process with the aim of placing management accounting in the context of strategic management to enable managers to use accounting information to support them in the decision-making process within the hospitality industry.

The chapters in Part 1 start with a review of the basic principles and practices. They include an introduction to the strategic management process and an overview of rudimentary accounting practices and techniques. These chapters are intended for those who have limited knowledge of financial accounting. The chapters within Parts 2 and 3 are designed to provide guidance on the processes of external and internal audit. The aim of Part 2 is to address the role of financial information in a strategic review of the environment. It examines the role of competitor accounting, strategic cost analysis and pricing. Part 3 covers the strategic process of internal appraisal, focusing on budgetary control, working capital control and performance measurement. Part 4 focuses on the determination of corporate strategy, providing chapters on financing, investment appraisal, risk assessment and cost of capital measurement. Part 5 concludes by considering the future of the hospitality industry and the impact, in particular, of globalization and information technology.

Generally, the approach adopted throughout the text is to demonstrate the financial technique under discussion with appropriate examples drawn from the hospitality industry. Some financial techniques have been given greater prominence than might normally be expected due to their particular relevance to the hospitality industry. Chapter 13, on business valuations, is such an example. Where possible the financial theories have been illustrated with real-life experiences based on published research drawn from the hospitality industry. Every effort has been made to quote the sources of copyright material and seek their permission to reproduce tables and diagrams concerned.

Finally, the book is intended for final-year undergraduate programmes and postgraduate courses in hospitality management and related disciplines.

To aid tutors and lecturers a free, looseleaf lecturers' guide has been prepared. It provides review exercises, discussion questions and sample assignments to accompany each chapter and is available from the Business Marketing Department, Cassell, Wellington House, 125 Strand, London WC2R 0BB.

Debra J. Adams
April 1997

PART 1
STRATEGIC PLANNING

INTRODUCTION

The aim of this first section is to provide an introduction to both the process of strategic management and to the basic elements of financial accounting in order to provide the reader with a basic level of understanding in these areas before embarking on the application of management accounting to the strategic management process. Chapter 1 reviews a variety of definitions of strategy and relates these to organizational structures and levels of decision-making by describing some of the processes and procedures involved. All organizations regardless of size, need to make decisions about the activities in which they wish to engage, the objectives they seek to achieve and the route that they intend to follow. These stages are introduced and discussed, providing the reader with a model to summarize the total process. The chapter concludes with a review of some of the key strategic issues facing the hospitality industry and specific issues relating to hospitality financial management.

Chapter 2 develops the link between effective decision-making processes and the role of the finance function as a provider of relevant and timely information. At this stage the changing needs of the business are emphasized using models to illustrate the life pattern of a business.

A review of the essential concepts in understanding the preparation of the key financial statements is contained in Chapter 3. The chapter reviews accounting practice and the preparation of the profit and loss account, balance sheet and cashflow statements in order to familiarize the reader with the presentation of financial information.

1

Fundamentals of strategic management

INTRODUCTION

For the modern hospitality business faced with the challenge of operating in increasingly diverse markets it is essential that the processes of strategic management are as effective as possible. All organizations need to make decisions about the nature of their business activities to ensure that the resources are put to the best possible uses while ensuring that customer needs remain satisfied. Strategic management, as defined by Ward (1992), is held to be 'the integrated management approach to combining the individual processes required for planning, implementing and controlling a business strategy'. It is important for every organization to review its activities continually in order to bridge the gap between where it is now and where it would like to be. This 'ideal position' is unique to each organization and is dependent on the long-term organizational goals and objectives which have been set over a period, during which the external environment will continue to change. As a result, achieving the end product of a chosen strategy cannot be guaranteed. Instead, the organization continually needs to monitor, control and adapt the business strategy, and this process is reliant on the provision of accurate and relevant accounting-based information. This chapter includes a discussion of the following key areas:

- The decision-making process
- Definition of strategy
- Organizational structures
- Organizational objectives
- Information needs
- Current strategic issues for the hospitality industry
- Critical success factors for the hospitality industry
- Key financial issues for the hospitality industry.

THE DECISION-MAKING PROCESS

Gore *et al.* (1992) describe the decision-making process as being concerned with the whole range of activities involved in arriving at a final decision. This includes everything from the initial recognition of a need for a decision through to the evaluation of the end result arising from having taken a decision. Having reviewed the work of numerous writers in the field of decision-making, Gore *et al.* propose a step-by-step guide to the decision-making process which is illustrated in Figure 1.1. Few writers include all the stages shown in this diagram but Gore *et al.* argue that each step is important in the overall process.

The process of strategic decision-making is clearly illustrated by a model proposed by Higgins (1982), which proposes a rational sequential approach imposed from the top of the organization. This model is illustrated in Figure 1.2 and is based on the comparison of required performance, based on organizational goals, with forecasted performance, enabling the likely performance gap to be clearly assessed. The forecasted performance is determined following a review of the organizational internal strengths and weaknesses coupled with an assessment of the effect of external forces.

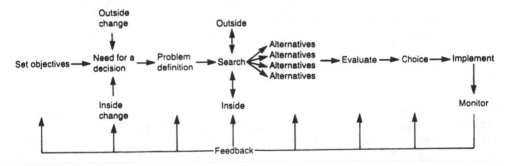

Figure 1.1 A decision-making process
Source: Chris Gore, Kate Murray, Bill Richardson *Strategic Decision Making*, 1992.

WHAT IS STRATEGY?

The work of Gore *et al.* (1992) provides a useful basis on which to establish a definition of the term 'strategy'. The conclusions drawn from this work are shown in Figure 1.3, which is a logically sequenced, interrelated framework for bringing together the varying approaches to strategy definition. The organization is viewed as providing an environment where individuals come together to share goals based on ensuring at least the survival of the organization in its current form and hopefully growth where there is efficient control of the internal activities in response to the demands of the environment.

The approach recognizes the organization as being a multi-decision-making system which requires a range of particular plans for particular types of problem. The range of related generic strategies are illustrated on the wheel shown in Figure 1.3.

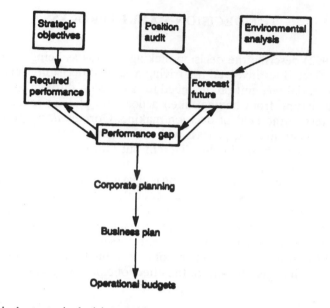

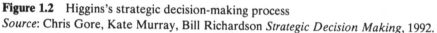

Figure 1.2   Higgins's strategic decision-making process
Source: Chris Gore, Kate Murray, Bill Richardson *Strategic Decision Making*, 1992.

ORGANIZATIONAL STRUCTURE

The term 'structure', used in the organizational sense, refers to the way in which capital and human resources are arranged and has considerable effect on the operation of the business. Organizational structures can be classified according to a number of characteristic features. The *classical* style is characterized by a strict hierarchy and clearly defined roles for each level. Such structures operate like a machine which is most effective under stable market conditions. However, such a structure lacks flexibility and is unable to react effectively in changing market conditions. The *behavioural* style places greater emphasis on personal responsibility and participation in decision-making and, as a result, tends to stimulate greater commitment to organizational goals. Every organization should have a clear vision of where it would like to see itself in the future and this is usually summarized in the mission statement.

In the smaller organization with a simple organizational structure, the mission statement can be developed into a set of relevant goals from which the objectives can then set. As the organization becomes larger the pursuit of these objectives becomes more difficult because organizations rarely function as total entities. Instead, the organization is made up of various functional activities such as operations, marketing, finance and personnel, and the long-term corporate objectives need to be broken down into separate strategies for each functional activity. As the organization becomes much larger and increasingly more diversified, the pursuit of corporate objectives becomes even more difficult. As a result the organization needs to subdivide into much smaller areas of responsibility. This can be achieved by splitting the organization into the functional areas (as described earlier) or into separate divisions. The separate divisions may then each have their own set of functional activities. Where managers have a considerable level of discretion these divisions are known as strategic business units (SBUs). Each SBU will normally have its own customers and market segment and the vast majority of strategic planning is undertaken at this level.

ORGANIZATIONAL OBJECTIVES

In the majority of organizations the setting of goals and objectives will be influenced by the people who control and work within the organization. It might initially be assumed

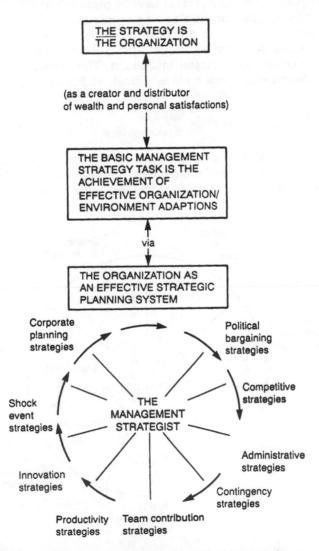

Figure 1.3   An integrated response to the question, 'So what is strategy?'
Source: Chris Gore, Kate Murray, Bill Richardson *Strategic Decision Making*, 1992.

that the organization has been created 'to achieve something'. However, this initial objective is often complicated by the actions of those internal and external to the organization with the result that the actual activities pursued do not always appear to be helping the organization to achieve its original objectives.

The profit motive

The reality is that the profit maximization motive is undermined by the objectives of those who are able to influence the organization the most. This book will concentrate on commercial operations with a profit motive. It is assumed, therefore, that the business is required to make a certain level of profit otherwise it will cease to exist. Economists argue that the pursuit of profit maximization in a competitive environment leads to economic efficiency. In practical terms, the performance of a business can easily be measured quantitatively using ratios such as return on capital employed, where profit is compared to capital investment. The practical measurement of efficiency and effectiveness is much more difficult and is often a matter of subjective judgement.

Stakeholders

The relevant stakeholders in a business will each influence the business strategy in a different way. The full range of stakeholder interests is illustrated in Figure 1.4. The relative power of each of these groups in relation to the other is very relevant and may change over time.

Figure 1.4   Stakeholders and their interests
Source: Chris Gore, Kate Murray, Bill Richardson *Strategic Decision Making*, 1992.

Quite clearly conflict can arise between the stakeholder groups, resulting in a business strategy chosen to meet the demands of the most dominant groups. This means that the resulting objectives of the organization are varied and certainly are influenced by factors other than profit maximization because each stakeholder is deriving a different reward from the existence of the business. Each of the stakeholders will now be considered in turn.

Shareholders

Shareholders investing in a large, international, well-diversified organization are essentially concerned with a competitive return on capital employed from their investment in the form of dividends and capital growth, that is the growth in the share price. Obviously, these are both functions of the profitability of the business and will therefore influence future business strategy. The need to pay out a reasonable dividend in relation to the investors' capital investment means that the business needs to make a level of profit sufficient to fund the dividend while allowing sufficient funds to remain within the business, in the form of retained profits, to finance growth. Failure to do this leads to shareholder dissatisfaction, with a possible fall in share price as investors disinvest, which undermines the market confidence in the company. The power of the shareholder group intent on pursuing the profit maximization objective has led some business operators to review their dependence on the equities market with the result that previously listed companies have returned to private ownership.

Managers

The management team have been engaged by the shareholders to maximize the profitability of the organization and are rewarded with a salary in return for achieving this. In practice, this concept is undermined by the interests of the individuals in the management team. Consequently, managers pursue a profit level which they perceive to be in excess of the minimum level acceptable to shareholders but which also allows them to achieve their own personal goals. The managerial theorist, Williamson, lists these personal goals as being not only salary, but also security, status, power, prestige and professional excellence. As a result, the pursuit of profit maximization through cost minimization is abandoned as expenditure contributes to gaining power, status and prestige. Many of the non-monetary rewards have the benefit of being invisible to others within the business, external shareholders and, of course, are not subject to taxation. The structure of the organization is also relevant as this determines the level of influence exerted by the management group, emphasizing the effect of ownership separate from control. The issues surrounding organizational structure are dealt with on pp. 114–17.

Employees

The strength of the employee group will depend on the nature of the workforce. Highly skilled permanent staff will have more power than a poorly skilled part-time workforce. A powerful group will pursue objectives which include increased salaries, improved working conditions and effective lines of communication.

Customers

The power of the customer centres on the products and services being offered and the perceived value for money, that is the relationship between the benefits of purchasing the goods and services against the price of acquiring them. The strength of the consumer group will depend on the market conditions in which the purchase is to be made. Suppliers and customers may also pay particular attention to any strategic threats which could arise from the company becoming involved in their own existing areas of trading.

Suppliers

This group is essentially interested in the long-term custom of the organization. At a practical level suppliers are able to exert pressure for quick repayment, thereby influencing business decisions relating to the management of working capital. The level of influence will depend on the reliance of the organization on a particular supplier.

Lenders

This group will require that the returns of the organization are sufficient to service the cost of the debt invested with the provision for capital repayments to be made in the future. The debt holder may also form part of the decision-making team to oversee the management of the debt, thereby influencing business strategy.

Society

The power wielded by society will depend on the strength of opinion of the collective group and the ability of the group to have a significant effect on the business. In recent times, for example, environmental issues have become more significant and organizations have been forced to adapt their policies and procedure accordingly. This has been the result of increasing public demand for change coupled with the desire to avoid negative publicity.

Governmental influence in the form of legislation may also effect the operation of the business. A recent example of governmental intervention in the hospitality industry has been the requirements of the Food Hygiene Regulations which have necessitated investment in equipment and training to meet government standards.

Incentives in the form of tax allowances or grants may serve to encourage investment in certain industries and locations. Local, or even national government may show interest and attempt to influence business decisions where strategy calls for large investment or the scaling down of operations resulting in widespread redundancies.

Goal congruence

It is possible for different stakeholder groups to have varied and possibly conflicting areas of interest in the organization and each group will try to influence business strategy accordingly. In an ideal world managers in the organization should aim to reflect the objectives of the shareholders and, to a certain extent, this does happen as managers who lose sight of their responsibilities to shareholders are likely to lose their position in an efficient financial market. Where the personal goals of managers reflect the shareholders' objectives, the implementation of business strategies to further these objectives is likely to be more successful. However, difficulties arise when managers' and shareholders' objectives are clearly in conflict. A situation can occur where shareholders wish managers to adopt a high-risk, high-growth strategy in order to produce additional profits. If the strategy fails and the business collapses, the shareholders may be able to offset those losses elsewhere with little personal risk. However, the managers in the business face high personal risk if the business fails and may therefore be reticent about pursuing such a strategy.

Goal congruence becomes even more difficult to achieve as the business grows in size and conflict may arise within the management group itself. Bowman and Asch (1987) believe that all businesses have to make a profit in order to survive but not all businesses typically *profit maximize*. The separation of ownership from control weakens the shareholders' influence over the firm's management, creating a situation where managerial objectives can be pursued. This relationship is illustrated in Figure 1.5.

INFORMATION NEEDS

Strategic management accounting in any industry should be a decision-support system, providing relevant information to the appropriate decision-maker. These decision-makers are situated not only at the very top of the organization, but also at various levels in the organization depending on the organizational structure. The business strategy has to be implemented all the way down through the organization and may result in several sub-strategies. The monitoring of the business strategy will take place at all levels in the organization, having been delegated to various managers at different levels. Therefore, the strategic management accounting system needs to provide information relevant to the needs of the user rather than raw data, and the information needs to be presented in an intelligible form in sufficient time to be of assistance in the

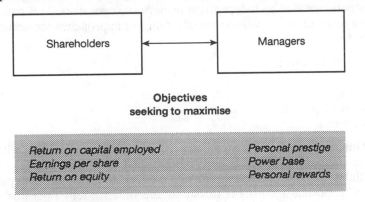

Figure 1.5 Business objectives

decision-making process. Essentially, it is balance between the cost of providing this information and the benefit to be accrued to the organization from taking a better financial decision. The increasing potential from computer power and new approaches to data transfer at lower cost mean that many organizations are able to achieve this objective.

CURRENT STRATEGIC ISSUES IN THE HOSPITALITY INDUSTRY

It is generally accepted by analysts that the level of growth in the hotel sector during the 1980s was exceptional, and unlikely to be repeated in the near future. Analysts at Kleinwort Benson Securities (KBS) have defined three key phases for industry development.

In the first, a period of slow growth, are the economies of Eastern Europe and the Far East, which are dominated by extractive and manufacturing industry. The UK is classified as being at the end of phase two, during which enormous growth has been driven by a growing service-based economy. The USA is well into phase three, where demand for service activities (including the hotel sector) is at a high level but is growing at a much slower rate. Industry experts forecast that during the next decade the international hospitality industry will be dominated by a handful of 'mega' hotel chains in the same way as the biggest airlines dominate travel.

Current issues facing hospitality organizations include:

- Changing industry structures and patterns of investment
- Opportunities arising from information technology
- Changing consumer demands.

These factors will now be considered in more detail.

Changing industry structure and patterns of investment

Traditionally, ownership in the hospitality industry has been very dispersed, resulting in an industry dominated by independent owners and operators. This pattern has been rapidly changing with the development of a range of approaches for achieving growth. These include:

- Acquisitional growth
- Branding
- Franchising
- Management contracts
- Joint ventures.

The first international hotel companies were formed in the late 1940s with the growth of American companies such as Hilton International, Inter-Continental and Sheraton. Large multinational hotel companies have continued to grow and to expand throughout the world, posing a constant threat to the independent operator who cannot compete in the key functional areas of marketing, information technology, purchasing power and financing. Organizational growth is not only achieved through the traditional path of acquisitions, but also through other means such as franchising, management contracts and joint ventures. In the USA it is estimated that 70 per cent of hotels are associated with a major brand name while in Europe it is only 30 per cent, but this figure is likely to increase rapidly.

Organizational development in the UK has been typified by the use of branding. Hilton International was among the first to create branded segments but many other groups have followed this example on a worldwide basis, including Ramada, Holiday Inn and Marriott. These brands often appear to the outsider to be separate operations or even separate companies, but traditionally companies have owned the brands they operate and in many cases this is still true. However, there is an increasing number of potential franchisees who are willing to pay a share of revenue received for the right to operate under brand names and some of them have grown into considerable hotel companies in their own right.

Recent trends have indicated that hotel ownership can have its penalties. Traditionally companies that have owned properties for many years are able to face recession in a strong position, having benefited from steadily appreciating assets. Recession in the early 1990s, however, was accompanied by a property market that was weaker than that in the early 1970s. Asset values of hotels often fell to values below the loans secured upon them, resulting in many properties falling into receivership. This in turn has resulted in the growth of the hotel management contract where the property remains in the ownership of the bank and the property is simply managed for a fee and possibly a share of the profits. Several of the major hotel operators now include managed hotels in their portfolio of properties. The nature of these arrangements means that the accounting information emphasis is focused on revenue and operating profit maximization as these are normally the two figures on which the management fee is calculated. Traditional ratios, such as return on capital employed, are obviously of less importance to the company managing the operation.

Opportunities arising from information technology

The past has already proven that hotel companies cannot afford to overlook the opportunities offered by the ever-increasing potential derived from the use of information technology. The most exciting development for the very near future must be the marketing opportunities offered by Internet. The Travelweb can provide the hotel company with a brochure which has no printing cost, no distribution cost and allows for the flexibility of frequent updates and changes. It is estimated that 10 per cent of the world's population already has access to the Internet and this figure is rapidly increasing, providing access to markets in a way which has never been witnessed before.

This section would not be complete without reference to the growing use of computerized Yield Management Systems, currently known as Revenue Maximization Systems. This import from the airline industry is tailored to carry out an activity which has always been performed by hotels and that is to maximize both revenue and occupancy. However, computerized systems replace the intuitive feel and allow for more complex computations of room rate and the effects on demand. As hotel groups make more confident use of this management tool it is likely that published tariffs will disappear and there will be a whole range of specific prices which will vary daily and will carry with them not only the class of room but also check-in and check-out restrictions as well as restrictions on access to service and facilities.

Changing consumer demands

The effect of a period of recession has been to sharpen the focus of the hotel industry on creating products and services that will win and retain customers. As a result the industry has witnessed the creation of features such as 'Executive Floors', all-day lounges, business centres, priority check-in and loyalty programmes. The customer outlook has also changed with the buyer having the experience and confidence to negotiate on price and quality. It is forecast that the era of mass markets is coming to an end and that instead there will emerge a series of market sub-sets which will provide products and services to meet the needs of a clearly defined market.

CRITICAL SUCCESS FACTORS FOR THE HOSPITALITY INDUSTRY

Using research published by the management consultants Pannell Kerr Forster (PKF), Croston (1995) has attempted to establish what can generally be considered to be the key critical success factors for the hotel industry. The findings indicate that those factors which have significant effects on hotel profitability can be categorized under the following headings:

- Operating efficiency
- Marketing
- Product specification
- Delivery of service.

These factors have been highlighted on the basis that the fundamental criteria for location, market and quality have already been met.

The first of these, operating efficiency, comprises several key components which include:

- Company philosophy and culture towards staffing and payroll costs
- Operating cost controls
- Competitor analysis
- Long-term planning.

The research indicates that company philosophy and culture are by far the most important factors for creating an environment in which all employees feel that they are actively involved in the control of costs. Payroll is the largest single controllable cost in most hotel operations and savings in this area will have a dramatic effect on profitability. Effective cost control throughout the business requires applying well-known techniques consistently and thoroughly in every aspect of the operation, and these techniques are discussed and developed in later chapters. Competitor analysis provides the opportunity to monitor not just 'how did we do' but also to track the performance of the competition in terms of revenues and market share. Medium and long-term planning is often a neglected activity in the hospitality industry. Traditionally, an incremental approach is adopted where last year's results form the basis of planning with a small increase added on to represent growth. Zero-based budgeting, that is budgeting from first principles as if for a new business, is described in detail later in the book.

The second critical factor identified by PKF is marketing and this highlights making effective use of global reservation networks and computer technology in the form of Revenue Maximization Systems. Again, these areas are discussed in detail later in the text.

The third critical success factor relates to the product specification and the physical experience of the guest. The most significant impact in terms of revenue and profitability can be attributed to the architectural style and decoration of the building. Grand or landmark buildings are able to charge a premium to guests staying in this type of operation but they also carry higher operational and maintenance costs, for example, payroll, food and beverage, property operation, maintenance and energy costs.

Finally, the fourth critical success factor identified is that of service. The guest experience is made up of the physical specification of the hotel plus service delivery. At the lower end of the star rating, physical expectations clearly assume greater priority in customer choice, but for four or five star operations service delivery has the greatest influence on pricing, performance and delivery. Evidence indicates that service excellence is a major contributor to increased profits because it supports higher revenue achievement in terms of both room-rate and occupancy.

KEY FINANCIAL ISSUES FOR THE HOSPITALITY INDUSTRY

There are a number of key financial issues which have particular relevance for the hospitality industry. These issues are specific to an industry which is dependent on the use of fixed assets and subject, as a result, to a high proportion of fixed costs. The issues include:

- Accurate valuation of property and assets
- Valuation of brands
- Planning and control to support global expansion arrangements
- Information needs arising from changing investment patterns.

These aspects are considered in later chapters.

CONCLUSION

The purpose of this chapter has been to introduce the concept of strategic management and to highlight the importance of tailoring information systems to provide relevant information to assist the manager in the decision-making process. The key strategic issues and critical success factors for the hospitality industry have also been introduced at this stage.

REFERENCES

Bowman, C. and Asch, D. (1987) *Strategic Management*, London: Macmillan.

Croston, F. (1995) Hotel profitability – critical success factors, in *Accounting and Finance for the International Hospitality Industry*, P. Harris (ed.), pp. 295–315. Oxford: Butterworth Heinemann.

Gore, C., Murray, K. and Richardson, B. (1992) *Strategic Decision Making*, London & New York: Cassell.

Higgins, J. (1982) Management information systems for corporate planning, in *Corporate Strategy and Planning*, B. Taylor and J. Sparkes (eds), pp. 299–310. London: Heinemann.

Ward, K. (1992) *Strategic Management Accounting*, Oxford: Butterworth Heinemann.

Williamson, O.E. (1990) *Organisation Theory: From Chester Barnard to the Present and Beyond*, Oxford: Oxford University Press.

2

Linking accounting and strategic management

INTRODUCTION

Virtually all business enterprises are required to monitor their financial activities and produce accurate audited accounts for external inspection. The disclosure require- ments for small businesses are fairly limited, whereas at the other end of the spectrum, the published accounts of the larger listed companies are required to be somewhat more detailed. It is this information which provides the potential investor with a limited insight into the strengths and weaknesses of the business and will affect the decision whether to invest or not. The published accounts are of little value, however, to the managers operating within the business because the key operating information, such as material and wage costs, are not clearly visible having been hidden through the process of consolidation. Instead, the manager is reliant on a series of internal reports, generated via the process called management accounting, which contain information tailored to meet the needs of that particular sector of the business. This chapter will consider the tools available to the manager to assist in the strategic management process and will examine the role of management accounting systems in supporting this process. The stages within the strategic management process have already been described as forming part of a continual process of analysis based on planning and control. Successful strategic decision-making requires the support of an efficient information system which should be designed to meet the needs of the individual organization and will be required to change as the strategy develops. This chapter will consider in particular:

- The nature of management accounting
- Tools for strategic planning
- Traditional accounting versus strategic accounting
- Strategic management accounting in the hospitality industry.

THE NATURE OF MANAGEMENT ACCOUNTING

The decision-making process centres upon choosing the best alternative from a possible range of different courses of action. It is possible, of course, that the alternatives may not all be known and the best decision is normally the choice with the highest overall benefit in relation to cost. Management accounting is the process of analysing, planning and controlling the business with the purpose of supporting the financial decision-making process. Financial accounting involves the actual recording of every financial transaction, and therefore operates in a historical framework. The end result is a set of published statements which are prepared to meet the demands of a legal framework provided by the Companies Act. The wide availability of the published statements means that companies will wish to keep to a minimum the information that they present in order to maintain a degree of competitive advantage. The emphasis in management accounting is to provide as much information as possible to assist the manager in controlling the business. Consequently, there are several differences between financial accounting and management accounting. Table 2.1 summarizes these.

The aim in management accounting is to help the manager run the business and, consequently, an effective management accounting system segments the business into key operating areas and the manager receives individually tailored reports containing the appropriate level of detailed information. The way in which the business is segmented is discussed further in Chapter 6.

TOOLS FOR STRATEGIC PLANNING

There are many approaches to strategic planning and various tools available. This section considers those most widely discussed, including:

- SWOT analysis
- Product life cycles
- Boston Consulting Group matrix
- General Electric matrix.

These techniques are known collectively as portfolio analysis.

	Strengths	Weaknesses
INTERNAL		
EXTERNAL	Opportunities	Threats

Figure 2.1 SWOT analysis
Source: Keith Ward *Strategic Management Accounting*, 1992.

Table 2.1 Financial accounting versus management accounting

	Financial accounting	Management accounting
Governed by	Company law, SSAPs	Needs of managers
Users	External	Internal
Time	Past and present	Present and future
Period	Usually one year	As appropriate
Coverage	Whole company or group	Divisions and sub-groups
Emphasis	Accuracy	Speed
Criteria	Objective and verifiable	Relevant, useful, understandable
Unit of account	Money	Money or physical units
Nature of data	Somewhat technical	For use by non-accountants

Source: M. Allen and D. Myddelton *Essential Management Accounting*, 1992, p. 7.

SWOT analysis

A simple approach for analysing the internal and external aspects of an organization is contained in the form of a SWOT analysis. SWOT stands for strengths, weaknesses, opportunities and threats and is often displayed in 2 × 2 matrix as shown in Figure 2.1.

The strengths and weaknesses refer to the internal aspects of the organization compared with the competition and the general expectations of the market place. Strengths are the special or distinctive characteristics which can be attributed to the organization. Weaknesses are aspects which make the organization less effective than other similar operations. The analysis should be performed honestly and the results compared to the aims of the organization as set out in the mission statement and goals. Techniques for performing the analysis, such as resource audits and performance measurement, are considered in Part 3. An analysis of the opportunity and threats should take account of all the external environmental factors and the relationships among them. An opportunity is any chance to follow a new or revised strategy that could benefit the organization. Opportunities may simply exist but more usually need to be created. Threats are possible events which have the potential to harm the organization's ability to achieve its goals and objectives.

A good SWOT analysis should highlight the critical success factors for a business and hence highlight those areas where a change in strategy is likely to have the most beneficial effect. However, a SWOT analysis is only an aid to strategic planning and the process should be carried out with considerable management judgement. There are other models which can also be used alongside this to provide a detailed analysis of the current position.

Michael Porter (1985) suggests a model which analyses the competitive environment facing an organization. This model categorizes competitive forces into five groups and the results can be linked with his later technique, a development of the added value concept, the value chain. The concept of value added refers to the contribution made by the organization to convert raw materials into the final product. The objective of the analysis is to highlight those areas which contribute most to the total value added, and subsequently to develop strategies to improve these areas. The techniques are explained in Chapter 4 in Part 2 in the context of competitor accounting.

Product life cycles

It is generally believed that products and services follow a 'life cycle' in terms of the current market and this has significant implications for the future strategic direction of the business. The concept has faced some criticism in recent times but the theory can still be usefully applied where common sense prevails. The theory separates the economic life of the product or service into a number of stages and these are shown in Figure 2.2.

Stage 1 is the initial development and launch of the product and the initial sales growth will be slow. This is a period of high risk as it is quite feasible that the product or idea will fail completely.

If the product is accepted by the market, there follows a period of rapid sales growth. This is **Stage 2**. Normally the potential level of sales is not infinite and eventually the rate of growth will slow down. It is quite possible that other companies will enter the market at this point and will benefit from the experiences of the pioneering company which has carried the high risk through the development stage. This point is particularly true in the hospitality and catering industry where the new product is available to all by simply purchasing the product or service. New ideas can be copied without the need to go through the development stage. A number of new companies may enter the market, rapidly increasing the volumes of the product available.

This rapid growth often coincides with the start of a fall in market growth. This is **Stage 3**. During this period there may be a period of shake-out when several competitors leave the industry or are taken over and the total capacity is rationalized.

Once a more stable position has been established, with sales demand approximately meeting product provision, a period of maturity ensues (**Stage 4**). This period may last for several years but eventually the demand for the product will start to fall as customer tastes change and other products have been introduced. It is possible to attempt to sustain the maturity period by making changes to the product or by seeking out new markets. The McDonald's concept is a good example of a company in the maturity stage of the product life cycle in Europe and the USA where additional products have

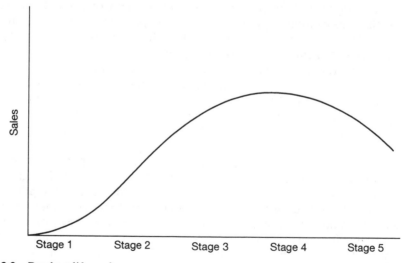

Figure 2.2 Product life cycle

been added to the menu to account for changing consumer tastes but the basic concept has remained the same. However, by seeking out new markets in former Eastern bloc countries, the product can be seen to be still in the growth sales stage in those regions.

Stage 5 is defined as the decline stage when sales are falling in a declining market.

	McDonald's Corporation
1948	McDonald brothers open first restaurant in the US
1954	Ray Kroc persuades the brothers to franchise the operation, giving him sole rights
1955	First franchise operation opened
1961	McDonald brothers sold the trademarks, copyright and formulas to Kroc for $2.7 million
1965	Chain goes public, floated on the Stock Exchange
1971	Expansion overseas
1974	3,000 units in operations at home and abroad
1984	Death of Ray Kroc; Fred Turner becomes Senior Chairman
1990s	Company introduces variations on the original theme. Expansion into new locations and new markets

Risk and the product life cycle

The overall level of risk facing an organization when it decides to launch a new idea is a combination of two types of risk. **Financial risk** is derived from the nature of the financing of the project and the cost structure of the business. Financial risk occurs when the project is funded by debt capital rather than equity capital with the risk arising from the fixed interest payments and the eventual need to repay the capital. Cost structure refers to the nature of the costs experienced by the business. Costs which have to be paid regardless of the level of trading are known as fixed costs and a high proportion of these renders a business as high risk. **Business risk** arises from the inherent nature of the product.

A business will try to achieve a balance by rejecting those projects with both high financial risk and high business risk. However, the combination of low business risk and high financial risk could provide very favourable returns for shareholders.

The stages of the product life cycle have different intrinsic levels of risk which the business has little control over as these are created by the outside environment. The launch stage is obviously the stage carrying greatest risk, but the risk is also high in the development stage when the potential size of the market is still not known. As the market matures the risk reduces and is dependent on the length of the maturity stage. The final stage is low risk as the demand for the product dies and the company's strategy is tailored accordingly. Risk and return are invariably linked with a positive correlation in that if risk increases, so must the return. This basic economic principle is illustrated in Figure 2.3.

During the growth stage the cost per unit may be high but this can be compensated by charging a premium for the product. The selling price is forced to stabilize or even fall in

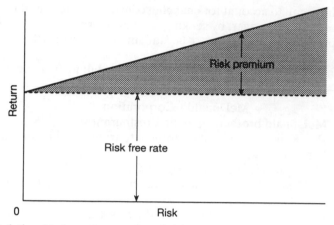

Figure 2.3 Relationship between return and risk
Source: H. Shaw *Strategic Financial Management*, 1994.

the maturity stage once the competition increases. During the maturity stage the emphasis falls on improving quality to justify a premium price or where products are homogeneous, reducing operating costs while maintaining quality at the same level. Strategic methods for reducing costs in the maturity stage are considered in Chapter 4.

The product life cycle and management accounting

The various stages of the product life cycle raise a number of issues for the provision of strategic management accounting information. The type of information required for strategic decision-making will vary depending on the stage of the product life cycle. The management accounting function can also be used to establish where the company is actually positioned in the life cycle, and whether it is about to enter a new phase. But note that the difficulty in pin-pointing the exact position is a commonly cited criticism of the product life cycle theory. Nevertheless, there can be little doubt that accounting information is useful for monitoring a company's position. Table 2.2 illustrates the change in emphasis required at each stage of the product life cycle.

Table 2.2 Separate stages of the product life cycle

PLC Stage	Launch	Growth	Maturity
Product	Unsophisticated	Range widening	Proliferation
Market	Narrow segment	Wider growth	Mass market
Competition	Low	Intensifying	High-cost producers exit
Price	High	Lower	Low
Profit	High/medium	Medium	Lower
Cash	Negative	Positive	Cash rich

Stages of the product life cycle

Each stage of the life cycle is now considered in detail in terms of:

- Cashflows
- Level of operating expenses
- Performance measures.

Launch stage. A critical feature of the launch stage is that the cashflow of the business will be negative because funds are being used to develop, test and launch the new idea. If the concept is perceived to be successful, more cash will be needed for fixed assets, working capital and launch marketing. Discounted cashflow techniques are normally used with new concept launches, with the potential cashflows being projected well into the future and a discount rate used for the analysis, which should reflect the perceived risk associated with the project, particularly in the early stages. However, at this stage the forecasted information cannot be sufficiently accurate to be of use for monitoring and controlling the project. Even if the initial evaluation of the project is positive, the business needs to consider how an appropriate set of financial control measures might attempt to monitor performance at this stage, given the level of uncertainty. Using the discounted cashflow technique, probabilities can be assigned to likely outcomes and the weighted average calculated. This approach is covered in more detail in Chapter 11, illustrating the advantages and disadvantages of such a technique.

Marketing expenditure will be crucial at this stage to establish the potential for the concept and, above all, the business should not be tempted to reduce marketing and research costs to earn short-term profits as this will undermine the business's long-term competitive position. It is likely at this stage that the operating costs will be fairly high and will remain so until the business is able to achieve cost reduction through improved operational techniques, the benefit of experience and sales volumes.

Traditional measures such as return on investment are wholly inappropriate at the launch stage. One of the primary objectives of a system for monitoring should be to collect information which reduces the risk associated with the project due to lack of knowledge. As a result, the project should be controlled using milestones based on the achievement of overall objectives. This depends on the project being broken down into visible stages and each stage being assessed for likely expenditure. If this can be achieved, the project can be assessed at each stage to check that it is worth continuing. In order to achieve this, accounting systems need to be designed to be able to cope with an ever-changing environment and, as a consequence, need to be flexible, informal and capable of rapid response.

Growth stage. Increasing marketing expenditure is still likely to be the key activity in order to create market growth as quickly as possible and to increase market share. At this stage it is common for the business to focus on product differentiation by emphasizing the particular product attributes. The marketing expenditure associated with this should be financially evaluated as a long-term investment by the business and the financial justification carried out using discounted cashflow techniques, much in the same way as it was performed for the launch stage. At some point the law of diminishing returns sets in and any further increases in marketing will not be worthwhile.

Once the product is successfully launched and the market begins to grow, financial measures become more important. Forecasting should now be considerably more accurate and the accounting measures should be able to pin-point the optimum expenditure level to avoid wasted expenditure. As the market for the product expands, the business needs to expand its own sales faster than the market to increase market share. Therefore, the management accounting system should be producing information to analyse the competitors' existing marketing strategies and potential responses to changes in the organizational strategy. Sales revenues will now have increased rapidly from those produced during the launch stage but the overall cashflow of the business may still not yet be positive as extensive investment is required to sustain the growth of the business. Profits should not be the main focus at this stage as the company should be reinvesting in marketing and research expenditure to maximize the opportunities in the market.

Maturity stage. Once the maturity stage has been established the management style should focus on control. It is at this stage that the overall profits can be maximized and cashflows turn positive. A typical feature of this stage is over-capacity in the market as the level of competitors increases. As a result, an extremely competitive environment is created and some operators will be forced out of business or will fall victim to takeovers and mergers. Further investment is now no longer necessary and marketing should be aimed at maintaining market share rather than attempting to increase it. The financial control process should focus on the shorter-term performance of the business, emphasizing profitability and cashflow generation. This is the most cash-positive stage of the business and the business should aim to maximize the benefit of these cash returns. Consequently, the control of costs at this stage is crucial and should be principally aimed at strategically reducing unit costs in relation to the competitors. Price competition will become more important at this stage, particularly if over capacity exists and the product is well understood by the customer. An alternative is to focus on a particular aspect of the product, such as levels of service or unique selling qualities.

At this stage it is appropriate to use a profit measure to control the business and return on investment is usually considered to be the most appropriate. To ensure this ratio is used effectively the profit margins should be monitored carefully and the manager will need information on cost structures in terms of fixed and variable costs and also, where possible, similar information for the competition. The strategic thrust at this stage is to maximize cost efficiencies and achieve maximum profitability.

A business needs to monitor the market carefully in order to predict accurately when the business is entering the maturity stage as a different strategic approach is required at this point. The maturity stage can be identified by reviewing the total market size and the market share held by the business. Care needs to be taken to ensure that the market really has matured and that it is not simply a temporary drop in market growth. Techniques for establishing market size and share are discussed in Chapter 5.

Decline stage. The decline stage of a particular concept will inevitably be reached as customer needs change. At this stage all costs which are no longer necessary should be removed with no further investment being necessary as the existing assets are worked until the end of their life. Financial measures such as return on capital and profitability are no longer valid as appropriate methods of financial control. The short-term measure of free cashflow is regarded as the best measure at this stage and the preparation of short-term cashflows is crucial. Cashflows may exceed profits due to declining requirements for working capital. In the hospitality industry the decline stage can be avoided by changing the nature of the business concept to match consumer needs. This is often achieved through the use of brands which are, for many organizations, transferable between products and concepts, so it may be necessary to remove the branding image from a declining concept and apply it to a more growth-orientated area.

Boston Consulting Group matrix

The Boston matrix is a general strategic planning concept which can be used with the product life cycle. The simplest version of this matrix is the one produced by the Boston Consulting Group (BCG). Other more complex models have followed but the majority are based on the principles demonstrated in the BCG matrix. It should be noted that all these models require managerial judgement and common sense to make them workable in a practical situation. The matrix illustrated in Figure 2.4 enables a business to plot the position of each of its products or brands in terms of relative market share and total rate of market growth.

The rate of market growth is an attempt to measure the level of attractiveness of the industry in terms of the rate of growth of the total market available for a product. Relative market share is a guide to the competitive strength of the business in the market place because companies with a dominant market share tend to produce higher financial returns. However, other factors such as service quality and operational efficiency, are also influential in determining the relative financial performance. The Boston Matrix can be used as a strategic planning device if the position of the company can be identified. There may be some relationship between the stages of the BCG matrix and the product life cycle although this is not always the case as they are based on different parameters (see Table 2.3).

| | | Relative market share | |
		High	Low
Market growth	High	Star	Question mark
	Low	Cash cow	Dog

Figure 2.4   Boston Consulting Group matrix

Table 2.3 Relationships between the BCG matrix and the product life cycle

Product life cycle	BCG matrix
Launch	Question marks
Growth	Star
Maturity	Cash cow
Decline	Dog

Like the product life cycle, the BCG matrix is more successfully used for charting past performance than for predicting future performance. The characteristics for each stage are illustrated in Figure 2.5.

The use of the BCG matrix leads to a focus on diversification strategies. The analysis tends to encourage the use of positive cashflows from business activities in the mature stage to fund new ventures and concepts. The positive aspect of this is that diversification reduces risk but in practice such a policy can lead to a lack of focus and increasing corporate costs arising from managing a diverse portfolio of activities.

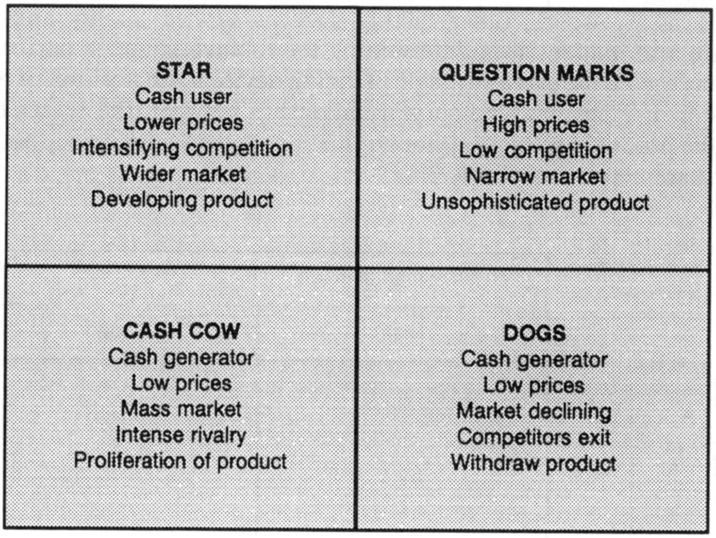

STAR	QUESTION MARKS
Cash user	Cash user
Lower prices	High prices
Intensifying competition	Low competition
Wider market	Narrow market
Developing product	Unsophisticated product
CASH COW	**DOGS**
Cash generator	Cash generator
Low prices	Low prices
Mass market	Market declining
Intense rivalry	Competitors exit
Proliferation of product	Withdraw product

Figure 2.5 Characteristics for the Boston Consulting Group matrix

General Electric matrix

This model, illustrated in Figure 2.6, is sometimes known as the directional policy matrix.

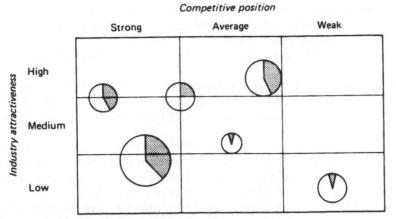

Figure 2.6 Nine-cell General Electric matrix
Source: Cliff Bowman and David Asch *Strategic Management*, 1987.

The matrix shows industry attractiveness on the vertical axis, which is the weighted average of a range of factors including size of industry, profitability, growth rate, nature of competition, business cycle and the ability to gain economies of scale. This is compared to competitive strength on the horizontal axis, which is the weighted average of a range of factors including market share, profit levels, management ability, production capability and technological strength. The aim is to plot each aspect of the business to illustrate how each relates to the other in terms of competitiveness and attractiveness.

TRADITIONAL ACCOUNTING VERSUS STRATEGIC ACCOUNTING

The majority of accounting systems are designed to process large volumes of data on a routine daily basis. This approach is certainly adequate where historical information is known to be a sound basis for future decisions. However, strategic decisions, which are designed to change the direction of the business, cannot be supported by information which has simply been produced by extrapolating the past performance to represent the future. Traditional accounting systems tend to focus on the past and financial planning is thus limited simply to an extension of the budgetary process. Shaw (1994) has highlighted the key areas for financial planning and control, identifying the differences between a traditional and a strategic approach. Table 2.4 is adapted from his recommendations.

Some strategic decisions require one-off evaluation, for example, a decision to open a new unit or revenue-generating area within an existing business. The financial evaluation requires assessing the net incremental impact on the business. Similarly, the cost of closing a business requires an evaluation of the opportunity costs of such an action. It may be necessary to consider the cost of, or benefit from, continuing, closing down or selling to another party. In order to support these types of decision the management accounting system needs to consider future incremental cashflows. This can present a problem to traditional management accounting systems which tend to focus on historical costs based on direct costs and indirect costs that have been apportioned across the organization. Consequently, the aims and objectives of each strategic decision need to be clearly stated and the information that is produced needs to be based on incremental costs only to monitor whether the targets are in fact being met.

A range of financial performance measures should be used which measure both the economic performance and the managerial performance of the business. The measures should be tailored to the particular strategies and may need to change in focus over time.

Economic performance focuses on the performance of the business in relation to the external environment in order to monitor the effect of all economic factors which are likely to affect the business regardless of management performance. Managerial performance can be assessed through the use of responsibility centres where an individual is monitored by evaluating only those revenues and costs which are controllable. The aim is to provide a system which motivates managers and clearly highlights good performance. The accounting system should produce information for internal use which is user-friendly in presentation and relevant to the needs of the user.

Table 2.4 Differences between a traditional and strategic approach to accounting

Activity	Traditional approach	Strategic approach
Corporate strategy	Generally, financial planning concentrates on the operational aspects of budgetary control	Financial planning is consistent with strategic aims and based on internal capabilities and resource availability
Capital structure	Capital is raised as and when it is needed, leading to a possible increase in cost of capital	Capital structure is intended to reduce cost of capital and minimize shareholder risk
Dividend policy	Dividend payment level is set to maximize shareholder wealth and raise share price in the short term	Dividends are paid only when all other more profitable uses of retained funds have been explored
Investment decisions	Reliance on profit is based on capital investment appraisal methods where profit is compared to investment	Management only invest in projects which provide positive discounted cashflows (net present value)
Profitability	General emphasis is on short-term profit maximization in order to improve earnings per share (EPS)	Management seek to improve the long-term profitability of the business and return on capital employed
Working capital	Focus is on profit flows	Focus is on internal cashflows
Pricing policy	Pricing is based on cost and profit per unit expectations	Pricing focuses on product and market considerations
Performance measures	Include a range of measures based on internal and external factors, including financial and non-financial values	Tend to be on a historical period-by-period basis, emphasizing internal operations

It is essential that the information produced by accountants is understandable by the managers who need to use it. Therefore reports should be tailored to meet the requirements of the user and this could include the use of graphs, pie charts and histograms to aid the less numerate manager.

The process of standard costing can be a useful element of a strategic management accounting system. A standard cost is an estimate of the cost of one unit of production, such as a bednight or a meal, and these can be used effectively for forecasting and for making comparisons with actual performance, which form the basis of budgetary control.

The following chapters of this text consider the traditional topics associated with financial and management accounting and in each case the processes described are illustrated with examples and recommendations for a strategic approach.

STRATEGIC MANAGEMENT ACCOUNTING IN THE HOSPITALITY INDUSTRY

The results of an extensive study by Collier and Gregory (1994), focusing on the practice of strategic management in hotel groups, concluded that strategic management accounting is being increasingly used in hotel groups for planning, evaluating market conditions and for competitor analysis. The research identified two main strategic management accounting areas, these being firstly the provision of information that assisted in the development of strategic plans, and secondly the monitoring of the market, competitors' price structures and competitors' costs. The development of strategic plans includes the preparation of long-range plans up to five years in advance, including profit and loss account, balance sheet and cashflow using spreadsheet technology for modelling. The monitoring of the market is made easier due to the open nature of the industry and the availability of some revenue and cost data. As a result, regular monitoring of the competition could be included in the remit of the accounting function. However, practice indicates that this aspect remains the responsibility of the marketing function.

CONCLUSION

Many businesses use traditional management accounting systems which focus on the internal aspects of the business and the regular production of routine data. A strategic approach to management accounting includes having an external focus to monitor changes in the environment while providing information which enables strategic decisions to be evaluated. Strategic decisions are made at all levels in the hospitality industry and the power of information technology can be harnessed to produce reports which are not only timely and relevant, but also enable sensitivity analysis and prediction modelling to take place. The remainder of this book will consider some of the modern approaches available to the hospitality industry to improve the decision-making process and the subsequent monitoring and control of those decisions.

FURTHER READING

Ward, K. (1992) *Strategic Management Accounting*, Oxford: Butterworth Heinemann.

REFERENCES

Allen, M. and Myddelton, D. (1992) *Essential Management Accounting*, New York: Prentice-Hall.
Bowman, C. and Asch, D. (1987) *Strategic Management*, London: Macmillan.
Collier, P. and Gregory, A. (1994) Strategic management accounting: a UK hotel sector case study, *International Journal of Contemporary Hospitality Management*, 7(1): 18–23.
Porter, M.E. (1985) *Competitive Advantage*, New York: Free Press.
Shaw, H. (1994) *Strategic Financial Management*, Oxford: Butterworth Heinemann.

3

Understanding financial statements

INTRODUCTION

The vast majority of business managers will need, at some point in their lives, to be able to understand and interpret financial information. The results of the business are usually summarized in three key statements – the balance sheet, the profit and loss account and the cashflow statement – and these are prepared at least once per year and in most cases several times per year. The aim of this chapter is to provide guidance for understanding these statements. There will be no attempt to illustrate the principles of double-entry book-keeping as this aspect is covered in a multitude of texts on the subject. Consequently, this chapter is concerned with the accounting principles which support the preparation of the financial statements, an overview of each statement and an explanation of the relationship between the statements. A more detailed review of the techniques for interpreting statements using ratio analysis is given in Chapter 8.

ACCOUNTING PRINCIPLES

The function of financial accounting is to record clearly every single financial transaction that the business is involved in and to classify and summarize these transactions for presentation in a series of published reports produced on an annual basis. These reports are then used by a range of external users who have access to very little other information. The external users include shareholders, banks and other lenders, government and tax authorities.

The statements contained in the published reports are required to give a fair and true representation of the business and in order to assist in the preparation of the statements to this standard there is a series of rules and regulations available. Some of these rules have been made into legal requirements but essentially it is the Companies Act which provides the statutory framework. The accounting principles which underpin the preparation of the financial statements in the UK were originally embodied in the Statements of Standard Accounting Practice (SSAPs). There were 25 of these statements, covering a range of issues, with the aim of providing guidance on the most appropriate technique for the preparation of the entries in the financial statements. The range of these statements is illustrated in Table 3.1.

Every major developed country has its own version of accounting standards and there is also an International Accounting Standards body. Originally the accounting standards in the UK and Ireland were established by the Councils of what were then six major accountancy bodies. The Accounting Standards Committee (ASC) was set up by the Council of the Institute of the Chartered Accountants in England and Wales with the objective of developing definitive standards on financial reporting. The result was a set of Standard Accounting policies.

The ASC has since been superseded by the Accounting Standards Board (1990) whose aim is to start a new era in accounting standard setting (the original ASC had lost much of its credibility). The SSAPs were perceived to be weak, and in many cases ambiguous, because they allowed for more than one treatment of a particular activity. As a result, there were ample opportunities for managers to indulge in creative

Table 3.1 Statements of Standard Accounting Practice

No.	Title
SSAP 1	Accounting for associated companies
SSAP 2	Disclosure of accounting policies
SSAP 3	Earnings per share
SSAP 4	The accounting treatment of government grants
SSAP 5	Accounting for value added tax
SSAP 6	Extraordinary items and prior year adjustments
SSAP 7	(Withdrawn 1978)
SSAP 8	The treatment of taxation under the imputation system in the accounts of companies
SSAP 9	Stocks and long-term contracts
SSAP 10	Statements of source and application of funds
SSAP 11	(Withdrawn 1978)
SSAP 12	Accounting for depreciation
SSAP 13	Accounting for research and development
SSAP 14	Group accounts
SSAP 15	Accounting for deferred taxation
SSAP 16	(Withdrawn 1988)
SSAP 17	Accounting for post-balance sheet events
SSAP 18	Accounting for contingencies
SSAP 19	Accounting for investment properties
SSAP 20	Foreign currency translation
SSAP 21	Accounting for leases and hire purchase contracts
SSAP 22	Accounting for goodwill
SSAP 23	Accounting for acquisitions and mergers
SSAP 24	Accounting for pension costs
SSAP 25	Segmental reporting

Table 3.2 Financial Reporting Standards

No.	Title
FRS 1	Cashflow statements
FRS 2	Accounting for subsidiary undertakings
FRS 3	Reporting financial performance
FRS 4	Capital instruments
FRS 5	Reporting the substance of transactions
FRS 6	Acquisitions and mergers
FRS 7	Fair values in acquisition accounting

accounting practices which helped to meet short-term profit and return on investment targets. The new body aims to produce a new set of accounting guidelines to improve upon the policies which have gone before. Table 3.2 shows the new Financial Reporting Standards (FRS) that have been produced to date.

The preparation of financial statements is clarified by the acceptance of accounting principles which should be uniformly applied. In practice, however, there is a considerable degree of user interpretation. The following notes provide a summary of the basic principles in statement preparation:

- **Consistency**. The accounting treatment of particular items should be the same from period to period. If this is not the case then the difference should be revealed.
- **Going concern**. An organization is assumed to continue in operational existence for the foreseeable future.
- **Matching**. The costs for the period should be matched with the appropriate revenue.
- **Materiality**. Changes in accounting practice are only permissible if the effect is not material.
- **Stated values**. Accounting records are kept for those events measured in monetary terms.
- **Prudence**. Provision should be made for all likely costs whereas profits should not be accounted for until realized.
- **Separate entity**. A business is considered to have a separate entity from its owners, which means that personal transactions are excluded from business accounts.

The effect of the accounting policies mentioned above is illustrated by comparing the cashflow and the profit and loss account of a business. The cashflow shows all revenues actually received and all costs actually paid. The profit and loss account recognizes both debtors and creditors. Debtors are those sales not yet received, although the transaction has taken place. Creditors are expenses which have been used but not yet paid for. Profit is calculated by considering all the sales for both cash and credit and matching these with all the costs of production.

A second item which does not appear in the cashflow is depreciation. The depreciation of a fixed asset is a measure of the 'wearing out' of the asset through use and this cost should be set against the profit for the period. There are different methods available for calculating the depreciation charge and profits will vary depending on which method is used. The following section provides guidelines for the more common approaches.

WHAT IS DEPRECIATION?

Depreciation is a charge made to the profits of the business to write off part of the value of a fixed asset. The more common forms of fixed asset are land and buildings, equipment and machinery, and motor vehicles. The first of these, land and buildings, may well remain unchanged in value over time or even increase. However, over the long-term perspective, the buildings will deteriorate and will require some maintenance. Equipment and machinery should be depreciated using an estimate of the useful life of the asset resulting in a nil value or simply a scrap value at the end of its life. Vehicles tend to depreciate more quickly in the early part of their life and it may be appropriate to depreciate the asset more heavily in the early years of its life to reflect this.

Straight-line method versus reducing balance

The total depreciation to be charged over the life of the asset is calculated by measuring the difference between the original cost and the residual value, that is the value of the asset at the end of its life or the period which is being considered. The straight-line method for calculating the annual depreciation charge is to simply divide this figure by the estimated life in years. This results in an equal charge each year. An alternative approach is the 'reducing balance' method which involves depreciating the asset by a fixed percentage each year, based on the year-end value of the asset. This results in higher levels of depreciation being charged in the early years of the life of the asset. The difference between the two methods is illustrated by the following example.

Kitchen equipment is purchased at a value of £10,000. The estimated life of the equipment is five years, when it is then considered to be worth zero. Calculate the depreciation charge using straight-line depreciation and a 50 per cent reducing balance depreciation charge.

Year	Straight-line	Year-end value	Reducing balance	Year-end value
	£	£	£	£
1	2,000	8,000	5,000	5,000
2	2,000	6,000	2,500	2,500
3	2,000	4,000	1,250	1,250
4	2,000	2,000	625	625
5	2,000	zero	313	312

There is some flexibility available when choosing a depreciation rate in terms of both the method and the period over which the asset is to be depreciated. This discretion can lead to the possibility where identical businesses could declare different profit levels as a result of adopting alternative depreciation methods. Additionally, a business which chooses to change its depreciation method from one accounting period to the next must declare in the published accounts that this has occurred as the profits may then be materially affected.

REVALUING FIXED ASSETS

Fixed assets, such as land and buildings, can experience both sharp rises in value during boom periods and falls in value during recession. As a result, the accounts of the company can become seriously out of line with the market value. The issue of asset revaluations is certainly a tricky one for the hotel industry where discrepancies in actual and book values have been considerable. The approach for estimating asset revaluations is dealt with in Chapter 13. The accounting treatment in the statements is to adjust the asset values in the balance sheet and to balance this with an entry in reserves.

ACCOUNTING FOR INFLATION

The problem of trying to show a true and fair view during periods of inflation has caused accountants to enter into fierce debate and the problem has never been clearly solved. SSAP 16: 'Current cost accounting' was issued in 1985 but was withdrawn in 1988 following widespread disapproval. The problem with inflation occurs when valuing assets as the book value will always fall short of the true value. This can distort performance measures such as return on capital employed where current profits are compared to out-of-date asset values. In periods of high inflation the relationship between sales and cost of sales is also distorted as the bought-in price of materials becomes out of date. The valuation of stock in particular can cause difficulty and this matter is now considered in detail.

STOCK VALUATIONS

There are four approaches to assessing what cost means when used for stock valuation purposes. The method used will affect the calculation of the cost of sales figures in the profit and loss account and will also affect the stock-held value in the balance sheet. The methods are:

- **First in, first out (FIFO)** where the cost of the most recently purchased items will be reflected in the valuation. During periods of inflation the earliest items with the lowest price will appear to be issued first, leading to a lower cost of sales calculation.
- **Last in, first out (LIFO)** where the latest and highest prices are charged to the profit and loss account, resulting in a higher cost of sales figure and lower profits, as well as a lower stock valuation.
- **Average cost** where the value of stock at any one time is the average of all items of cost.
- **Replacement cost** which is the present cost to replace the asset or stock item.

The following example illustrates the effect of each method on profitability.

The following table provides a summary of the inflows and outflows of a typical commodity recording the date of receipt and the purchase price and the date of issue. This information is then summarized in a second table to illustrate the differences in closing stock value depending on the method used.

Date	Units received	Purchase price (£)	Units used	Market price (£)
1/1	600	10.00		10.00
5/1	200	12.00		12.00
10/1			300	12.00
15/1			400	13.00
20/1	100	14.00		14.00
30/1			50	15.00

Method	Date	RECEIVED (ISSUED) Quantity	Price (£)	Value (£)	BALANCE Quantity	Value (£)
FIFO	1/1	600	10.00	6,000	600	6,000
	5/1	200	12.00	2,400	800	8,400
	10/1	(300)	10.00	(3,000)	500	5,400
	15/1	(300)	10.00	(3,000)	200	2,400
		(100)	12.00	(1,200)	100	1,200
	20/1	100	14.00	1,400	200	2,600
	30/1	(50)	12.00	600	150	2,000
LIFO	1/1	600	10.00	6,000	600	6,000
	5/1	200	12.00	2,400	800	8,400
	10/1	(200)	12.00	(2,400)	600	6,000
		(100)	10.00	(1,000)	500	5,000
	15/1	(400)	10.00	(4,000)	100	1,000
	20/1	100	14.00	1,400	200	2,400
	30/1	(50)	14.00	700	150	1,700
AVERAGE (£)	1/1	600	10.00	6,000	600	6,000
	5/1	200	12.00	2,400	800	8,400
	10/1	(300)	10.50	(3,150)	500	5,250
	15/1	(400)	10.50	(4,200)	100	1,050
	20/1	100	14.00	1,400	200	2,450
	30/1	(50)	12.25	613*	150	1,838*

* Rounded

The FIFO method produces the highest closing stock valuation at £2,000 and this serves to reduce the value of cost of sales and therefore increases profitability. The LIFO method produces the lowest stock valuation at £1,700, thereby increasing the cost of sales and reducing profitability. As a result, for many businesses the average value or the replacement value provide the most consistent result. The management and control of stock levels is considered in detail in Chapter 7.

ACCOUNTING STATEMENTS EXPLAINED

The accounting statements are produced in order to convey the financial performance of the business. There are three in total and the aim of this chapter is to provide the manager with an understanding of the basic principles underlying each statement. This understanding will enable the manager to interpret the financial position of any organization. The following chapters will develop this understanding further by providing additional tools for analysis such as ratio calculations using figures drawn from the financial statements.

The balance sheet

The balance sheet can be described as a snapshot of the business at a particular moment in time. It is based on the simple equation that the total value of what the company owns will equal the financial claims on the business, that is the total liabilities:

Assets = Total liabilities

It should be remembered that the balance sheet is always out of date; it does not refer to the present position or to the future and it should always balance. The items that the company owns are referred to as assets and these can be subdivided into those which are long-term or fixed in nature and those that are current.

Fixed assets are typically items such as land, buildings, equipment, machinery, computers and motor vehicles. These are all assets which are normally introduced into the business with the purpose of enabling the business to function in order to make profit. They are described as being 'tangible' assets because they can be seen and touched. Fixed assets which cannot be physically accounted for are called 'intangible' and the most common of these is goodwill. This arises when a business is purchased for a value which exceeds the net value of the physical assets. Purchases of fixed assets are called 'capital expenditure' items, and this area will be discussed in Chapters 10 and 11.

Current assets include stock which may be subdivided into raw materials, work in progress and finished goods, as well as outstanding sales known as debtors and cash balances. The current assets normally have a short life and are used up in the operation of the business.

There are several types of liability which are classified in terms of the long term and short term. Long-term liabilities include loans from external parties who have lent to the business and who receive interest in return. Owners' capital or equity is also a type of liability in that it remains the property of the owners. Returns are paid in the form of dividends and are related to the performance of the business. Alternatively, the profits could be reinvested in the company and are known as retained profits or reserves. Short-term or current liabilities include bank overdrafts, taxation and outstanding balances owed to suppliers. It is now possible to expand the initial equation to read:

Fixed assets+Current assets = Long-term liabilities+Short-term liabilities

The balance sheet is produced as a result of a process known as double-entry book-keeping. This forms the basis of accounting procedures and works on the basis that for every transaction there are two equal entries. All of the business entries are recorded during the period using this method and at the end of the period the entries are checked using what is known as a trial balance to ensure that both sides are still equal.

The layout of the balance sheet can vary and the level of detail will depend on whether the statement is for internal or external reporting. Published balance sheets are subject to legal constraints to standardize the layout. The sample format is known as the vertical format where the two balancing sections lie above and below each other rather than side by side. The vertical format is based on the equation:

$$\text{Fixed assets} + \text{Current assets}$$
$$- \text{Long-term} + \text{Current liabilities} =$$
$$\text{Capital} + \text{Reserves}$$

Capital and reserves are known as owners' equity. This may be made up of share capital, which might be issued solely to the owners or to the public at large. There are various types of shares in issue, the most popular of which are ordinary shares. The types of shares available for issue are discussed in more detail in Chapter 9.

Reserves are funds accumulated from internally produced profits. Profits may be paid out as dividends or they may be retained to further expansion, which is when they become known as reserves or retained profit. Reserves may stay in the form of cash but it is much more likely that they will be used to purchase fixed assets. Other types of reserve are generated by certain activities. As an example, a revaluation reserve is created when fixed assets are revalued either above or below their book value. If there is a change in the fixed asset value in the balance sheet then the reserve provides the balancing entry.

The share premium account is also a type of reserve and is created when ordinary shares are sold to the public for more than their nominal or original value. The following example illustrates how this reserve is created.

XYZ Ltd is to raise additional capital through the sale of unissued ordinary shares which have a nominal value of £1.00 each. The issue price is to be 10 per cent below the market price of £2.20. Prior to the sale the extract from the balance sheet looked like this:

		£ million
Assets		3
less long-term loans		1
		2

Share capital	Authorized	Issued
	£ million	£ million
Ordinary shares (£1 each)	2	1
Reserves		1
		2

After the sale of the remaining shares the balance sheet will show an increase in assets due to the cash being received for the sale and a change in the share capital layout:

		£ million
Assets		5
less long-term loans		1
		4

Share capital	Authorized	Issued
	£ million	£ million
Ordinary shares	2	2
Share premium		1
Reserves		1
		4

One million shares have been sold for £2 each which represents £1 nominal value and £1 share premium per share.

Working capital

Most businesses require funds to be available on a daily basis in order to allow the business to operate. These funds may be used to purchase stock in advance of trading and to pay staff. Consequently, at any moment of time a business will have money tied up in stocks and in debtors, that is those customers who have received the product or service but who have not yet paid. Too much cash tied up in these areas may deprive the business of funds for profit-generating expenditure on fixed assets. Additionally, large volumes of stocks and debtors may result in losses through inefficient management. Therefore it is essential to keep current assets as low as possible. The definition of working capital is:

Working capital = Current assets − current liabilities

This term provides a measure of the balance between short-term funds and short-term assets. There are various approaches to monitoring working capital, ranging from those measures which focus on the total amount in relation to sales to individual measures for the components of working capital. These are considered in more detail in Chapter 7.

Investments

A company may well consider investing in activities outside the scope of the existing business. Cash surpluses may be used to invest for both the short term and the long term. A short-term investment will provide a lower return but can be converted quickly back into cash should the need arise. Long-term investments should provide the highest possible return available while suiting the long-term plans of the company. The business might consider making long-term loans to other operations in return for interest, buying shares in other companies in return for dividends or purchasing other companies in total.

The profit and loss account

The balance sheet has already been described as a useful summary of the business position frozen at a moment in time. However, this does not reveal what the business has achieved over a period of time. The profit and loss account provides a summary of revenues and costs occurring over a given time span. Published accounts produce the statement on an annual basis but the statement may be produced as frequently as is desirable. There is generally no single layout used for the statement and published accounts aim to produce the minimum of information required to meet statutory guidelines. A sample statement taken from the published accounts for Queens Moat House plc is shown in Figure 3.1.

The statement starts with the net sales (gross sales less VAT) figure for the period which includes all sales transactions for both cash and credit. This is matched with the costs and charges for the period to reveal different levels of profit. These levels of profit are now described in detail.

- **Gross profit**. The difference between net sales and the cost of the materials for producing the sales. (Some companies may include wage costs at this point.)
- **Trading profit**. Sales less all costs of production.
- **Operating profit**. Trading profit less fixed costs such as rent and depreciation.
- **Net profit before tax**. Operating profit less interest payable.
- **Net profit after tax**. Net profit before tax less taxation.
- **Retained profit**. Net profit after tax less dividends to be paid to shareholders.

Each of these profit levels can be used as useful measures of profitability depending on the users' needs. However, it should be remembered that the statement is prepared based on the interpretation of the accounting standards and therefore the profit figure could vary for two identical companies depending on the methods used. An abbreviated format is used for external reporting under the Companies Acts.

Internal accounts will be considerably more detailed and should be tailored to suit the needs of the business and area of responsibility. The Uniform System of Accounts for Hotels provides guidelines of a format suitable for hotel operations and variations on this are widely used in the hospitality industry.

Uniform System of Accounts for Hotels

The UK version of the Uniform Accounting System was developed by the Hotel and Catering Economic Development Council in 1969. However, it is the US system, the Uniform System for Accounts in Hotels, that is more widely used and this was first published by the Hotel Association of New York City in 1926. The current version is the ninth edition which was revised in 1996. The Uniform System may be defined as a manual of instructions for preparing standard financial statements and schedules for the various operating and productive units which make up a hotel.

The purpose of the manual is to provide a simple formula for the classification of accounts which can then be adapted by any hotel regardless of size or type. The basic aim of the system is to enable users within the industry to manage their properties more effectively with the information provided and to enable users from outside the industry to understand the industry more readily since all the statements they are reading are similar and comparable.

The guidelines for the profit and loss account include three key operating areas and these are defined as rooms, food and beverage. The layout of the statement provides for several control levels as illustrated below.

		1994 £m	1993 £m
2	**Turnover**		
	Continuing operations	426.6	354.4
	Discontinued operations	–	26.9
		426.6	381.3
3	Net operating costs	(334.6)	(304.6)
	Trading profit	92.0	76.7
3	Rents payable	(20.1)	(18.4)
3	Depreciation	(36.7)	(39.9)
2	**Operating profit**	35.2	18.4
	Operating profit		
	Continuing operations	35.2	14.7
	Discontinuing operations	–	3.7
		35.2	18.4
	Exceptional items – continuing operations		
6	– Net surplus on revaluation of tangible fixed assets	7.0	26.0
6	– Restructuring costs	(15.0)	–
6	– Profit on disposal of fixed assets	3.6	–
6	– Loss on disposal or closure of businesses	(0.5)	–
6	– Amounts written off investments	–	(0.3)
	Interest receivable	3.4	5.7
	Profit on ordinary activities before interest payable	33.7	49.8
6	Foreign currency (losses)/gains – exceptional items	(23.4)	13.9
6	Interest payable – exceptional items	(7.7)	–
7	Interest payable	(97.8)	(110.1)
	Loss on ordinary activities before taxation	(95.2)	(46.4)
8	Taxation	(4.8)	2.0
	Loss for the financial year	(100.0)	(44.4)
	Dividends and appropriations		
9	– Preference shares (non-equity)	(14.7)	(14.7)
20	**Retained loss for the year**	(114.7)	(59.1)
10	**Loss per ordinary share**	(12.4)p	(6.4)p
10	**Loss before exceptional items per ordinary share**	(8.5)p	(10.7)p

Figure 3.1 Consolidated profit and loss statement for Queens Moat House plc (for year ending 1 January 1995). *Source*: *Annual Report and Accounts*, 1994.

	Rooms	Food	Beverage	Total
Net sales				
Less cost of sales				
Gross profit				
Less wages and staff costs				
Net margin				
Less allocated expenses				
Departmental operating profit				
Less service departments and general expenditure				
Hotel operating profit				
Less repairs and maintenance				
Hotel net operating profit				

The system also provides for the use of a balance sheet, cashflow and industry tailored operating ratios. However, the most commonly used are the profit and loss accounts and the operating statistics. There are a variety of measures which can be drawn from the profit and loss account to aid interpretation and these are discussed in detail in Chapter 8.

Profit versus cash

A business may forecast to be profitable but success will ultimately depend on there being sufficient cash available to generate sales. The difference between cash and profit is due to the timing differences incurred on the receipt of sales and on the payment of expenses, as well as depreciation. Current depreciation charges do not represent a cash outflow and therefore the cashflow value will always be different from the profit figure. Cashflows also include capital items such as financing and fixed asset expenditures, neither of which would appear in the profit and loss account. The cashflow is considered to represent a more factual representation of the state of the business and it is this rather than profit which is used to appraise long-term investments. Discounted cashflow techniques are discussed in detail in Chapter 10.

The cashflow statement

The principal aim of the cashflow statement is to measure the liquidity of the business. The cashflow statement is required to be produced in the company reports and this is shown as a historical picture summarizing how funds have been generated and how they have been utilized. Unlike the profit and loss account, the statement includes

		1994 £m	1993 £m
a	**Operating activities**		
	Net cash inflow from continuing operating activities	65.4	62.8
	Net cash inflow from discontinued operating activities	–	10.7
	Net cash inflow from operating activities	65.4	73.5
	Returns on investments and servicing of finance		
	Interest received	3.6	4.9
	Interest paid	(76.6)	(103.1)
	Interest paid on finance leases	(15.7)	(18.4)
	Preference share dividends paid	–	(0.3)
	Net cash outflow from returns on investments and		
	servicing of finance	(88.7)	(116.9)
	Taxation		
	UK corporation tax paid	(1.8)	(4.0)
	Overseas tax paid	(0.1)	(0.8)
	Tax paid	(1.9)	(4.8)
	Investing activities		
	Purchase of tangible fixed assets	(14.6)	(24.2)
	Disposal of tangible fixed assets	30.0	12.6
	Acquisition of businesses – deferred consideration paid	(8.8)	–
	Disposal of businesses	–	3.8
	Disposal of current and fixed asset investments	–	0.2
	Net cash inflow/(outflow) from investing activities	6.6	(7.6)
	Net cash outflow before financing	(18.6)	(55.8)
	Financing		
	Increase in borrowings	47.2	59.2
b	**Net cash inflow from financing**	47.2	59.2
c, d	**Increase in cash and cash equivalents**	28.6	3.4

Figure 3.2 Consolidated cashflow statement for Queens Moat House plc (for year ending 1 January 1995). *Source*: *Annual Report and Accounts*, 1994.

operating activities, sources of capital and capital expenditure items. The format of the published statement is regulated by Financial Reporting Standard 1 (FRS1). This supersedes the Statement of Accounting Practice (SSAP) No. 10, Statement of Source and Application of Funds. A sample layout taken from the accounts for Queens Moat House plc is shown in Figure 3.2.

The statement explains the increase or decrease in the cash balances over the year in terms of the cash inflows from operating activities, sale of fixed assets, and the raising of additional finance compared to the cash outflows for interest and dividend payments, taxation, and the purchase of fixed assets. The revised style of cashflow has the advantage that cash is the critical element rather than working capital changes; this can easily be reconciled with the movements in the cash book.

Preparation of the published cashflow

All the information required for this statement can come from the profit and loss account and the balance sheets for the opening and the close of the year. Consider the following example:

Treetops Hotel		
Balance sheet	**Yr ended**	
	19x4	**19x5**
	(£000)	**(£000)**
Fixed assets		
Freehold premises	65	100
Equipment and furnishings	84	126
Less depreciation	22	42
Net fixed assets	127	184
Current assets		
Stocks	66	72
Debtors	42	48
Cash balance	14	11
Current liabilities		
Creditors	45	56
Taxation	22	28
Dividend	15	20
Net current assets	40	27
Total assets	167	211
Less long-term liabilities	—	20
Capital employed	167	191
Financed by		
Ordinary shares	100	100
General reserve	41	51
Retained profits	26	40
Capital employed	167	191

Profit and loss account for the year ending 19x5		£000
Sales		250
Cost of sales		<u>128</u>
Gross profit		122
Operating costs		
Wages and administration	28	
Depreciation	<u>20</u>	
		<u>48</u>
Operating profit		74
Interest payable		<u>2</u>
Net profit before tax		72
Corporation tax		<u>28</u>
Net profit after tax		44
Proposed dividend		<u>20</u>
Retained profit		<u>24</u>

The first step is to calculate the net cash inflow from operating activities. Companies are required to show this calculation as a note attached to the statement in the published accounts.

	£000
Operating profit	74
Add back depreciation	20
Adjust for changes in working capital by comparing the two balance sheets	
(Increase) or decrease in stocks	(6)
(Increase) or decrease in debtors	(6)
Increase or (decrease) in creditors	<u>11</u>
Net cash inflow from operating activities	<u>93</u>

An increase in current assets (stocks and debtors) represents an outflow of cash and this reduces the cash inflow value. An increase in creditors represents a cashflow inflow as creditors are being used as a source of funds. From these workings the cashflow statement can then be prepared.

Cashflow statement for year ending 19x5		£000
Net cash inflow from operating activities		93(+)
Returns on investment and servicing of finance		
Interest paid	2	
Dividend paid (taken from previous year)	<u>15</u>	
		17(−)
Taxation (figure actually paid)		22(−)
Investing activities		
Freehold premises	35	
Equipment and furnishings	<u>42</u>	
		77(−)

Financing
   Issue of long-term loan   20(+)
Decrease in cash   3

The change in the cash figure should reconcile with the cash balances shown in the two balance sheets.

Balance at 31/12/x4	14,000
Balance at 31/12/x5	11,000
Decrease in cash	3,000

The cashflow statement has an important role to play as an internal control statement where it will be produced in the form of a forecast as regularly as is required. This is commonly on a monthly basis although weekly and even daily may be used. To illustrate the preparation of the cashflow the following information is to be used.

A hotel is to start trading on 1 July. The following is the forecast trading data and expenditure for the first four months from 1 July to 30 October.

Sales	£300,000
Pattern of sales	July 35%
	August 20%
	September 15%
	October 30%
Credit sales	80% of each months sales, payable in the following month
Cost of sales	50% of total sales, payable in the following month
Wages and staff costs	30% of total sales, payable in the month incurred
Fixed costs	
Salaries	£5,000 per month
Insurance	£10,000 for the year of which £2,500 is payable in July and £7,500 payable in October
Property tax	£5,000 payable in September
Depreciation	£1,250 per month
Interest	£6,000 paid in October
Other costs	£1,250 payable on a monthly basis
Opening balance at bank	£(10,000) negative.

The forecasted cashflow is shown below:

	July	August	September	October
Sales – cash	21,000	12,000	9,000	18,000
Sales – previous month	nil	84,000	48,000	36,000
Total inflow	21,000	96,000	57,000	54,000
Costs incurred				
Cost of sales	nil	52,500	30,000	22,500
Wages and staff	31,500	18,000	13,500	27,000

Salaries	5,000	5,000	5,000	5,000
Insurance	2,500			7,500
Property tax			5,000	
Interest				6,000
Other costs	1,250	1,250	1,250	1,250
Total outflow	40,250	76,750	54,750	69,250
Net flow	(19,250)	19,250	2,250	(15,250)
Opening balance	(10,000)	(29,250)	(10,000)	(7,750)
Closing balance	(29,250)	(10,000)	(7,750)	(23,000)

The profit for the period is £9,000. This can be reconciled to the cash balance by adding back the non-cash items, including depreciation and cost of sales, and deducting the credit sales.

A review of the above figures indicates that although the business is just profitable, there is a cashflow difficulty leading to an increasing overdraft and the cost of this overdraft has not been included in the figures.

The above example illustrates that it is possible to be profitable but still experience difficult trading conditions due to a lack of cash. As a result, for many businesses the forecasted cashflow is an essential tool for predicting the future success of the business.

LEGAL REQUIREMENTS

Most businesses are required to publish a set of financial statements. These should be presented in the standard format in order to meet the requirements of the Companies Act and the guidelines embodied in the Statements of Standard Accounting Practice. Consequently, most businesses are required to produce a balance sheet, a profit and loss account, a cashflow statement and also a directors' report, auditors' report and detailed notes to explain and expand upon the information presented.

The directors' report should contain information such as the level of dividends to be paid, the names and interests of the directors as well as information regarding the nature of the business and details of employee policies and development. There is also a number of additions to the information disclosed that is required by the Stock Exchange to enable a full listing to be given.

CONCLUSION

This chapter has introduced the basic principles of accounting practice to provide the reader with an insight into the underlying principles of financial statement preparation. The balance sheet provides a historical snapshot of the business at a given moment in time and, although this is useful for analysis purposes, it should be remembered that the business is never static. There are essential differences between the profit and loss account and the cashflow statement which must be clearly understood in order to use these statements effectively. The profit and loss account shows the profitability of the business over a given time period whereas the cashflow emphasizes liquidity. The way in which these statements are used is summarized in Table 3.3.

Table 3.3 Summary of the three financial statements

	Past	Present	Future
Profit and loss account	Published statement	Management accounts	Budgeted
Balance sheet	Published statement		Budgeted
Cashflow statement	FRS 1	Management accounts	Period basis

FURTHER READING

McLaney, E. (1994) *Business Finance for Decision Makers*. London: Pitman Publishing.
Mills, R. and Stiles, J. (1994) *Finance for the General Manager*. London: McGraw Hill.

PART 2
EXTERNAL ANALYSIS

INTRODUCTION

An informed view of environmental influences and competitive forces is an essential part of strategic planning. There are a number of techniques which can be used to assist in the process of environmental analysis including:

- PEST analysis
- Portfolio models
- Competition analysis.

An understanding of the environment enables the business to develop a strategy to meet the demands of the future environment. The first stage of a formal analysis is to examine the global macro-environment, sometimes referred to as PEST analysis. The aspects to be reviewed with this analysis are summarized below.

PEST	
Political	Political systems, laws and regulations, political stability and risk.
Economic	Rate of growth, pattern of consumption, rate of exchange, monetary and fiscal policy, interest rates, inflation, taxation levels and labour skills.
Social	Demographics, culture, social factors, education and nationalism.
Technological	Levels of innovation and application to a range of areas.

The chapters in this section consider how accounting information can be utilized to develop strategies to create sustainable competitive advantage. In order to do this a series of portfolio models, based on the work of Porter, are described to provide a range of tools for evaluating the competitive environment. The accounting role is critical for producing information on competitors that will help the business to select its own strategy. The comparison of competitors' relative costs and investments will provide valuable information which can be used in the setting of pricing strategies. Ward *et al.* (1992) asserts that the key to a cost comparison exercise lies in correctly predicting future levels of cost and not in the measurement of historic relationships. This will enable the business to establish whether competitors are setting prices at levels which are sustainable in the long term. It may be that competitors are setting prices below their true cost levels in order to dominate the market and drive out local competition before increasing selling prices to improve profitability. However, the competitive situation is far more serious if competitors have already achieved long-term cost reductions and are able to offer lower prices for similar products or services without eroding the profit level per unit. Consequently, there is certainly potential for the management accounting information system to assist in the provision of information that will help in the development of competitive strategies with the intent of pursuing competitive advantage, although evidence suggests that this is not widely understood in practice.

The following two chapters consider the importance of cost control and revenue maximization in the hospitality industry in the context of maintaining competitive advantage.

4

Managing costs

INTRODUCTION

The effective management of costs is a major challenge for any organization. The benefits are obvious in that a reduction in costs will lead to an increase in the profit to sales ratio and an improved return on capital employed. Yet for many hospitality organizations the need for cost controls is only highlighted when costs have already started spiralling out of control or when revenue levels are falling during periods of intense competition or recession. This chapter considers firstly how routine performance can be monitored and controlled, and then subsequently provides suggestions for a long-term approach to strategic cost reduction with the purpose of improving a business's opportunities for competitive advantage. The specific aspects to be covered are:

- The nature of costs
- Costs for decision-making
- Monitoring routine performance
- Investigating the cost base
- Cost leadership
- Competitive analysis
- Porter's approach to achieving competitive advantage.

THE NATURE OF COSTS

A common way of reviewing costs is to consider their behaviour in relation to revenue or volume. This is done by defining two basic cost types:

- Fixed costs
- Variable costs.

Fixed costs are those that remain unchanged in total over a given period of volume of activity whereas variable costs change proportionately with a change in the level of activity. In cost-per-unit terms this means that the cost per unit falls in terms of fixed costs as volume increases whereas the variable cost per unit remains the same regardless of volume. Classifying costs in this way provides a powerful tool for decision-making in that the *contribution*, which is the interim profit before fixed costs are deducted, can be used for a series of decision-making activities, as well as being the essential determinant of *breakeven point*. The key relationships are:

Sales revenue − Variable costs = Contribution

Contribution − Fixed costs = Profit

This can then be used with the relationship fixed costs divided by the contribution per unit to establish a breakeven point in units, that is the level of trading where neither a profit or a loss is made. For example:

Given the following information:

	Per unit £
Sales	10
Variable costs	4
Contribution	6
Fixed costs	60,000 in total

We can immediately see that the breakeven point must be 10,000 units because each unit provides a contribution of £6 towards the total fixed costs. The proof is:

Sales	10,000 × £10	100,000
Variable costs	10,000 × £4	40,000
Contribution	10,000 × £6	60,000
Fixed costs		60,000
Profit/(loss)		nil

A certain level of required profit can also be built into the equation. If an operation requires a level of profit of, say, £20,000, possibly to meet a return on equity considerations, then this figure can be used with the cost information to establish the required level of sales, as the following workings demonstrate.

$$\frac{\text{Required profit + fixed costs}}{\text{Contribution per unit}} = \text{Required volume of sales}$$

Using the previous data

$$\frac{20,000 + 60,000}{£6} = 13,333 \text{ units}$$

The reality for many hospitality organizations is that a combination of products is sold, each with its own cost structure and resulting contribution per unit. The overall contribution and resulting breakeven point then becomes dependent on the actual sales mix achieved, as the following example demonstrates.

The Cascade Hotel has prepared the following budget for the forthcoming year:

Total sales	£400,000	
Sales mix	Rooms	50%
	Food	30%
	Beverage	20%
Cost of sales	Food	40%
	Beverage	35%
Other variable costs	Rooms	£40,000
	Food	£45,000
	Beverage	£35,000
Fixed costs		£170,000

In this situation it is not possible to calculate the contribution per unit because each department will be selling numerous products, each with their own selling price and resulting contribution. Instead, we use the relationship between total sales and total contribution, which is known as the *C/S ratio*. To calculate the overall C/S ratio and the resulting breakeven point from the above data the following workings are required:

	Rooms	Food	Beverage	Total
Sales	200,000	120,000	80,000	400,000
Cost of sales	——	48,000	28,000	76,000
Gross profit	200,000	72,000	52,000	324,000
Variable costs	40,000	45,000	35,000	120,000
Contribution	160,000	27,000	17,000	204,000
Fixed costs				170,000
Net profit				34,000
C/S ratio	80%	22.5%	21.25%	51%

The resulting breakeven point is calculated using the fixed costs as follows:

$$\frac{170,000}{51\%} = £333,333 \text{ in sales}$$

If the sales mix were to change to:

Rooms	40%
Food	40%
Beverage	20%

then the resulting C/S ratio would change and a new breakeven point would need to be calculated. A simple approach to calculating the new weighted C/S ratio is by using the percentage points as follows:

	C/S ratio (%)	Sales mix (%)	Percentage points	
Rooms	80	40	32	(80 × 40%)
Food	22.5	40	9	(22.5 × 40%)
Beverage	21.25	20	4.25	(21.25 × 20%)

The new weighted C/S ratio is the sum of the percentage points: 45.25%.

The resulting breakeven point is:

$$\frac{170,000}{45.25\%} = £375,690.60 \text{ in sales}$$

This approach is known as *Cost-Volume-Profit* (CVP) analysis and provides a powerful tool for assessing the viability of a business. The difficulty often falls not in the analysis but in the initial classification of costs into those which are fixed and those which are variable in nature. However, there are a number of simple, as well as more sophisticated, statistical techniques available to assist in this exercise and the reader is recommended to review the additional reading.

The following example demonstrates the *High–Low* approach to cost analysis.

The following sample of costs and activity levels were recorded for a food servery.

	COVERS 1800	2400
	£	£
Labour	9,000	11,400
Food costs	12,600	16,800
Administration costs	6,000	6,000

Labour costs are analysed by dividing the difference between the costs:

$$\frac{11,400 - 9,000}{2,400 - 1,800}$$

$$= £4$$

This isolates the variable cost per unit. From this we can calculate the variable costs as being:

$$2,400 \times £4 = £9,600$$

and so the fixed costs must be:

$$11,400 - 9,600 = £1,800$$

Food costs are proven to be totally variable:

$$\frac{16,800 - 12,600}{2,400 - 1,800} = £7 \text{ per unit}$$

Administration costs are purely fixed costs.

The CVP approach can also be used to help explain why some businesses are more risky in nature than others. Consider the following CVP graphs in Figure 4.1.

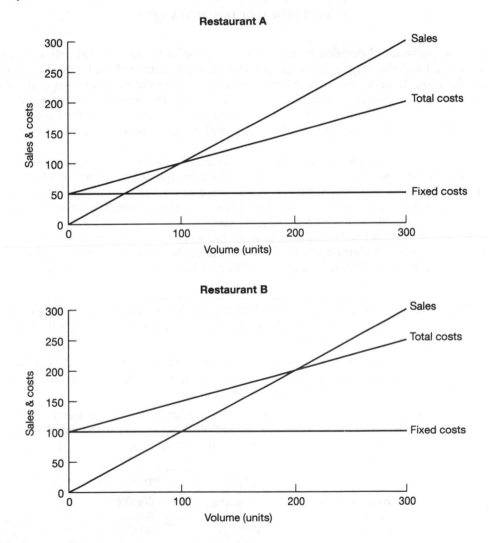

Figure 4.1 CVP graphs for restaurants A and B

Restaurant A illustrates an operation with lower fixed costs and hence a lower breakeven point. This means that lower sales are required to achieve a profit and if sales revenue falls the loss will be relatively small. Restaurant B illustrates a high fixed cost operation where the breakeven point is much higher, but once this has been achieved the resulting profitability will be much higher. The traditional approach to investment in the hospitality industry, that is direct equity investment, means that many operations have substantial fixed costs in terms of salary costs, property operation and maintenance costs and the servicing of finance. The high-risk nature of this type of investment has led to the growth of other forms of expansion, using techniques which serve to reduce risk, and these are discussed in further detail in Chapter 10.

COSTS FOR DECISION-MAKING

For the purposes of decision-making, it is often useful to consider the *relevant costs* associated with the project. These are costs which will be incurred as the result of taking the decision. In many cases the relevant costs are in fact the variable costs and these may be used in the decision-making process. In reality, the variable costs may only be used in the short term and in situations where spare capacity exists. In the long term it is likely that both fixed and variable costs will need to be considered as relevant costs.

In most decisions it is also necessary to consider the nature of the *opportunity cost*. This can be defined as the benefit foregone as a consequence of taking an alternative course of action. No cash exchanges hands; the cost results from foregoing an alternative which requires no transaction. These costs are often not clearly understood and are then left out of the decision-making process.

Finally, a *sunk cost* is defined as one which has already been incurred and cannot be recovered. It is considered to be irrelevant in the decision-making process and should be left out. In the following example the different types of cost are identified.

XYZ is a food manufacturer specializing in cook-chill meals. An unexpected order has been received for which labour and production-line capacity is available. The two main ingredients required are:

Ingredient A which is used regularly in the existing process and 1,000 kgs are required for this order. The existing stock holding is 1,500 kgs purchased at 85p per kg. The current replacement cost is 90p per kg.

Ingredient B is currently in stock with a stock holding of 500kg purchased at 60p per kg. This order requires 300 kg to be used. Without the order the entire stock would be either wasted or sold off as pig food at 30p per kg.

	Ingredient A	Ingredient B
Relevant cost	90p/kg	30p/kg
Sunk cost	85p/kg	60p/kg
Opportunity cost		30p/kg

MONITORING ROUTINE PERFORMANCE

This is most usually carried out as part of the budgetary control process, where variances are used to compare actual performance with budgeted values, and will be covered in more detail in Chapter 6. The essential requirement for effective budgetary control procedures is a system for analysing costs incurred in the organization. This normally means breaking the organization down into areas of responsibility known as budget centres or cost centres. Responsibility is then assigned to individuals for the management of the sales and costs in those areas. The three types of budget centre are:

- Cost centre
- Profit centre
- Investment centre.

Typically, an organization will comprise of *cost centres* where only servicing activities take place, such as marketing, personnel, and training and administration, and *profit centres* where trading activities take place. The performance of a profit centre is based on a comparison of revenues and costs. An *investment centre* is often the complete operation, where overall profitability can be compared with the investment. Variances are normally considered in terms of cost types such as materials, labour and expenses, and the comparison with the budget is normally made on the basis of the cost of the resource (price per unit) and the volume used in the process. The budgeted figures are based on standard costing procedures to forecast the spend at a given volume and the actual results are then compared with this. It may then be useful to prepare a flexible budget statement, which reflects actual volumes at standard or target cost, to provide a means of effective comparability with the actual results. This is illustrated in Chapter 6.

The system of flexing is certainly useful for monitoring performance but often the data required to produce the flexed statements is not available and variances in practice are often calculated simply by comparing original forecasts with the actual performance.

INVESTIGATING THE COST BASE

Costs which provide the greatest scope for improvement are often the indirect or overhead costs which are most often fixed in nature. These are often the greater proportion of costs in any case and deserve further attention. It is often assumed that because they are fixed in nature they cannot be effectively controlled or reduced. In practice, other costs, which are directly attributable to revenue levels, are much harder to reduce without reducing the quality of the product or service, although considerable management time is spent in tracking them. To reduce variable costs effectively a long-term view of the production process is required (see pp. 56–58).

The nature of overhead costs can be investigated using techniques such as *zero-based budgeting* (ZBB), a technique which has its origins in the public sector. This technique requires the relevance of all costs to be questioned during the budgeting process, rather than relying on an incremental approach where last year's performance is the starting point for setting this year's budget. It is described in more detail in Chapter 6 with its relevance to the hospitality industry. ZBB can produce substantial benefits but it is a time-consuming activity and requires considerable expertise on the part of the operational manager to be used effectively.

An approach which has attracted considerable attention in recent years, particularly in the manufacturing sector, is that of *activity-based costing* (ABC).

Activity-based costing

This approach focuses on indirect costs and attempts to establish links between expenditure and the activities carried out by the organization. It contrasts with the traditional approach of allocating overheads arbitrarily to departments on the basis of revenue, floor space, head count or any other base deemed to be appropriate. ABC has its origins in the manufacturing sector but is now being more widely applied in many different types of organization. The process requires the identification of the key activities which take place in the organization and establishing a cost centre for each of those activities. The next step is to determine what is known as the *cost driver* for that activity. That is the events which can be described as the significant determinant of the cost of the activity. Finally, a unit cost should be derived for each activity and these are assigned to each product on the basis of the demand for the activity.

This is probably better understood if it can be applied to a practical situation. In the case of a hotel, some of the major activities that are performed include receiving reservations, checking in, room servicing, billing and checking out. Examples of cost drivers that might be appropriate to these activities include: number of reservations received, number of guests arriving at the front desk, number of guests in-house, and the number of point of sales transactions.

The next stage is to divide the cost by the total number of driver units in order to calculate the cost per unit of activity. Finally, the cost of activities is traced to products, according to a product demand for activities, by multiplying unit activity costs by the quantity of each activity that a product consumes. Hence the process attempts to measure as accurately as possible the *total* actual cost of each activity in the organization rather than focusing specifically on direct or variable costs.

COST LEADERSHIP

For companies competing on price, it is important to achieve cost leadership as it enables the operation to gain increased market share by providing the best value for money to the customer. It also enables the operation to strengthen its position of competitive advantage by utilizing the higher financial returns to improve quality, customer service and product innovation. Cost leadership means that a business seeks to achieve the status of being the lowest cost supplier to the market. This does not mean that the business is the lowest priced supplier, but that there is the potential to reduce prices during periods of intense competition. Michael Porter has written extensively on this theme and says that:

its cost position gives the firm a defence against rivalry from competitors, because it can still earn returns after its competitors have competed away their profits through rivalry. (Porter, 1980)

Porter argues that there are only two alternative routes to competitive advantage – cost leadership or differentiation – and that there is little advantage in being the industry average competitor pursuing a 'stuck in the middle position'. The alternative competitive positions are illustrated clearly in Figure 4.2.

Lowest cost competitor	Industry average competitor	Highest price competitor
Cost leadership	Stuck in the middle	Differentiator

Figure 4.2   Alternative competitive positions

Other writers argue that such a polarized approach is a dangerous strategy to pursue and that practice suggests that it is possible to be both cheaper and better. However, focus strategies can assist a business in determining its competitive position and assist in planning a route forward.

The pursuit of cost leadership can also be achieved through economies of scale and establishing experience cost curve advantages. The nature of the experience curve is illustrated in Figure 4.3.

The assumption is that the cost benefit is derived from the length of time the business has been operating and is related to the product life cycle. In Figure 4.3 the business experiences lower cost per unit derived from experience and economies of scale based on higher volumes. However, the basis of this theory can be immediately eroded by the introduction of new technology which may provide immediate cost advantages to a new business entering the arena. Achieving long-term cost leadership requires a strategic

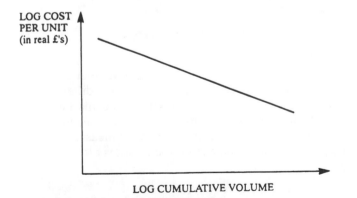

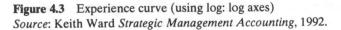

Figure 4.3   Experience curve (using log: log axes)
Source: Keith Ward *Strategic Management Accounting*, 1992.

approach in that the long-term nature of costs needs to be considered. Short-term measures for cost reduction, such as operational cuts in staffing levels, material costs and operating costs, normally cannot be sustained and inevitably lead to a drop in product and service quality. Instead, a long-term approach is needed, based on a 'spend to save' policy.

The key areas for investigation are centred around the components of the *value chain* as defined by Porter (1980). These are discussed in detail on p. 61. Conventional approaches to cost analysis tend to be based on an historical analysis of costs, focusing on a single accounting period at a time. The approach tends to be introspective, operations-based and reactive to short-term crises. A strategic approach has a wider focus and is forward-looking, analysing costs as they change throughout the product life cycle. The aim should be to consider the external environment, that is the competition, in addition to internal factors, and to be proactive in analysing information.

A limited approach to cost management often occurs because the responsibility for cost-cutting usually lies solely with operating managers rather than being part of the strategic planning process. Frequently, costs are only managed during crisis situations and many important costs are ignored. All too often employees hold negative perceptions of the cost-cutting activity and personal relationships and emotions stand in the way of objective action. As a consequence, exercises in cost reduction are neither followed up nor maintained, while the wrong costs are often cut first because they are the easiest to eliminate.

To summarize, the obstacles most likely to prevent costs being managed in a strategic way are:

● Top management attitudes
● The dominance of return on investment as a measure of performance, preventing further investment spend
● The failure to recognize the importance of spending to save.

The key sources of cost reduction as applied to the value chain are to be found in investing in new plant and equipment, the application of new technology and realizing the benefits to be derived from economies of scale and organizational learning based on experience.

COMPETITIVE ANALYSIS

The process of competitive analysis includes assessing a number of key characteristics for a business. These include the external attractiveness of the different products and/or market opportunities measured, using the growth in the market in total and the competitive position of the individual business in terms of current market share and relative cost levels. These characteristics are often hard to measure in practice although a profiling approach, which is based on a matrix analysis, is often used.

Market development

The nature of competitive strategy is very much influenced by the stage of development of the product in the market place. The stages are defined as:

- Stage 1 – Product launch
- Stage 2 – Sales growth
- Stage 3 – Competitive shake-out
- Stage 4 – Maturity
- Stage 5 – Decline

Techniques for analysing how each stage might be identified were discussed in Chapter 2.

During the launch stage, competitive advantage is established by virtue of the fact that a new product and/or service has been launched in the market place ahead of the potential competition. The focus for competitor analysis at this stage will be on the relative levels of development and launch costs. However, this type of information is often difficult to obtain.

As the industry moves into the rapid growth stage, the key factor becomes the growth in market share and the focus switches to monitoring marketing expenditure. This information is more readily available in that the level of marketing activity is easily visible and it is therefore more simple to evaluate.

Once the product has reached the mature stage, the basis of competition analysis is frequently the selling price and the key success factor in obtaining competitive advantage is in the effective management of costs to ensure that in a highly price-sensitive market profit levels are maintained. This exercise is obviously vital to many business operations in order to sustain competitive advantage throughout the maturity stage which, in practice, is proportionately considerably longer than the other stages of the product life cycle.

The competitor analysis should not be simply limited to relative cost comparisons however. Relative selling prices and customer perceptions should also be monitored. Products or services which are perceived to a higher value in the eyes of the customer do not need a lower cost base because the premium selling price compensates the resulting profit levels. Therefore, relative cost comparison exercises should start from an appreciation of the strategic product positioning that the competitor is seeking to achieve.

Sources of competitive information

The problem of achieving effective competitor analysis lies in obtaining good, reliable and meaningful information. It is not always necessary to obtain absolute values. Quite often relative financial data, that is data relative to one's own business, is sufficient. The management accountants within the business should be sufficiently experienced to be able to apply their own knowledge of cost structures to develop data drawn from the competition. The overall aim is to build up a comprehensive database about the competition that is continually being updated. The information contained within the database can be drawn from a number of sources without in any way resorting to unethical forms of industrial espionage. A varied range of sources are listed in Table 4.1.

PORTER'S APPROACH TO ACHIEVING COMPETITIVE ADVANTAGE

Michael Porter (1985) offers a three-step approach to achieving competitive advantage.

These are:

- Analysis of industry structure
- Choosing a competitive strategy
- Implementation of strategy.

These will now be considered in more detail.

Analysis of industry structure

The structure of the industry is determined by the pressure from five competing forces acting upon the business. These are:

- The threat from new entrants
- The bargaining power of suppliers
- The bargaining power of buyers
- The threat of substitutes
- Rivalry between existing competitors.

This can be illustrated diagrammatically, as shown in Figure 4.4. Each force will now be analysed in detail.

The threat from new entrants

The threat of entry by new competitors is often influenced by the economies of scale, brand loyalty and cost advantages already being achieved by the existing players in the

Table 4.1 Sources of competitor information

Library research	Annual reports
	Press/journal material
	Investment analysts' reports
	Government reports
	Published market intelligence
	Company literature
	Company history
	Academic case studies
	Computer-based information service
	Competitor advertising
Interviews	Journalists
	Academics
	Others with specialist knowledge
Direct contact	Visits to other establishments
	Physical observation
	Physical analysis of product
Conferences	Industry associations
Primary market research	Consumer surveys
	Industrial market research
Soft information	Own staff and management
	Mutual suppliers
	Mutual customers

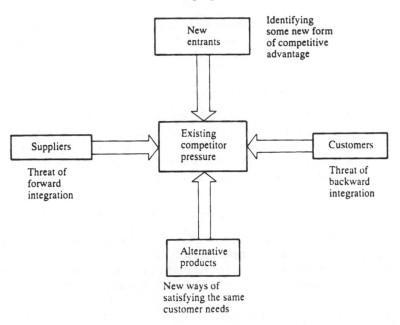

Figure 4.4 Current and potential competitor analysis (using the Porter model as a basis)
Source: Keith Ward *Strategic Management Accounting*, 1992.

market, along with the capital required for entry. This force can have significant effect in the hospitality industry where all of these conditions can apply.

An entry barrier is anything which represents a significant economic disincentive for a business to invest in a particular industry. In the hospitality industry it is often the size of the investment that is required to set up the business that acts as a significant barrier to possible new entrants. The cost structure may also serve as a barrier, particularly when fixed costs are high and higher volumes are required to achieve profitability. Finally, another commonly used barrier is through the use of heavily marketed brands to try to create customer loyalty.

The power of suppliers

The power of the suppliers is derived from the availability of resources and may have more significant effect for, say, operations setting up in developing economies. The conditions which make suppliers more powerful include those situations where there are no substitute products available for the buyer to switch to or the cost of switching supplier is too high to be viable.

The power of buyers

The power of buyers is derived from the level of supply and demand and the homogeneity between product suppliers. The power that buyers can exert is increased when a number of buyers unite or when a number of suppliers exist and costs are incurred in switching supplier. The threat from buyers is also increased when there is a real risk that the buyer will consider backward integration, that is expanding by buying out a supplier in an attempt to achieve satisfactory prices and quality.

The threat of substitute products

To identify the level of threat from substitute products it is necessary to identify those products and services which perform the same function. Often these products are situated in industries which seem quite remote from the industry in question. For example, within the leisure industry there is a whole range of leisure activities, each vying for a limited customer leisure time and spend.

Rivalry between existing competitors

Rivalry among existing firms can occur in a number of ways which can include price competition, new products and increased levels of customer service. The degree of rivalry depends on a number of features related to industry structure. Numerous or equally competitive businesses may cause instability by attempting to make strategic moves while hoping to remain unnoticed. Where there is low market growth the level of competition can intensify as businesses attempt to expand by capturing market share from other businesses. This intensifies still further where there is little opportunity for product differentiation. High levels of competition often means that profitability is eroded but high exit barriers can prevent firms from moving into other more profitable areas.

Exit barriers arise when the business is supported by high-cost dedicated assets which have limited alternative uses, such as hotels. Exit costs might also include redundancy settlements and wasted material costs.

The level of rivalry is also dependent on the market position and is most intense during the mature stage of the product life cycle. It results in a condition called shake-out, that is when the less profitable operations are forced to retire.

Consequently, the higher the pressure from the five forces, the less attractive the industry, as profit levels are constantly being reduced and it is increasingly difficult to maintain market position.

Choosing a competitive strategy

The next stage in Porter's approach to achieving competitive advantage is to decide upon a competitive strategy. Porter suggests that there are only two generic competitive positions – cost leadership or product differentiation. *Cost leadership* involves achieving competitive advantage through overall lowest cost compared to competing firms. *Differentiation* involves identifying those product or service characteristics which customers perceive as valuable and meeting those needs better than any of the competition. As a result, a premium charge can be made.

Implementation of strategy

The final stage of Porter's model is the implementation of the strategy. Porter has produced what is known as the *value chain* model to illustrate how this final stage can

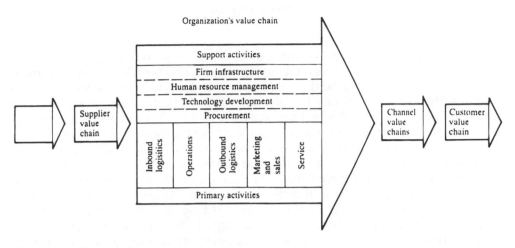

Figure 4.5 Value chains
Source: Michael Porter *Competitive Advantage*, 1985.

be achieved. The value chain comprises a grouping of the primary and secondary activities of the organization that improve the product or service (or both) provided to the customer. This is illustrated in Figure 4.5.

A business can be described as having a collection of activities that are performed to design, produce, market, deliver and support its product. The way in which an organization does this is a reflection of the organization's history, structure, past strategies and the nature of the activities themselves. It may be useful to illustrate how the chain might apply to a hotel operation.

Inbound logistics. These are the activities concerned with receiving, storing and distributing the input resources in the system. Practical examples include bookings received from customers using a variety of reservation capture methods.

Operations. This stage converts the inputs into the final products and/or services of the organization, that is the management of the whole experience which converts needy customers into satisfied customers.

Outbound logistics. This stage is concerned with the collection, storage and distribution of products and services to the customers, that is the service distribution points such as room service, restaurants etc.

Marketing and sales. These are activities designed to attract further purchases during the period of the customer stay.

Service. These activities ensure that customers enjoy their purchased goods and services which are associated with customer care and after-sales service.

Porter's approach has been designed with the intention of providing a framework for classifying the various areas of the organization in order to understand how the various activities interrelate and contribute to the firm's competitive position. The aim is to understand what resources exist in the organization and how they might be used more effectively.

CONCLUSION

The management of costs is an essential part of any business and should be carried out throughout the life of the business and not just in times of crisis. The routine control of costs can effectively be achieved through the use of budgetary control systems based on assigning areas of responsibility to individuals and monitoring the variances which occur between expected and actual performance. In the long term a strategic view of cost management is required which may mean moving away from the traditional approaches to cost monitoring. A strategic view means that all levels of managers in the organization should be reviewing the cost base and should be seeking ways of achieving long-term cost savings which are sustainable. This may mean incurring expenditure in order to save in the long term, thereby insuring that the organization can achieve competitive advantage through control of the cost base. Monitoring the competition can provide a wealth of information to assist an organization in establishing its position in the market place. A formal approach to mapping the competitive environment is illustrated below.

Techniques for monitoring the competitive environment

It is not necessary to monitor every competitor in the market place and indeed it is highly unlikely that this would be achievable. Instead, monitoring just a handful of competitor operations can provide useful information about the competitive position of a business. Data based on sales can be analysed in the following manner.

	Sales £000s	Market share (%)	Relative market share (%)
Firm A			
Year 1	700	19.4	
Year 2	1,000	20.4	
Year 3	1,200	20.8	
Firm B			
Year 1	1,400	38.9	2.0
Year 2	2,200	44.9	2.2
Year 3	1,200	50.0	2.4
Firm C			
Year 1	1,000	27.8	1.4
Year 2	1,200	24.5	1.2
Year 3	2,000	23.6	1.1

Firm D			
Year 1	500	13.9	0.7
Year 2	500	10.2	0.5
Year 3	400	5.6	0.3
Total			
Year 1	3,600	100.0	
Year 2	4,900	100.0	
Year 3	7,200	100.0	

Relative market share is calculated by dividing each competitor's market share percentage by that for Firm A.

The main points which arise from this analysis are:

(i) Firm A's sales are increasing from year to year by 42.9% in Year 2 and by 50% in Year 3.
(ii) Firm B is maintaining its proportion of the market.
(iii) Firm B is achieving higher market growth by capturing market share from Firms C and D.

Therefore, Firm A needs to ensure that its own market share is not likely to be eroded by the strategy pursued by Firm B. It may well then be possible to characterize Firm B's strategy in terms of Porter's cost reduction focus or differentiation focus strategies. Firm A needs to ensure that it is not stuck in the middle. Consequently, such an analysis yields very useful information for Firm A without requiring the entire market to be defined and analysed.

REFERENCES

Harris, P. and Hazzard, P. (1992) *Managerial Accounting in the Hospitality Industry*, Cheltenham: Stanley Thornes.

Partridge, M. and Perren, L. (1993) Achieving competitive advantage, *Management Accounting*, November.

Pearson, G. (1990) *Strategic Thinking*, London: Prentice-Hall.

Porter, M.E. (1980) *Competitive Strategy: Techniques for Analysing Industries and Competitors*, New York: Free Press.

Porter, M.E. (1985) *Competitive Advantage*, New York: Free Press.

Ward, K. (1992) *Strategic Management Accounting*, Oxford: Butterworth Heinemann.

Ward, K., Hewson, W. and Srikanthan, S. (1992) Accounting for the competition, *Management Accounting*, February.

5

Managing pricing strategies

INTRODUCTION

This chapter reviews the various pricing methodologies available to the hospitality industry for the pricing of accommodation, food, beverages and other activities. The review of accommodation pricing techniques considers formulistic approaches to pricing, such as the 'rule of thumb' method and the Hubbart formula, and then reviews in detail the demand-driven approaches such as Yield Management. Food and beverage pricing is considered with specific reference to sales mix and approaches to menu analysis for maximizing gross profit in percentage and cash terms. In theory, price setting appears to be a simple task, but in reality the pricing process is complicated by market, economic and psychological influences and, as a result, the pricing decision requires input from financial, marketing and operational managers in order to ensure that the resulting pricing policy is based on the correct information. The principle aim of any pricing policy should be to increase revenue without sacrificing volume, while increasing profitability and ensuring long-term business value. It should also aim to change customer buying behaviour by responding to influences from the competitive environment.

COST-BASED APPROACH TO PRICING

The principle aim of an effective pricing policy is to ensure that the profit per product is maximized while maintaining a perception of value for money in the eyes of the customer. Despite this aim, the traditional approach to pricing tends to be based on cost plus techniques where a mark-up is added to the cost of producing the product. The cost of the product can range from simply analysing the food cost, in the case of menu pricing, through to attempting to achieve a total cost per product. However, this level of detail is reliant on adequate information being available to enable fixed or indirect costs to be allocated to individual products in a satisfactory manner, which can be difficult in practice particularly where there are several products being provided.

When the pricing policy is based solely on direct costs or on material costs, the difference between the selling price and those costs must be sufficient to cover all other costs and provide an adequate level of profit. The following example illustrates a mark-up policy of 200 per cent on cost in a restaurant.

A restaurant produces one dish which is made from food costs to the value of £3. The restaurant has forecasted to sell 10,000 of these dishes over a set period with forecasted variables at 25% of sales and fixed costs of £12,000.

Selling price	=	£3 plus 200%
	=	£9

Therefore

Sales	=	£90,000
Food cost	=	£30,000
Variable costs	=	£22,500
Fixed costs	=	£12,000
Net profit	=	£25,500

The profit required to meet investors' target returns is often used as the basis for establishing the total revenue for an operation where costs can clearly be predicted. The required profit is added to the estimated cost figures to produce a value for total sales. This figure is used with volume forecasts and sales mix predictions to arrive at selling prices for individual products and services.

PRICE SETTING

The economic theory of supply and demand argues that as an item becomes more scarce its price should increase and that there is a direct relationship between price and demand. In the hospitality industry this simple relationship is complicated by the seasonality of the business, giving rise to differing demand patterns and the multiple number of products available in a restaurant, for example, where sales are inter-related.

The hospitality industry also differs from the manufacturing industry in terms of the product. Although products may be very similar, no two establishments offer the exact same product. There will always be some difference in terms of the product itself and the nature and quality of service. This factor means that it is difficult for operators to use the competition prices as a guideline but it does also give the operator far greater scope for achieving product, and therefore price, differentiation.

One approach might be deliberately to charge more than the competitors and use product differentiation to justify the higher price. However, the cost of raising quality should be considered in relation to the increase in selling price, and continual monitoring is required to ensure that the customer still perceives the product to be good value.

Alternatively, an operation may choose to price the product at a level below the competition. This tactic can be dangerous in that unless real cost savings can be made without undermining quality, the profit per product will drop without a sufficient corresponding increase in sales volume. This in turn may lead to a price-war situation with a downward spiral of price-cutting which leads to profit reduction for all operators and even the possibility of bankruptcy. Although the economic principle of supply and demand and price elasticity apply to the hospitality industry, generally a fully booked restaurant does not increase its prices on a Saturday night when it is fully booked, preferring instead to turn customers away.

The accepted pricing practice is to set the published prices at the maximum and then, particularly in the case of rooms, to discount prices to maximize utilization during the poor trading periods.

ACCOMMODATION PRICING

Managing the room resource in hotel operations requires achieving a careful balance between maintaining room rates and achieving maximum occupancy where a relatively small increase in room rates may be worth a drop in occupancy in terms of profitability. However, room occupancy percentage remains the critical determinant of success for many operators, particularly where substantial sales can be generated in other trading areas within the hotel.

Hotel occupancy levels are commonly viewed to be directly related to the size of the hotel, average room rates, conference facilities, hotel ownership and location. Severe discounting may serve to maintain volumes in a period of recession, but it can also have a dramatic downward effect on profitability and the cashflow levels of the operation.

Hoteliers throughout Europe have faced difficult trading conditions throughout the early 1990s, with falling average room rates and occupancy volumes. To compensate for this it is natural that management attention should turn to cost-cutting and improving cost controls in order to maintain profitability. Staff costs are often the first to be cut. As a result, even during the poorest trading years of the early 1990s some hoteliers managed a small increase in operating profit.

There are various approaches to setting the room rate, ranging from those which are simply formulistic to those that require an extensive analysis of target profit levels and costs. These will be discussed in detail below. However, a successful approach to rooms pricing requires an accurate knowledge of the markets to which the product is attractive and a clear knowledge of price elasticity patterns. The Yield Management (YM) approach to pricing does just this and, with the widespread use of computerized reservation systems, is now being more widely used. As a result, a detailed discussion of this approach will follow later in the chapter. But first, the following discussion considers the alternative approaches that are practised for setting room rates.

Rule of thumb method

In an operation where the majority of income is derived from room letting, one approach is to base the average room rate calculation on the capital cost for building one room. It should be reasonable to assume that there should be a fairly direct relationship between the cost of the building and the room rate to be charged. The rule of thumb states that £1 of room rate should be charged for each £1,000 invested in building the room. If a room costs £100,000 in capital costs to build, the average net room rate is calculated to be £100. This relationship is based on the assumption that the hotel is fairly large (several hundred bedrooms), has other departments such as food and beverage, and that the operation will achieve 65–70 per cent average room occupancy.

This approach is used as a very general guide only and can lead to incorrect pricing strategies where the emphasis is purely on historical costs.

Profit-based pricing techniques

This approach is sometimes referred to as the 'bottom-up' approach to pricing or the 'Hubbart formula' and was originally developed for the American Hotel and Motel Association. This method is based on accurate forecasts for operating costs and for room occupancy. The sales figure is calculated by adding the target profit to the fixed and variable costs. The total figure is then subdivided to arrive at different rates for different room types. The following example demonstrates the method in practice.

Forecasted projections for a 100-bedroom hotel operation are given below.

Investment details

	£
Fixed assets	500,000
Working capital	50,000
Total net assets	550,000
Financed by:	
Owners equity	200,000
10% mortgage debenture payable 199x	350,000
	550,000

Trading forecasts   – average of 65% occupancy
           – forecasted profits for other departments £40,000
           – owners require a 20% return on equity invested.

	£
Net profit required (based on after-tax target percentage return on equity)	40,000
Corporation tax (at 25% of profit before tax)	13,333
Profit before tax	53,333
Interest (relating to mortgage debenture)	35,000

Depreciation	50,000
(10% straight-line method on fixed assets)	
Insurance and licence	20,000
(forecasted)	
Property operation	120,000
(forecasted)	
Administration	55,000
(forecasted)	
Management salaries	120,000
Less profit from other departments	(40,000)
(forecasted)	
Operating expenses for accommodation	145,225
(forecasted at 26% of revenue)	
Accommodation revenue required	558,558

Forecasted rooms sold annually

The forecasted room occupancy percentage should be an accurate forecast for the likely number of rooms sold, based on current achievable levels in similar operations. An accurate forecast will improve the reliability of the rate-setting calculation.

$$100 \text{ rooms} \times 365 \text{ nights} \times 60\% \text{ occupancy} = 21,900$$

$$\text{Average room rate required} = \frac{558,558}{21,900}$$

$$= \text{£}25.50$$

The rate calculated from this approach is simply the average room rate before VAT. From this, rates for room types and market segments will need to be calculated.

Setting the room rate

Single and double rates can be calculated by considering historical double and single occupancy rates. Using the data generated in the example given above, if twin occupancy is 60 per cent of rooms sold and single occupancy is then 40 per cent and a 20 per cent difference is required between twin and single rates, the calculation would be:

(60% × 60% × 100 rooms × 365 × 1.2R) +
(40% × 60% × 100 × 365 × R) = 558,558

where R represents the single rate. This solves to:

15,768R + 8,760R = 558,558

$$R = \frac{558,558}{24,528}$$

= 22.77

The double rate will be £27.32.

This type of algebraic formula could be expanded to include other room types and market segments as long as the occupancies for each type of room could be forecasted.

Room pricing options

The simplest approach would be to offer all rooms at one rate. The advantage of this approach is that it is easy to administer and to communicate to customers. However, the approach fails to respond to peaks and troughs in demand by recognizing customer price sensitivity and, as a result, fails to maximize revenue.

Alternatively, room rates can be set by room type, depending on the room characteristics. This approach is also fairly simple to administer but is useless where all rooms are uniform. Even if the hotel has different room types it is still limited by the stock of each of those room types and consequently the approach becomes product-led rather than market-led.

Another approach is to use price segmentation, that is to introduce logical restrictions on the booking in return for a discounted rate. This allows customers to have access to lower rates in return for reduced flexibility, and differentiates those who are willing and able to pay higher prices from those who are willing to change their behaviour in exchange for a lower price. Such an approach enables the hotel to penetrate new markets without encouraging existing business to trade down. It is more difficult to manage than the other approaches and requires the support of a rooms management package such as a Yield Management system.

ACCOMMODATION MARKETS

The transient hotel market, excluding groups, may be crudely classified into two – leisure and business – and each market has its own booking pattern characteristics.

Leisure travellers
- Advance bookings
- Quality required varies
- Destination flexible
- Highly price sensitive
- Stay longer

Business travellers
- Short booking lead times
- Tend to require high quality
- Destination predetermined
- Relatively less price sensitive
- Short-term stay avoiding weekends

Hotel pricing strategies should take advantage of these differing market characteristics by attempting to expand the price elastic markets while ensuring that inelastic business revenues are maintained. Practically, this means managing the hotel's capacity to ensure that an appropriate number of rooms is left available at high rates to accommodate the late booking business market. The industry has long been at ease with charging different rates to different markets and although business customers may feel that they are subsidizing the holiday market, any rate that exceeds the variable cost of providing the product ensures a contribution towards fixed costs.

The strategy of matching rates to customer behaviour has been less well received, particularly where customers who pay one rate later realize that they could have negotiated a cheaper rate. Obviously, the key to success with this strategy is to ensure that the rules are clearly structured and logical. This approach to pricing is likely to become more popular, particularly where the increased use of technology means that customer markets can be defined by the guest arrival and departure patterns rather than by status.

ROOM RATE DISCOUNTING

Discounting is a widespread practice in the hotel industry and is particularly suited to a product based on minimal variable costs and substantial fixed costs. Providing that a room is sold at a price in excess of variable costs, some contribution to fixed costs will be made. This knowledge has led to an almost unchecked approach to room rate discounting by some operators. Often there is no methodology at all to determining how discounts are to be offered and the customer is forced to enter into a haggling procedure in order to achieve the best rate. Rate-cutting can generate more revenues but this is not always transferred to the bottom line when operating profit per occupied room is falling due to expenses increasing at the rate of inflation.

The technique Yield Management provides a formal approach to room discounting which focuses on price and market segment using technology to develop a room pricing policy. More recently, this technique has become known by the term 'revenue maximization'.

YIELD MANAGEMENT

The process of Yield Management (YM) involves controlling the rooms inventory to maximize sales by adjusting room rates in response to the level of rooms booked for a future arrival date. Most hoteliers are well practised at lowering prices to stimulate sales when demand is low, but generally the process of discounting is not supported by any clear methodology. This can result in disgruntled customers and lower revenues. The practice of YM broadens the scope of the price-setting process by focusing on the rooms available and rooms pricing.

The concept of a method for maximizing occupancy and revenue is not new. The airline industry has used the technique for many years with a great deal of success. When airlines cannot fill all of the seats on an aircraft with full-fare customers, they try to fill them with customers paying discounted rates. An empty seat represents a lost opportunity, owing to the perishable nature of the product. The airline must decide how many fares to discount while making sure it has enough seats left to sell to late-booking full-fare-paying customers in order to maximize the possible revenue. Consequently, YM techniques have been essential for managing a fixed capacity efficiently.

Comparisons can easily be drawn between the management of airline seats and hotel rooms, where fixed capacity also exists and the products are sold in segmented markets with variable levels of demand and often well in advance of the consumption date. The cost structures of the two industries are also similar in that they are both capital intensive with high fixed costs, while the marginal cost of selling one more airline seat or one more hotel room is minimal. Yet despite the similarities in the two industries, the hotel industry has been slow to accept the advantages that YM can offer, although evidence now suggests that more and more operators are examining the potential of the technique.

Calculating room yield

The two main factors that managers use to measure performance in room revenues are occupancy and average room rate. Both of these should be maximized to ensure that the full potential rooms revenue is achieved. The yield is an integrated statistic based on actual potential revenue and is calculated using the following example.

Hotel A has 100 rooms and a rack rate of £100. The following sales mix represents the pattern of business for one night.

Rack rate	25% at £100
Corporate rate	15% at £80
Walk-in trade	3% at £50
Travel agency	3% at £45
Groups	10% at £30

This results in total revenue of £4,285, an occupancy of 56 rooms or 56% and rate per available room of £42.85. The 'yield statistic' is expressed as follows:

$$\text{Yield} = \frac{\text{Realized revenue}}{\text{Potential revenue}}$$

Potential revenue is the maximum sales that could be obtained if all the available rooms are sold at full rack rate; realized revenue is the actual sales generated.

The yield statistic for the previous example would be:

$$\frac{£4,285}{100 \text{ rooms} \times £100} = 42.85\%$$

In terms of room sales, many combinations of occupancy and achieved room rates could generate equal revenue and yield percentages, as the following figures for Hotel A illustrate:

Average room rate	Occupancy (%)	Realized revenue (£)	Yield (%)
100	42.85	4,285	42.85
90	47.61	4,285	42.85
80	53.56	4,285	42.85
70	61.21	4,285	42.85
60	71.42	4,285	42.85
50	85.70	4,285	42.85

The yield statistic can also be expressed as a combination of occupancy percentage and average room rate. It can be calculated by multiplying the average rate ratio by the actual room occupancy percentage where the average rate ratio is calculated by expressing the average rate as a percentage of the average maximum potential rate. Given the data in the example above:

$$53.56\% \text{ occupancy} \times \frac{80}{100} = 42.85\% \text{ yield}$$

This simple statistic provides a single value for measuring a hotel's performance and forms the basis of YM. The purpose of the approach is to maximize room yield by managing both the room rate and the occupancy percentage so that when demand exceeds supply the customer pays more and when demand is low the price is discounted, while ensuring each customer pays the maximum possible price.

Critics of YM have identified the fact that not all these combinations of occupancy and rate (as illustrated in the above example) produce the same level of profitability. By introducing the marginal cost of servicing a room, of say £10 per room, the hotel contribution to fixed costs can be calculated.

Occupancy (%)	Realized revenue	Servicing cost	Contribution
42.85	4,285	429	3,856
47.61	4,285	476	3,809
53.56	4,285	536	3,749
61.21	4,285	612	3,673
71.42	4,285	714	3,571
85.70	4,285	857	3,428

The rooms contribution can be seen to fall as occupancy increases and rates fall. However, the effect of the fall in rooms contribution arising from discounted room prices may well be outweighed by the resulting increase in food and beverage revenue derived from increased volumes.

Yield Management system requirements

In order to use the system effectively, it is essential to have a clear understanding of the markets in which the business operates. This will be achieved by analysing historical data in terms of the patterns of demand, the market segments and price elasticity. Demand analysis is essentially based on clearly defining the product and differentiating the main market segments in order to identify the levels of demand from each market segment at different times of the year, thereby predicting the number of rooms needed to meet each segment's needs.

Specifically, the system must contain information relating to customer booking patterns and behaviour, and the timing of demand in each market segment. This will need to be supported with data relating to the policy and volumes of overbooking and a clear knowledge of the impact of price changes on demand patterns and occupancy. Producing this level of information is a task of enormous complexity but expert system packages can be used to aid the process. These are software packages containing a 'knowledge base' which allows the system to approach and solve problems by interpreting the 'facts' based on decision rules written into the software.

Problems specific to hotels

In certain circumstances YM practices that have been translated directly from the airline industry may fail to adjust to the complexities offered by the hospitality industry. The key problem arises when a guest, having stayed one night, decides to extend the stay for one or more nights. If the first night's stay is determined to be a low demand, low-rate reservation problems will arise if the ensuing nights of stay are during high demand periods. Similar problems arise when a customer wishes to stay through a period of both low and high demand. The solution in this case might be to offer an average of the high and low rates generated.

Resistance to change

In practice, there are still a limited number of operators making the maximum possible use of YM systems. Research by Jones and Hamilton (1992) identified two major problems in the usage of the technique. First, there is a tendency for the complexity of the system to overwhelm the user so that the concept of the system is never clearly understood and, as a result, the human interface with the system is often ignored. The key to success is in ensuring that everyone in the organization understands what the process is about (including both managers and operators). This can be done by simplifying the jargon which is often associated with running the system.

Secondly, the effective use of the system depends on the accuracy of the forecasted data and although technology can effectively plot the historical trends, the final forecasts should also be reviewed by the management team to ensure that the forward projections for demand are as accurate as possible. Existing reward systems that are based on sales volume, occupancy and average room rate may be inappropriate. Instead, it may be possible to introduce rewards to those personnel who implement the new techniques and suggest improvements for the operational use of the system. This may serve to overcome the potential for employee demotivation arising from the perception that the reservation or sales task has been deskilled.

Customer perceptions

The airline industry has successfully used differential rates for many years and customers appear to be used to the fact that they are charged different rates for the same flight. However, the issue of fairness can affect the maximization of profits. Generally, customers feel that price rises are fair when costs increase and the price rise has been incurred in order to maintain profits and not to increase them. In order to convince customers of the fairness of the system, while maximizing price, one approach is to increase the reference price, that is the rack rate, in the knowledge that virtually all customers will pay less than this.

Research drawn from surveys on hotel guests has established that customers express satisfaction with Yield Management practices when information on the different pricing options is available, when a substantial discount is given in return for cancellation restrictions and, finally, when different prices are charged for products which are perceived to be different. This would indicate that improved communication with the customer is necessary to ensure complete acceptance of the approach. Research has indicated that customers perceive unacceptable practices to include offering insufficient benefit in return for booking restrictions, imposing severe booking restrictions such as non-refundable, non-changeable restrictions on discounted rooms and not informing customers of the availability of discounted rates.

The future for Yield Management

Developments in external computerized reservation systems (CRS) will clearly have a significant effect on the use and extension of YM applications. It is already possible to interface YM systems to external CRSs, thus widening the potential for the use of YM systems. However, many organizations are some way off this position and still need to up-grade their internal systems to match the standards inherent in external CRSs. In the longer term, the application will need to be interfaced with Market Segment Profit Analysis (MSPA) which enables decisions to be made on the basis of profit rather than revenue maximization. The MSPA approach identifies the costs within each 'activity centre' in the hotel, enabling profit values and margins to be calculated for each market segment. The development of this approach requires further research and more advanced technology, but it is already clear that an emphasis on profit rather than revenue will, in the long term, realize the full potential of a YM system.

FOOD AND BEVERAGE PRICING

Restaurant management has traditionally been based on unsophisticated techniques for pricing menu items and the most commonly used approach has been simply to multiply the food cost by a factor of three or even four to produce a target gross profit percentage. Alternatively, the average spend per customer can be determined in the same way as average room rates by using a bottom-up, profit-based approach. Again, the problem with a cost-based strategy lies in the accurate forecasting of costs and volumes.

Pricing menu items

A common approach to menu pricing is to calculate the standard cost to produce one of each menu item. The cost is then multiplied by a factor to achieve the target gross profit, as the following example demonstrates.

Standard cost	£1.00
Multiplication factor	3
Selling price	£3.00
Gross profit %	67%
Gross profit £	£2.00

Naturally, this is a mechanistic approach and in reality the price should be set to reflect what the market will pay. As a result, some items will have a higher gross profit percentage than others, and the combination of products sold (the sales mix) then becomes important.

It is also important not to rely solely on gross profit percentage. Often it is the cash gross profit figure that is vital, as the figures in Table 5.1 demonstrate.

It would be preferable to sell more of menu item 1 than menu item 2 despite the lower GP percentage.

Table 5.1

Menu item	Cost price	Selling price	GP (%)	GP (£)
1	£5.00	£10.00	50	5.00
2	£2.00	£6.00	67	4.00

Sales mix

This is defined as the combination of menu items sold from the menu. The sales mix will influence the average spend per cover and the resulting gross profit percentage, as Table 5.2 demonstrates.

Table 5.2

Menu item	Quantity sold	Selling price (£)	Total sales (£)	Cost price (£)	Total cost (£)	GP (%)
1	10	4.00	40.00	2.00	20.00	50
2	15	3.00	45.00	1.00	15.00	67
3	20	2.00	40.00	1.50	30.00	25
4	10	1.00	10.00	0.20	2.00	80
5	5	1.00	5.00	0.30	1.50	70
Total	60		140.00		68.50	51

This combination of menu items produces an average spend of £2.33, a gross profit percentage of 51 per cent and gross profit in cash terms of £71.50. If the sales mix were to change, the effect would be that shown in Table 5.3.

These variables make the setting of food menu selling prices particularly complex and the problems are equally valid for establishing beverage prices. This in turn makes the process of controlling gross profit percentage a time-consuming exercise in practice, and for many operations the exercise can never be accurately completed due to the range of information required.

Fixed-price menus

British restaurants have been slow to introduce fixed-price menus where the customer pays one price for a three-course meal without choice or a reduced price for two courses. The practice has been common in Europe for many years with fixed-price menus available in all types of operation. However, many top London hotel restaurants are now benefiting from offering a set-priced lunch menu based on buffet items or limited choice. The reasoning is that customers prefer to know what the maximum price will be without being caught out with cover charges, service charges and separate charges for bread, vegetables and coffee. For many operations the appeal of fixed menus is a full restaurant at lunch time, which improves staff morale and is good for the image of the hotel.

Table 5.3

Menu item	Quantity sold	Selling price (£)	Total sales (£)	Cost price (£)	Total cost (£)	GP (%)
1	15	4.00	60.00	2.00	30.00	50
2	15	3.00	45.00	1.00	15.00	67
3	15	2.00	30.00	1.50	22.50	25
4	5	1.00	5.00	0.20	1.00	80
5	10	1.00	10.00	0.30	3.00	70
Total	60		150.00		71.50	52

Demand-based menu pricing

Increasing profits can either be achieved by reducing expenses, the usual targets being food and labour costs, or by raising the selling price. In recessionary times the latter option may appear to be out of the question. However, the reality is that for a high fixed-cost operation a one per cent increase in price will have a considerably more substantial effect on profitability, as the following example illustrates.

Selling price	£10
Variable cost	£2
Volume	2,000 units
Fixed costs	£10,000

	Original data	Increase selling price by 10%	Reduce costs by 10%
Sales	20,000	22,000	20,000
Variable costs	4,000	4,000	3,600
Fixed costs	10,000	10,000	9,000
Net profit	6,000	8,000	7,400

These figures clearly illustrate where possible selling price should be maximized by considering the most that a customer is likely to spend on that item before the value/price relationship is lost. This approach can be developed further using techniques described as menu analysis.

Approaches to menu analysis

An approach to menu analysis, called menu engineering, was proposed in 1992 by Michael Kasavana and Donald Smith. This is a portfolio approach whereby menu items are classified in terms of those with the highest contribution margin and highest sales volume. Contribution margin is defined in this case as the difference between selling price and direct costs. Menu items could then be plotted in terms of a grid as shown in Figure 5.1 and managers could choose those menu items with the lowest direct costs.

The bias in this approach may result in favouring highly priced items which maximize contribution, resulting in a strategy which eventually decreases demand and profitability.

Similar approaches using different variables have been proposed by Miller (1980), using food cost percentages, Pavesic (1983), using the combination of food cost percentage, contribution margin and sales volume, and Hayes and Huffman (1995), using individual profit and loss statements for each menu item based on direct and allocated costs. Pavesic's approach, using a combination of three variables, attempts to overcome the bias inherent in the earlier approaches. The target is to achieve a sales mix that optimizes the cash contribution margin (defined by Pavesic as sales less food costs) and total sales revenue while achieving the lowest food cost percentage. The menu items are then classified into the following groups:

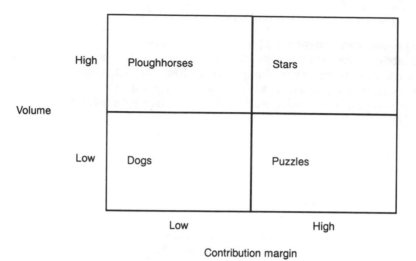

Figure 5.1 Kasavana and Smith's approach to menu analysis
Source: M. Kasavana and D. Smith *Menu Engineering*, 1992.

- Standards: High contribution margins, high food cost percentages
- Primes: High contribution margins, low food cost percentages
- Sleepers: Low contribution margins, low food cost percentages
- Problems: Low contribution margin, high food cost percentages.

Pavesic offers the following explanation. Primes are often the speciality dishes which can be priced at whatever the market will bear, while standards are often popular items that are offered on most menus and need to be priced keenly. The sleeper category includes new items that are being test-marketed to see how the clientele responds to them. The final group is made up of the 'problem' items and these should be eliminated from the menu. Pavesic suggests that maximum contribution will be achieved when the predominant sales mix is made up from primes and standards while sleepers are used to diversify the menu and attract new clientele to the establishment.

The approach offered by Bayou and Bennett (1992) is different from those previously offered in that instead of using average cost, each menu item is individually costed in full. However, the cost allocation task is not simple when numerous sales mix possibilities exist. An approach to segment profitability, as described by Bayou and Bennett, can be a useful approach to ensuring that all menu items are priced to achieve minimum levels of profitability. Profitability analyses can be performed at several levels ranging from: (a) the entire restaurant; (b) individual business operations such as breakfast, lunch, dinner and banqueting; (c) product groups; and (d) individual menu items.

Decisions based on contribution margin are useful for pricing short-term decisions, such as bidding for a banquet, where knowledge of contribution levels can suggest the lowest bidding strategy. Any selling price in excess of variable costs will provide a contribution towards fixed costs. Completion of the above analysis may indicate that one segment is not profitable. However, it may be decided that pricing to achieve a loss in one segment is acceptable when that segment draws custom to the restaurant.

CONCLUSIONS

This chapter introduces the reader to the various pricing methodologies that are available to the hospitality industry. All pricing strategies need to consider both internal factors such as cost and target returns as well as external factors such as the competition and market demand.

FURTHER READING

Brotherton, B. and Mooney, S. (1992) Yield Management – progress and prospects, *International Journal Hospitality Management*, 11(1): 23–32.

Cross, R., Hanks, R. and Noland, R. (1992) Discounting in the hotel industry: a new approach, *Cornell H.R.A. Quarterly*, February.

Kelly, T., Kiefer, N. and Burdett, K. (1995) A demand-based approach to menu pricing, *Cornell H.R.A. Quarterly*, February.

Relihan, W. (1989) The yield management approach to hotel room pricing, *Cornell H.R.A. Quarterly*, May.

REFERENCES

Bayou, M. and Bennett, L. (1992) Profitability analysis for tableservice restaurants, *Cornell H.R.A. Quarterly*, April.

Hayes, D. and Huffman, L. (1995) Menu analysis: a better way, *Cornell H.R.A. Quarterly*, February.

Jones, P. and Hamilton, D. (1992) Yield Management: putting people in the big picture, *Cornell H.R.A. Quarterly*, February.

Kasavana, M. and Smith, D. (1992) *Menu Engineering*, Detroit: Hospitality Publishers.

Miller, J. (1980) *Menu Pricing and Strategy*, New York: Van Nostrand Reinhold.

Pavesic, D. (1983) Cost/margin analysis: a third approach to menu pricing and design, *International Journal of Hospitality Management*, 2(3): 127–34.

PART 3
INTERNAL APPRAISAL

INTRODUCTION

An essential part of the strategy process is to compile a position audit or capability profile which includes considering the conditions that exist inside the firm. The primary objective of internal appraisal is to establish a clear picture of the organization in terms of its resources and capabilities. This requires identifying and tabulating resources and also evaluating the management utilization of those resources. Internal appraisal involves reviewing the main functional areas of the business: accounting and finance, marketing, operations, personnel and research and development. The financial area is an important aspect of internal appraisal in that a review of the key financial data provides an immediate insight into the health of the company. Generally, the first area for inspection is the historical financial results of the company which are analysed through ratio analysis. Although the results are retrospective, they are important in that they demonstrate the effectiveness of past management decisions. The internal analysis should also encompass a review of current resources and existing accounting procedures for budget setting and control and performance measurement. The following three chapters focus on these important aspects of internal appraisal – budgeting procedures, cash management and performance measuring mechanisms.

6

Making budgets work

INTRODUCTION

This chapter considers the role of the budgeting process as a key factor in implementing the strategy of an organization. Budgeting has an essential role to play in converting all elements of the strategic plan into actual financial statements so that a standard for performance for the short-term future can be set in the context of the long-term aims and objectives of the organization. If used correctly, the process ensures that the organizational resources, such as capital and labour, are allocated efficiently and effectively, and at the same time provides a vehicle for departmental co-ordination and communication. This chapter considers the role of budgeting with reference to the following issues: the planning process; motivation; and improving the effectiveness of the budgeting activity.

BUDGETING AND THE STRATEGIC PLANNING PROCESS

The budget provides a short-term plan for the organization and is normally prepared for the year ahead. The plan should be drawn from the long-term objectives of the organization and should provide a scheme for the implementation of the organizational goals and objectives. The budget should be more than just an extension of last year's actual results with incremental increases for revenues and costs. However, for many organizations the budgeting process is reduced to this basic exercise which ensures that each year more and more slack and inefficiency is built into the budgeted values. Instead, the budget-setting exercise should reflect the current activities of the business and allow for a distinction between two types of activity:

- Maintenance activities which are a continuation of existing activities
- Development activities which can be considered to be new opportunities in terms of products or markets or both.

A maintenance budget reflects an organization pursuing well-established activities whereas a development budget should reflect changes in strategic direction such as divestment or changes in product or market base. A budget for a business planning to launch a new product or concept will need to allow for capital expenditure and high levels of marketing costs, whereas a business in the mature stage or entering the decline stage of the product life cycle will need to budget for substantially reduced marketing and investment costs and will focus on the cutting of critical costs.

PURPOSE OF BUDGETS

The successful implementation of the budgeting process should achieve a number of aims. These include enabling the organization to:

- **Quantify future plans**. The budgeting process compels operational managers to look ahead and set short-term targets. This enables shortfalls in sales and resources to be identified and provides the opportunity for measures to be implemented to overcome these difficulties.
- **Set performance objectives and targets**. The budgeting process provides the opportunity to set targets to raise operational performance by increasing management motivation levels.
- **Co-ordinate departmental activities**. The preparation of the sales budget for each trading department forces the different departments to co-ordinate with each other. This is particularly true in a hotel where the restaurant sales budget is dependent on the forecasted room occupancy levels.
- **Communicate plans and objectives**. The budgeting process provides a formal opportunity for higher level managers at divisional regional levels to set targets based on the long-term objectives of the organization.
- **Control business performance**. The process provides a standard based on expected revenues and costs to which actual performance can be compared. Variances between actual and planned performance can then be identified and inefficiencies targeted and eliminated.

However, the budgeting process in its entirety can be time-consuming and therefore costly in terms of management time and resources. Critics of the process argue that the cost and time involved is not justifiable because the end result is based on many unknown factors and the actual performance is almost certainly likely to be different. This criticism needs to be considered in the light of the overriding benefit of the budgeting process which is that it forces managers to consider all the factors that are likely to affect the business and this requires both an internal and an external analysis.

Finally, it can be argued that the budgeting process encourages managers to spend up to budget. Certainly, it is true that this can occur towards the budget year end when managers note that they have not utilized the full value of their expense budget for, say, stationary, and are tempted, as a result, to spend more than is required. This effect can be minimized, however, through communication and participation in an effective budgeting process.

DETERMINATION OF GOALS AND OBJECTIVES

The budget is the translation of the organizational business and financial goals into actual values. The nature of organizational objectives has already been discussed in Chapter 1, and there it was concluded that goals may range from profit or revenue maximization to simple survival tactics. The short-term planning in the organization should aim to achieve long-term objectives but invariably conflict can arise. For example, maximizing return on capital employed in the short term may mean that the long-term future of the business is compromised. Emphasizing the maximization of this ratio means that there is a temptation to increase profits artificially by cutting expenditure in areas such as maintenance, training and marketing, while plans for further investment in assets are curbed. Therefore, it is far better to use more than one yardstick for setting targets and assessing performance. The planning process is based on three types of objective, all of which are closely related. These are known as business, operational and financial objectives and may be described as follows:

- **Business objectives** relate to markets, economic and business conditions, organizational style and personnel policies.
- **Operational objectives** are based on realistic levels of activity given the supply of resources available. A limiting factor is a scarce resource which impedes the operation or growth of business activities.
- **Financial objectives** are incorporated into the budget and are used to evaluate actual performance. They directly relate to the budget-setting process and may be expressed in a variety of forms which might include targets set as follows:
  - absolute terms, e.g. sales to reach £2 million
  - relative terms, e.g. sales to increase by 10 per cent on the previous year
  - a range, e.g. stock to sales to be between 10 and 15 per cent
  - a ratio, e.g. return on total assets to be 16 per cent
  - a maximum, e.g. debt to equity ratios not to exceed 50 per cent
  - a minimum, e.g. dividend cover to be at least twice.

Allen and Myddelton (1992) provide a summary of what a financial budget must aim to provide and identify the main areas that a business must consider when trying to improve its performance. These are illustrated in Figure 6.1.

Planning to achieve organizational goals

Most organizations aim to produce a series of budgets for all levels in the operation. The typical hotel unit is made up of a number of departments, some of which are classified as trading areas, such as the restaurant or the rooms division, and others that provide support services such as marketing, personnel and maintenance. Each of these areas is required to produce a budget, from which a master budget may be prepared. A master budget is the set of consolidated budgeted statements for all the areas within a unit and these may then be consolidated with other units to produce an overall master budget for a division or for the business in total depending on its structure.

Consequently, for the majority of organizations where there are a number of scattered units, it is usual to operate a decentralized system where control is devolved

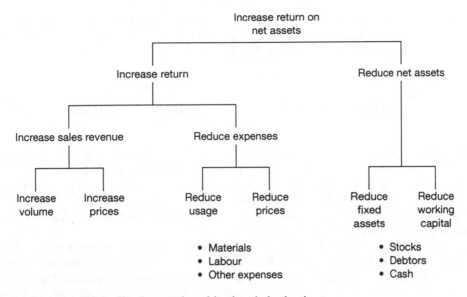

Figure 6.1 Financial split of operating objectives in budgeting
Source: Allen and Myddelton *Essential Management Accounting*, 1992.

to the budget centres. These can be defined as areas in the organization where responsibility has been devolved to a manager and the accounting reports and information have been tailored to match the responsibilities of that manager. Budget centres can be categorized into three types: investment, profit and cost centres. These are defined as follows:

Investment centre is an area where the manager is responsible for revenues, costs and assets employed, for example a hotel division within a large group. The traditional measures of performance for this group include return on capital employed, asset turnover and profitability to sales.

Profit centre is an area where the manager is responsible for both revenues and costs, for example the restaurant within a hotel operation.

Cost centre is an area where managers are responsible for costs only, such as the marketing, personnel and maintenance departments.

Normally the responsibility for a department is assigned to an individual manager who must accept responsibility for that area and, as a result, receives regular reports, known as management accounts, containing details of all the controllable costs. Successful implementation of this process for responsibility accounting can lead to much higher actual performance, particularly where participation and communication are encouraged. Many of the larger hotel companies assign profit centre responsibilities to individual unit managers with investment responsibilities being held at area or divisional management level. However, with the increased emphasis in the 1990s on decentralization and empowerment, this is likely to change as unit managers take on more responsibility for investment decisions.

Responsibility accounting will not be successful where managers are held to be responsible for costs over which they exert no, or only partial, control. This situation can occur in organizations where costs are allocated or apportioned to departments from the centre or where a system for transfer pricing exists. Solutions for overcoming these problems are discussed in more detail in Chapter 4.

ADMINISTRATION OF THE BUDGETING PROCESS

Having established areas of responsibility within the organization the administrative control of the budgetary process should be considered. This requires a key person in the organization, such as the accountant, taking responsibility for the budgeting process throughout the period of preparation. This involves setting guidelines to ensure that the budget is prepared to a standard format in the appropriate timescales. A typical sequence of activities is shown in Figure 6.2.

It is generally considered desirable for individual managers to participate in the budgeting process. In some organizations the budget is imposed from the top without participation from or consultation with those managers who will execute the budget. This is generally considered to be a less effective approach for raising performance levels compared with an environment where managers can engage in participation and negotiation. However, where managers are given the freedom to participate, time should be allowed for the negotiation process.

The budget period

This may vary from one organization to the next but is usually one year in length and is often dependent on the natural business year. In the hospitality industry the seasonal

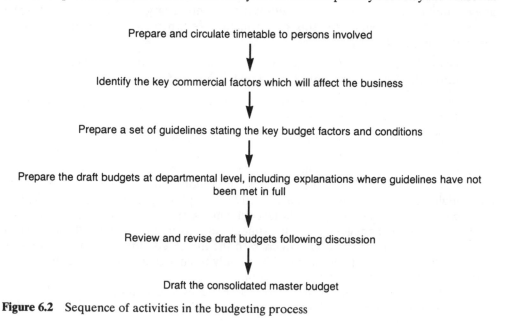

Figure 6.2 Sequence of activities in the budgeting process

nature of trading means that the control periods within the budget will need to be accurately determined. Traditionally, the budget period is split into twelve periods coinciding with the calendar months. The disadvantage with this procedure is that the periods are of different length and will straddle the weeks, with one budget period often ending mid-week. An alternative approach is to use thirteen budget periods each of four weeks in length. A business which is reliant on virtually all seasonal trade would then need to split the budget month down further into a week-by-week budget to take account of factors such as Bank Holidays. Traditionally, one year is planned in detail and this year is then worked through almost to completion before the next budget is considered. This results, firstly, in an intensive period each year when the budget is being prepared and, secondly, a period at the latter end of the year when the manager is working without a short-term plan. The use of a rolling budget provides the solution where a month or quarter is continually being prepared to add to the budget year while the current month or quarter drops out of the timeframe.

The process of communication

Each responsibility centre is required to prepare its own forecast of what it hopes to achieve and the resources it intends to employ. In order to harmonize the forecasts of the various centres and to avoid inter-departmental conflict, a budget committee should be constituted. The various heads of department form the membership and the accountant assumes the role of budget officer or budget co-ordinator. This process ensures that individual budgets complement each other and that the lines of communication between departmental heads are open. In order to standardize the budget procedure many organizations find it useful to set out the responsibilities of the persons involved and the layout of the forms to be used, in a budget manual. Typically, it is important to communicate the following points to those involved in the budgeting process.

- A statement of the objectives of budgetary control and the procedures to be used to ensure uniformity of approach
- A definition of responsibilities for each person involved
- A timetable for the preparation of the budget
- The budget and control periods
- The responsibility centres for the preparation of each budget
- The cost codes to be used for cost collection and classification
- The standardized report layouts to be used by each unit to assist in consolidation.

Information technology can have a vital role to play in providing a medium for the distribution of standardized forms for data entry. These are often distributed on packages containing a spreadsheet which, with the use of preset formulas, can be of tremendous assistance in the forecasting process as well as providing a standard layout and good presentation. The process of consolidation at head office can be a lengthy exercise but again, with the use of spreadsheet packages, the time involved can be greatly reduced.

PREPARATION OF THE BUDGET STATEMENTS

There are potentially three budgeted statements which can be prepared. These are:

- The trading account or operating budget
- The cashflow
- The balance sheet.

However, it is not always necessary for all responsibility centres to prepare all three statements. Centres termed as profit centres may only need to prepare the operating budget while the investment centre, of which the profit centre forms a part, will find all three statements of value. In the larger multi-unit organization it is often the case that individual units prepare the operating budget and the other statements are only prepared at a higher level in the organizational structure. This may well be appropriate in an organization where much of the accounting activity takes place centrally, such as the payment of suppliers and the receiving of outstanding monies from customers. However, self-accounting units should also prepare a forecasted cashflow and balance sheets.

Budget layouts

Many hospitality operators use a version of the layout recommended by the Uniform System of Accounting when preparing their budgeted statements. This system is described in detail in Chapter 3 and is essentially a uniform accounting system which was introduced in 1969 by the Economic Development Council particularly for hotels and caterers. The standard system provides a basic layout for the profit and loss accounts, the balance sheet and the cashflow statements and distinguishes three operating departments: rooms; food; and liquor and tobacco. In order to control the financial operation of the hotel several levels of control are suggested by the system. The system is described in more detail in Chapter 3.

Forecasting revenue

The starting point for the budget in a commercial organization is normally to estimate the sales revenue for the period. There are numerous factors to be taken into account, both internal and external to the organization. These include:

- Past actual figures, based on volumes, selling prices and the sales mix
- Current anticipated trends, and consequently it is important not to start the budgeting process too early so that the most up-to-date information can be used
- Economic factors, such as trading conditions, inflation rates and unemployment levels, in addition to details regarding planned local activities and events
- The competition, including general information and projections as well as current advance bookings
- Capacity restraints, which will limit the sales budget by the level of capacity and resources available (known as limiting factors). It is important that these factors are clearly identified and their effects reduced or eliminated entirely.

There are several key resource constraints relevant to the hospitality industry. The most obvious is in the form of physical constraints which may hinder sales growth, such as total room availability, total bed night availability, total restaurant covers and bar space. These might be coupled with constraints relating to labour, such as shortages of skilled staff and limited management skills, as well as equipment capacity restraints and limited capital available for expansion.

Sales trend analysis

This approach to forecasting future sales is based on the use of product demand curves or the product life cycle. A description of the principles of the product life cycle is included in Chapter 2. In order to predict the trend in future sales, past sales figures are collected and plotted onto a graph against time. This shows the sales trend and indicates the stage in the product life cycle that has been reached. This methodology can be improved with the use of time series analysis which attempts to eliminate the seasonal nature of past data and seeks to establish the underlying trend through averaging.

Preparation of the operating budget

Having determined the likely level of sales for the budget period, the next step is to determine the level of resources required to service those sales. An important requirement in forecasting costs is an understanding of cost behaviour. Once this has been established the problem of predicting the future level of the cost item is almost solved. An inspection of past records will clearly highlight those costs which are variable and those which are fixed, but the difficulty arises when attempting to classify semi-variable costs, that is those with both a fixed and a variable element. A number of methods is available for assisting in this process, ranging from the simple high–low method to the more complex techniques such as multiple regression analysis. The first of these methods is illustrated in Chapter 4. The reader is advised to consult the further reading at the end of this chapter for references to a statistical-based approach.

The cash budget

A knowledge of the company's cash cycle is essential to the success of any business. Many unit managers within large hospitality organizations feel that the cash budget is unimportant and requires little attention as the company as a whole will always have plenty of cash to support cashflow problems at individual sites. However, in order to produce a company cashflow forecast, the requirements of individual sites need to be consolidated to produce an overall picture. A small change in debtor days at each operation in a large multinational organization will have a significant effect on the company's overall cashflow, as will a change in strategic direction in terms of the customer base, say from individuals to company business. To summarize, the cashflow statement assists in the management of the company's finance by disclosing the peaks and troughs within the budget period, indicating where extra funds will be needed. Short-term needs maybe met from short-term sources such as overdrafts but normally long-term funding is preferable, even for supporting the working capital needs of a seasonal business.

The corporate cashflow sheet will contain all or many of the following transactions:

- Net funds generated from operations
- Sales and purchases of fixed assets
- Issue and redemption of equity
- Long-term borrowings and redemption of debt
- Changes in working capital.

Balance sheet

The asset budgets serve several purposes by ensuring that all assets, both fixed and current, are planned for in the budget. Charges are made to the operating budget in respect of depreciation for new assets acquired or coming on-stream during the budget year, and when new facilities start to trade the related income and costs are to be incorporated into the operating and cash budgets. The relationship between the components of the budgeted balance sheet can then be monitored using ratio analysis. Working capital ratios and asset management ratios can be used futuristically when applied to the budgeted values to ensure that the financial targets being forecast are both realistic and efficient.

BUDGETARY CONTROL PROCESS

Having prepared and agreed the budget for the forthcoming period, a key factor in the success of the budgeting process is the level of monitoring which then takes place in order to compare actual results to those that were planned. This level of control is supported by what is known as a system for variance accounting where the planned activities of the organization are compared to the actual results and the differences analysed. Broadly speaking, there can be many potential causes for variance. These range from those which have occurred due to external factors such as economic, social, legal and political changes, changes in competition and changes in supply conditions, to those which have arisen due to changes and inefficiencies in the operating systems. Effective variance accounting is based on establishing individual unit selling prices and costs in a process known as standard costing. This enables performance to be monitored in terms of both price and volume changes.

Standard costing

Standard costing provides a method for identifying the causes of the variation between actual and budgeted results and can exist only where firm standards of performance are capable of being set. A fast-food outlet is a good example of an operation where standardized products are sold and where it is possible to establish standard ingredient costs that are designed to hold constant over a determined period. The process of standard costing requires the setting of five standards:

- Purchase prices, where each unit has a set selling price
- Purchase specifications, where each ingredient is clearly specified
- Portion sizes, where each dish is specified in terms of size
- Yields, where weight changes in the cooking process are identified
- Recipes for production, to ensure a uniform procedure is followed.

The standard cost of the final recipe represents what the cost should be if there is minimal waste, maximum efficiency and the supporting standards are followed. The use of such an approach has distinct advantages in that by presetting the standard the best methods and materials for the product are determined and variances may be produced which indicate where the actual costs have varied against the standard. It may also mean that targets are set against which employee performance may be measured and this can assist in the training of staff. Such activity focuses management attention on the shortfalls and is known as *management by exception*. Finally, the process can also improve the quality of pricing decisions because the business has accurate information about costs.

However, standard costing can be a difficult system to administer in practice. It is time-consuming to set up in the first instance as all dishes need to be costed and it is essential that all records are maintained for the system to work effectively. Computer technology can certainly assist where purchasing and inventory control packages can be linked to menu costing options to provide up-to-date costed dishes.

The operational restraints imposed by standard costing may be disliked by employees as procedures and products are mostly preset, leaving little scope for personal development. As a consequence, standard costing is used most effectively in fast-food style operations with semi or unskilled labour. Alternatively, the skilled workforce may be redeployed following the introduction of standardized products.

FLEXIBLE BUDGETING

A budget prepared in advance of the trading period and set at an assumed level of activity is called a fixed budget. This original budget can then be used in comparison with the actual data. However, the comparison is less meaningful when actual activity is significantly different from the budgeted activity. Where standard unit costs are available or where the proportions of fixed and variable costs have been calculated, it is possible to calculate a revised budget based on the actual level of sales using the budgeted levels of costs. This revised budget is called a *flexible budget*. This approach can be used to monitor variances caused by changes in volume, changes in sales mix and operating cost inefficiencies. The following example illustrates the use of a flexible budget.

The following figures have been extracted from the fixed budget for the Bay Restaurant for Period 5.

Budgeted covers	3,200
Average spend	£12.00
Gross profit	60%
Labour and expenses	30%
Fixed costs	£2,500

The actual results were:

Covers	4,500
Average spend	£10.00
Gross profit	£27,900
Labour and expenses	£13,000
Fixed costs	£2,900

The following table illustrates how the results might be analysed.

Variance	Fixed budget	Flexible budget	Actual	
Covers	3,200	4,500	4,500	
Average spend	£12.00	£12.00	£10.00	
Sales	38,400	54,000	45,000	9,000A
Gross profit	23,040	32,400	27,900	4,500F
Labour and expenses	11,520	16,200	13,000	3,200F
Fixed costs	2,500	2,500	2,900	400A
Net profit	1,340	2,900	1,200	1,700A

The variances can be summarized as follows:
Variance due to volume   2,900 − 1,340 = 1,560F
Variance due to operations 2,900 − 1,200 = 1,700A
Variance overall   1,340 − 1,200 = 140A
A = Adverse   F = Favourable

USING BUDGETS TO MOTIVATE

The budgeting process is often used not only to plan ahead, but also for target setting and for raising individual performance. Traditional theories of motivation focus on the identification of specific factors such as pay systems, working conditions and self-fulfilment as being associated with producing increased levels of motivation. There have been various studies conducted across a range of industries on the theme of employee motivation and performance with relation to budgets. Generally, these have concluded that difficult goals produce either very good or very bad results compared with goals of normal difficulty, and that difficult goals lead to reduced effort on the part of those managers who are less mature and experienced and who have less self-confidence. Results from a variety of sources of research indicate that:

- Budgets have no motivational effect unless they are accepted by the managers involved as their own personal targets.
- Up to the point where the budget target is no longer accepted, the more demanding the budget target the better the results achieved.
- Demanding budgets are also seen as more relevant than less difficult targets, but negative attitudes result if they are seen as too difficult.
- Acceptance of budgets is facilitated when good upward communication exists. The use of departmental meetings was found helpful in encouraging managers to accept budget targets.
- Manager reactions to budget targets were affected both by their own personality and by more general cultural and organizational norms.

The relationship between budget difficulty and the ensuing level of performance can be shown graphically and is illustrated in Figure 6.3.

It shows that a budget level which is perceived as being more likely to be achieved will motivate a lower level of performance. Consequently, in order to improve performance the budget level should be set in excess of the average performance likely to be attained.

IMPROVING THE EFFECTIVENESS OF THE BUDGETING PROCESS

The effectiveness of budgeting relies on reducing slack or bias by ensuring that forecasts are accurate during the budget preparation stage and by ensuring the timeliness of the reporting of the actual results. Bias in budgeting is a major problem and detection in the budget-setting process can sometimes be impossible. Bias occurs when a manager incorporates a certain amount of slack into the budgeted figures. There are various reasons for doing this but it occurs mainly when the managers' performance is being assessed against the budgeted targets. Slack may be built into sales, by understating what is possible, or into costs, thereby masking potential overspends. Alternatively, in tough environments, managers may set unachievable budgets to divert attention away from current poor performance. Delays in reporting the actual results against budget would lead to delays in the taking of corrective action, which may in the long term reduce management motivation. Consequently, a system of 'flash' reports may be useful. These report rough numbers relating to sales and key costs such as materials and wages within a few days of the end of the budget period with the complete results coming no more than a week later.

The incremental approach to budget setting is widely used and is based on the assumption that a budget will grow each year as a result of inflation or with the provision for 'natural growth'. As a result, gradual changes in the business may be overlooked. These may be basic changes such as differences in the cost structure or the customer base. Even without such changes occurring, the traditional approach ensures that previous overspends and inaccuracies are compounded each budget period. An alternative is zero-based budgeting – an approach which challenges the existence of all items in the budget.

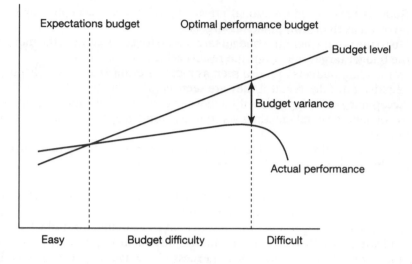

Figure 6.3 The effect of budget difficulty on performance

Zero-based budgeting

The concept of zero-based budgeting (ZBB) relies on the assumption that levels of expenditure in previous periods does not justify a continuation of that spending in future periods. Instead, all spending must be justified each year. This approach is most useful in the control of indirect, overhead costs such as marketing, maintenance and training. Each activity in the organization is scrutinized and the expected outcome determined. These activities are then ranked based on the following criteria:

- The objectives of the activities in relation to the organization's overall objectives
- The required budget for the activity
- Justification for the outcomes of the activity against cost.

The main differences between normal and ZBB are summarized in Table 6.1 which has been adapted from the work of Allen and Myddelton (1992).

The number of units required varies depending on the size of the organization. A large organization would expect to have several units for each type of overhead

Table 6.1 Normal budgeting versus zero-based budgeting

	Normal budgeting	**Zero-based budgeting**
Frequency	Annual	Every 3–5 years
Time and effort	Often significant	Very substantial
Starting point	Last years budget/actual	Zero
Basis for budget	Last year +/− percentage	Separate decision packages
Amount	Single sum	Range of cost benefit options
Involves	Manager and boss	Cross-functional team
Needs awareness of	Function	Whole business
Priorities	Not stated	Ranks 'mosts' and 'wants'
Alternatives	Not stated	Detailed review

expense. Each unit should contain just one or two employees and the associated costs. Once the decision units have been established, the department head must prepare an analysis for each separate unit in his or her responsibility. For each decision unit the following will need to be documented:

- The unit's objective
- The unit's present activities
- Justification for the continuation of the unit's activities
- A list of alternative ways of carrying out the unit's activities
- Selection of recommended alternatives
- The budget required.

Ranking process

In order to determine how money will be spent in the organization, it is necessary to rank all activities in order of importance to the organization. This may be achieved using committees who may approve automatically the first 50 to 60 per cent of all activities and the remainder are ranked by middle and top management. The completed ranking process and approved expenditures constitute the new budgets for those areas or departments.

Advantages of zero-based budgeting

The detail required to complete zero-based budgeting successfully is obviously extensive and therefore time-consuming, requiring a management team who knows the whole business very well. This may present difficulties in an industry where staff and management turnover is traditionally very high. However, the advantages of ZBB are that the process:

- Concentrates on the cash value of each department's activities and budget and not on percentage increases
- Can reallocate funds to the department or activity providing the greatest benefit to the organization
- Provides a quality of information about the organization that would otherwise not be available
- Involves all levels of management and supervision in the budgeting process
- Obliges managers to identify inefficient or obsolete functions within their areas of responsibility.

CONCLUSIONS

The preparation of a detailed budget will be of value to most operations by helping to quantify the short to medium-term objectives and plans. This will then provide a benchmark against which actual performance can be compared and action taken to improve future results. A checklist for effective budgeting will include:

- Establishing attainable goals or objectives
- Planning to achieve these goals or objectives
- Comparing actual results with those planned and analysing the differences
- Taking corrective action if required
- Improving the effectiveness of budgeting.

FURTHER READING

Emmanuel, C., Otley, D. and Merchant, K. (1990) *Accounting for Management Control*, London: Chapman and Hall.

Ezamel, M. and Hart, H. (1987) *Advanced Management Accounting*, London: Cassell.

Harris, P. (1994) *Managerial Accounting for the Hospitality Industry*, Cheltenham: Stanley Thornes.

Otley, D. (1987) *Accounting Control and Organisational Behaviour*, London: Chartered Institute of Management Accountants.

REFERENCES

Allen, M. and Myddelton, D. (1992) *Essential Management Accounting*, New York: Prentice-Hall.

7

The management of working capital

INTRODUCTION

A key feature consistent with many of the business failures during the 1980s in the UK has been the fact that businesses have been too late in realizing the importance of short-term and long-term cash availability. Obviously, achieving profit is important, but maintaining sufficient cash funds for financing the payment of suppliers (trade creditors) and for financing long-term management decisions is the successful route to achieving strategic objectives. When there are insufficient funds in the form of cash the business may, at worst, face liquidation if creditors are not being paid, but such a shortage also limits the ability of a business to pursue a strategy of expansion through revenue growth. This chapter considers the management of working capital in total as well as a review of the key aspects of each of the components including:

- Working capital cycles
- Measures for managing working capital
- Managing debtors
- Managing creditors
- Inventory control
- Cash management.

WORKING CAPITAL

Working capital is normally defined as the cash value of current assets less the current liabilities. When the assets exceed the liabilities this is known as positive working capital. Current assets are funded partly from the current liabilities such as trade creditors and bank overdrafts and also from long-term sources of funds such as bank loans or equity. Negative working capital arises when current liabilities exceed current assets. In this case current liabilities are funding both current assets and a proportion of long-term assets.

Generally, a business should seek to minimize the level of each type of current asset held, such as stock, debtors and cash, and maximize the benefits from short-term financing arising from the delayed payment of creditors. However, other factors influence the working capital policy, such as the possibility of lost sales through not offering credit to potential customers, lost sales through holding insufficient stocks and increases in operating costs due to poor supplier relationships. The management of working capital should be based on achieving a balance between these factors. The problem lies in the fact that the level of funds required is constantly changing, particularly where there are seasonal sales which will affect stock, debtor and creditor levels. As a result, forecasting working capital requirements becomes difficult in cases where the level of future sales and the timing of cashflows is not known with accuracy. However, it is essential that every attempt is made to predict accurately the business cash requirements, and the increasing importance of monitoring the levels of cash generated in a operation is now widely recognized.

A business can increase profits through cost-cutting or creative accounting but there is no corresponding increase in cashflows following these activities. Therefore, the monitoring of cashflows and not profits is, in many cases, the true measure of the health of the business. There are various approaches to monitoring cash levels and working capital requirements and these will now be considered.

WORKING CAPITAL CYCLE

Unfortunately, to maintain liquidity the level of available current assets must be kept sufficiently high to cover payments to outstanding suppliers when they fall due. These cash balances mean that the business incurs an opportunity cost for interest lost or the earnings that could have been made if the cash had been invested elsewhere. The exact amount of idle cash held can be managed effectively by understanding and controlling the cash operating cycle. This specifies the period taken in days between the cash payment to suppliers for goods and the cash being received from customers for sales. In a manufacturing business a large portion of the cash cycle will focus on days required to manufacture the finished product from the raw materials and the incomplete finished goods are known as work in progress. The usual cash operating cycle is illustrated below:

Days raw materials held in stock	x days
Days needed to produce goods	x days
Days finished goods held in stock	x days
Days debtors take to settle accounts on receipt of goods	x days
less	
Days taken to pay trade suppliers	x days
equals	
Cash operating cycle	x days

The typical hotel operation requires stock for almost instant usage and the emphasis is not on the management of the stock cycle but on ensuring that sufficient stocks are held for service without incurring the costs associated with overstocking. The chain of events (in simplified form) in a hotel operation which will affect the working capital cycle is shown below.

Days raw materials held in stock	x days
Days debtors take to settle accounts on receipt of goods	x days
less	
Days taken to pay suppliers	x days
equals	
Cash operating cycle	x days

Whenever a business is able to gain credit from suppliers this, in effect, finances part of the cash operating cycle. Consequently, large businesses such as hotel chains can operate with shorter operating cycles if they are able to secure better credit terms. Any delay in the time taken to receive cash from outstanding customers or in the credit terms offered will increase the length of the cycle. This will eventually lead to the running down of cash resources and may lead to liquidation. The problem for manufacturing businesses lies in the length of time taken for stock to be sold. This is obviously less of an influencing factor for a hotel organizations where stocks are of a lower value in cash terms and are fast-moving.

The key factor for successful control of the working capital cycle for a service-type operation is in the management of debtors and creditors. However, in the case of large-scale production kitchens, there are obviously similarities with the traditional manufacturing approach, as the following example illustrates.

The Canford Kitchen produces a range of speciality meals using cook-chill processes. It distributes these meals to a number of different brands of fast-food restaurants. The table below gives information extracted from the accounts for the past three years.

	Year 1 £	Year 2 £	Year 3 £
Sales	864,000	1,080,000	1,188,000
Cost of goods sold	756,000	972,000	1,098,000
Purchases	518,400	702,000	720,000
Debtors (average)	172,800	259,200	297,000
Creditors (average)	86,400	105,300	126,000
Raw material stock (average)	108,000	145,800	180,000
Work in progress	75,600	97,200	93,360
Finished goods (average)	86,400	129,600	142,875

Internal appraisal

Assume all sales and purchases are on credit terms. Days taken is worked out as follows:

	Year 1	Year 2	Year 3
$\dfrac{\text{Raw materials}}{\text{Purchases}} \times 365$	76.0	75.8	91.3
$\dfrac{\text{Work in progress}}{\text{Cost of sales}} \times 365$	36.5	36.5	31.0
$\dfrac{\text{Finished goods}}{\text{Cost of sales}} \times 365$	41.7	48.7	47.5
$\dfrac{\text{Debtors}}{\text{Sales}} \times 365$	73	87.6	91.3
$\dfrac{\text{Trade creditors}}{\text{Purchases}} \times 365$	(60.8)	(54.8)	(63.9)
Total length of cycle	166.4	193.8	197.2

The scale of working capital

In order to establish the significance of working capital it is useful to review the relative importance of working capital in a sample of balance sheets taken from a range of hospitality companies. These are illustrated in Table 7.1 showing working capital as a percentage of total capital employed.

Over trading

This is a term used when a business is financing too high a level of sales activity with insufficient working capital. The situation can occur where sales are increasing faster than the cost base through rapid growth or when costs are rising quickly due to inflation. In each case the business faces a cash shortfall situation. Over trading is more likely to affect the business selling on credit terms than for cash-orientated businesses.

MEASURES FOR MANAGING WORKING CAPITAL

There are a number of performance evaluation techniques for monitoring the level of working capital. These include the calculation of a range of ratios based on the relationships that exist between the different types of current assets and current liabilities, and also specific ratios for managing each type of asset. When calculated using internally reported values drawn from management accounts the results provide

Table 7.1 Comparative balance sheets for a range of industrial classifications

	Services			Manufacturing			Hotels			Eating establishments			Alcoholic drink establishments		
	1991	1992	1993	1991	1992	1993	1991	1992	1993	1991	1992	1993	1991	1992	1993
Land & buildings	9.2	9.1	8.4	7.6	7.8	7.2	41.6	41.7	40.5	22.0	20.2	19.1	30.5	32.5	30.5
Fixture & equipment	24.2	23.2	22.7	23.5	22.6	22.3	28.8	28.5	29.9	32.6	34.0	33.8	33.3	32.7	34.4
Intangibles	1.1	1.2	1.2	0.9	0.9	0.9	1.2	0.9	0.9	3.5	4.0	4.2	2.7	2.7	2.3
Other non-current	2.3	2.5	2.6	2.0	2.1	2.4	3.3	3.7	4.3	2.9	2.9	3.0	3.3	2.4	2.0
Stock/WIP*	6.6	6.6	6.5	17.2	16.8	16.5	3.5	3.7	3.6	6.6	6.3	6.3	6.5	7.1	6.6
Trade debtors	28.4	28.2	29.1	32.9	33.1	33.8	6.9	7.1	6.9	13.0	12.8	13.3	6.2	6.4	7.1
Other debtors	6.7	5.8	3.4	4.5	4.0	2.1	5.4	4.3	2.0	5.6	4.8	2.9	5.5	4.6	2.3
Cash	16.3	17.1	17.8	9.0	9.2	9.5	6.9	7.2	7.2	10.0	10.7	11.0	9.1	8.3	9.3
Other current assets	5.2	6.4	8.4	2.6	3.4	5.3	2.4	3.0	4.8	3.9	4.3	6.4	2.9	3.3	5.6
Total assets	100.0	100.0	100.0	100.0	100.0	100.0	100.0	100.0	100.0	100.0	100.0	100.0	100.0	100.0	100.0
Trade creditors	9.2	8.7	8.3	11.1	10.7	10.4	3.9	3.6	3.1	9.5	9.0	8.6	7.3	8.6	8.2
Bank loans overdrafts	9.7	8.8	7.6	8.7	8.4	7.5	12.7	13.1	12.8	12.9	12.1	10.8	11.3	11.0	8.5
Taxation	6.4	6.3	5.8	3.7	3.5	3.3	2.3	2.4	2.5	6.6	6.4	5.9	4.7	4.5	4.0
Loans payable	13.2	13.0	12.0	8.8	8.9	8.3	9.9	11.2	9.2	11.9	11.7	11.5	16.6	12.4	13.0
Other current liabilities	40.5	43.3	44.2	32.4	34.0	35.4	23.1	24.5	24.4	37.4	41.1	41.0	28.7	33.7	38.8
Share capital	7.3	8.1	8.7	6.9	7.8	8.3	6.9	8.4	10.5	9.5	10.0	11.6	5.7	6.6	6.3
Retained earnings	(7.7)	(9.7)	(7.7)	(4.0)	(8.0)	(8.1)	(4.0)	(7.8)	(8.2)	(23.5)	(26.5)	(24.9)	(13.8)	(20.6)	(21.5)
Reserves	5.0	4.9	5.0	4.5	4.5	4.7	15.4	14.2	14.3	7.6	7.5	7.4	8.3	7.9	8.8
Deferred taxation	0.4	0.3	0.3	0.7	0.6	0.5	0.7	0.7	0.6	0.4	0.5	0.4	0.4	0.4	0.4
Long-term liabilities	15.9	16.3	15.9	13.0	13.5	13.5	29.1	29.7	30.8	27.7	28.2	27.7	31.0	35.6	33.5
Total liabilities & equity	100.0	100.0	100.0	100.0	100.0	100.0	100.0	100.0	100.0	100.0	100.0	100.0	100.0	100.0	100.0

*Work in progress

Source: The Guide to British Performance, Dun & Bradstreet International, 1995

a useful tool for monitoring and evaluating performance. However, when taking values from the published balance sheet it is important to remember that the financial statements are drawn up following a number of conventions and rules and that the asset values are simply those at that point in time and that the relationships may have considerably changed since that date.

The current ratio

This provides a measure of the balance between the assets and liabilities. Usually a business would seek to achieve a ratio in excess of 1 to 1 as this would communicate confidence to short-term creditors by confirming the ability of the business to meet all its short-term debts. Many textbooks on accounting advocate a ratio of 2 to 1, that is current assets at twice the value of current liabilities, as being a safe measure. In practice, the trading patterns of the business will dictate the level of a 'safe' ratio. In restaurants, for example, current assets will consist of cash and fast-moving stocks with possibly little or no debtors. Therefore, all assets are in fairly liquid state and it would not be unusual to see a consistent ratio of 1 to 1 or less with no working capital difficulties being experienced. Alternatively, a hotel operation may well have a considerable level of debtors and slow-moving stocks, and the most efficient ratio will be much higher than 1 to 1.

A range of values drawn from different sectors of the hospitality industry is illustrated in Table 7.2.

The acid test ratio

This ratio provides a measure of the balance between liquid assets and liabilities. Liquid assets are normally taken to be debtors and cash whereas stock may take longer to realize. However, it may also be relevant to exclude some of the debtors as well if the outstanding balances are difficult to realize. The target for the ratio is normally about 1 to 1 but, again, differences in industry operating practice means that these benchmarks should not be adhered to rigidly.

MANAGING DEBTORS

Ideally, if all sales could be for immediate cash payment, liquidity problems would be less likely to occur. Unfortunately, in many sectors of the hospitality industry it is expected that credit will be available and in many cases this serves as a marketing tool to attract further business. The optimum level of debtors outstanding is established by achieving a balance between the cost of giving credit and the additional profits to be generated from credit sales. The cost of granting credit to a customer includes:

- **Loss of interest**. The supplier is, in effect, giving the customer an interest-free loan during the period in which the amount is outstanding.
- **Reduced purchased power**. During the period that the debt is outstanding the supplier may suffer from insufficient funds to buy stock or pay staff.

Table 7.2 Working capital ratios for a range of industrial classifications

Median values	Services			Manufacturing			Hotels			Eating establishments			Alcoholic drink establishments		
	1991	1992	1993	1991	1992	1993	1991	1992	1993	1991	1992	1993	1991	1992	1993
Acid test	0.7	0.7	0.7	0.7	0.7	0.7	0.1	0.1	0.2	0.2	0.2	0.2	0.1	0.1	0.1
Current ratio	1.0	1.0	1.0	1.1	1.1	1.1	0.4	0.4	0.4	0.5	0.5	0.5	0.4	0.4	0.4

Source: The Guide to British Performance, Dun & Bradstreet International, 1995

- **Administrative costs**. Maintenance of a sales ledger will incur costs for record-keeping and staffing.
- **Cost of bad debts**. Such costs occur when an outstanding debt is not paid. The greater the length of debtor days, the greater the risk of bad debts occurring.

However, costs are also incurred when credit is denied, the most significant being the loss of customer goodwill and sales.

In the hotel industry credit is extended at various levels, ranging from the house accounts where credit is extended during the guests' stay until the point of check-out when payment is made, to authorized credit which is extended to customers where the balance outstanding is shown on the sales (city) ledger. Credit is also extended when a guest pays by credit card where billing is made to the credit card company, usually incurring commission charges.

Credit policy

To avoid excessive bad debts an effective policy for giving credit should be established. This should be communicated to staff through training sessions and company manuals and there should be standard forms for collecting credit information. The company policy regarding credit should include guidelines for who should be granted credit, what references are required, how much credit is to be granted and the length of credit period to be extended. The credit application form should be the most accurate document on customer details available and is, therefore, worth reviewing carefully. When preparing a credit application form the following checklist should be considered:

- Are these reasonable questions?
- Would I give out such information?
- Is it necessary and relevant?
- Will the customer find it easy to answer?

In addition to the credit application form there are many sources available for gathering information about customer creditworthiness. These include:

- Credit ratings supplied by credit agencies such as Dun and Bradstreet
- Banks
- Trade associations
- Own company experience.

To ensure that debtor management is efficient, it is important to monitor that invoices and statements are sent out promptly and accurately. The sooner the invoice is sent out the sooner the customer will deal with it. An accurate, clear invoice will also improve the speed with which it is paid. Payment terms should be clearly worded. Terms such as '30 days net' mean payment on the 30th day without taking discount, but this is not very clear to the customer. A more accurate message to the customer would be: 'Please pay within 30 days of the invoice date' or 'Please ensure payment reaches this office by the 25th of the month following the month of the invoice'.

A courteous but firm system of reminders and collection procedures should be operated and the sending of statements, reminders and telephone contact calls should all be logged.

The monitoring of debtor levels can be greatly assisted with the use of computer technology and for many hotels this was one of the first areas to undergo computerization. Most computer packages should be able to produce an ageing analysis of debtors, list of accounts that have exceeded their credit limit and an average debtor payment period calculation. With this information available, it is important to ensure that debtor information is conveyed to other departments, such as reservations, to prevent credit terms being continued when large debts are already outstanding.

Late payment of bills is clearly damaging to any type of business, but it particularly affects the smaller business. These types of business are often at the mercy of much larger companies who deliberately delay payment for financial advantage. To avoid the problems associated with collecting debts it may be relevant to consider debt factoring and offering discounts for prompt payment.

Debt factoring

In recent years there has been a growth in the usage of external debt collection agencies and there are various services available, depending on the needs of the individual business. The more common arrangement is one where the factoring organization will pay invoices immediately up to an agreed percentage of the sales ledger, say, 80 per cent, and receive, in return, a fee which may be say, 1.5 per cent of the invoice total. Consequently, the business receives an immediate injection of cash. But there are some disadvantages to debt factoring that should be considered. The most significant disadvantage is that the outstanding customers will be contacted by the factoring company and this may give the wrong impression to the customer. Also, some contracts revert the debt to the company after, say, 60 days. However, the advantages of factoring should not be dismissed because the process relieves the supplier firm of the administrative and financial burdens of granting credit, but obviously at a cost. In order to evaluate the cost effectiveness of factoring it is necessary to evaluate the benefits which might include reduced overdraft costs, reduced bad debts and reduced administration costs, and compare these with the cost of the factoring service.

Cash discounts

Discounts off the total amount outstanding maybe offered to the customer for early payment but care should be taken to ensure that the customer really is eligible. The offering of a cash discount is becoming less frequent and has never really been adopted by the hotel industry, and in many cases the cost of discounting may mean that this is not a viable approach to reducing debtors. If a customer is offered terms of say '2/30, net 60' this means that payment is due within 30 days and will result in a 2 per cent discount, otherwise the full amount is due within 60 days. The customer has two options, he can either pay less 2 per cent on day 30 or he can pay the full amount on day 60. The extra 30 days credit costs the customer 2 per cent. This works out at approximately $360/30 = 12$ times per year or an annual interest rate of 24 per cent. The calculation can be worked out more precisely using the following formula:

I (interest rate) = (1 + discount rate) − 1

that is

I = (1 + 0.02) − 1 = 26.8%

Unless the supplier's cost of borrowing is more than this figure, it is uneconomic to offer this level of discount. The following example illustrates a cost benefit analysis calculated from the view point of the creditor.

The following details relate to a debt of £1,000 owed by Sunshine Food Products to a food wholesaler. The terms are payment within 10 days to receive a discount of 5% or full payment within 30 days. The food company has an overdraft facility on which interest is payable at 15%. Should the food company take up the offer of the discount for early payment?

Benefit if the cash discount is accepted is a saving of £50 arising from
£1,000 × 5%.

Benefit if the discount is rejected is a saving in overdraft costs because the business would have 20 more days use of the money which represents:

£950 × 20/365 × 15% = £7.81

Therefore the benefit of discount outweighs the cost of the overdraft incurred.

Interest charges

The reverse of offering a discount for early payment is to make an interest charge for late payment. The difficulty of this method in practice is in enforcing the payment of the interest. As mentioned earlier, it is often smaller businesses who suffer most from the late payment of invoices.

Bad debts

The cost of offering additional credit should be compared to the benefits of incurring additional sales. The following example illustrates the cost benefit analysis.

The current level of sales is £20,000 per month with an average credit period of one month. If the credit period is lengthened it is anticipated that sales will increase and some bad debts will be incurred. There are considered to be three options, the first of which is to continue with the existing policy.

Increase in credit period	Increase in sales above £20,000 per month	Percentage of bad debt
nil	nil	nil
1 1/2 month	£4,000	1
2 month	£10,000	10

The bad debt is only incurred on the new sales. The variable costs are known to be 60% of sales. Fixed costs are £50,000. There will be no increase in stocks required. Total investment in net assets, excluding debtors, will be fixed.

	Current situation £	Increase by 11/2 months £	Increase by 2 months £
Sales	20,000	24,000	30,000
Sales pa	240,000	288,000	360,000
Variable costs	144,000	172,800	216,000
Contribution	96,000	115,200	144,000
Bad debts	———	480	11,000
	96,000	114,720	143,000
Fixed costs	50,000	50,000	50,000
Profit	46,000	64,720	93,000

Despite the bad debt increase extending credit to 2 months, this does provide an increase in profit.

The additional investment in debtors at cost is as follows, assuming the cost of capital is 15%:

Debtor level	20,000	36,000	60,000
Value at cost	12,000	21,600	36,000
Opportunity cost	1,800	3,240	5,400

It is still worth offering additional credit to increase sales.

Debtor ratios

Ratios can also be used for debtor management and probably the most widely used is the debtor collection period. This is calculated as follows:

$$\text{Debtor days} = \frac{\text{Average debtors} \times 365}{\text{Annual credit sales}}$$

This value indicates the average time between the sale being recorded and payment being received. The ratio may be calculated annually or on a weekly or monthly basis substituting the relevant number of days. Most businesses calculate an average for the debtors in total and also values for individual accounts. The following time scales are averages of the periods normally used.

0–40 days	acceptable credit period
40–60 days	chase letter normally sent
60–90 days	second chase letter and personal calls made to the company

The average length of days for debtors in the UK is considered to be approximately 45 days with the very large businesses taking much longer. Beyond 90 days it may be possible to retrieve bad debts through the courts but this is normally not worth the time and cost involved. It is better, therefore, to operate an effective credit policy to minimize the possibility of debtors being written off as bad debts in the first place.

MANAGING CREDITORS

The process for paying suppliers is influenced by three important factors:

- Interest costs
- Administrative costs
- Supplier relationships.

Creditors are an important source of short-term finance and it is obviously beneficial to delay payment. Discounts may be offered by some suppliers as an attempt to improve payment settlement times. However, these should only be considered where the discount is greater than the opportunity cost of early payment as demonstrated by the previous example.

Large companies often take more than 30 days to settle an invoice and this is due partly to administrative factors, particularly where invoices for individual units are settled centrally. Invoices for each supplier may be processed on a certain day each month and where the payment day is missed the supplier will need to wait until the following month. However, delay in payment may well be intentional with companies taking advantage of suppliers who fail to follow-up on outstanding invoices. Failure to pay on time may well damage supplier relationships and this could result in less co-operation from suppliers, increased prices, and delayed or erratic deliveries. A different approach to creditor management, based on Japanese management principles, focuses on the relationship with suppliers where communications are fostered in order to improve service and to reduce the need for extensive stock-holding. Businesses which have taken this approach have reduced the number of suppliers used and have involved the supplier in strategic decision-making processes.

The management of creditors is achieved through the production of regular reports containing the credit payment period ratio which is calculated as follows:

$$\text{Creditor days} = \frac{\text{Average or period end creditors} \times 365}{\text{Total purchases}}$$

The value calculated gives the number of days for which credit is taken.

INVENTORY CONTROL

Stock or inventory may be defined as any current asset held for conversion into cash. In manufacturing industries stock-holdings may account for almost half of the total assets employed and consequently stock management will require careful planning and control. In these types of business the stock is classified into three types:

- Raw materials. This is stock held in the state in which it was purchased without any work having taken place.
- Work-in-progress. This is stock which has been partially converted into the final state and the value is made up of raw material costs plus labour and expenses.
- Finished goods. These are completed goods awaiting delivery or service to the customer.

In typical hospitality organizations the stock-holding levels are likely to be much lower and are often held solely in the raw material state with the transition to finished goods taking place at the point of consumption.

The levels of stock-holding for different types of hospitality organizations are illustrated in Table 7.3.

Table 7.3 demonstrates that overall stock-holdings are a small element of the total assets employed. Stock will comprise food and beverages which will be fairly fast-moving, but also items such as disposables and stationery. The overall objective of inventory control is to minimize the costs associated with stock-holding without losing potential sales through not having sufficient stock available. The cost of stock comprises three elements: the purchase price, the holding costs and the cost to the business of being out of stock. The cost of holding stock includes costs associated with the following:

- Lost interest on money tied up in stock
- Storage space
- Staffing, insurance costs
- Risk of obsolescence and pilferage
- Purchasing costs.

The cost of being out of stock is difficult to calculate accurately. It is not easy to quantify the cost of the loss of customer goodwill and potential lost sales when insufficient stocks are available. Other costs may be incurred where production is halted in other areas, causing a delay in services, through the loss of flexibility which exists when there is buffer stock and the administrative costs incurred from placing lots of small orders.

Stock management should include the use of models where appropriate and also stock turnover ratios. The use of these methods will depend on the nature of the stock; an effective stock control system will not necessarily classify stock items in the same way.

Both the Pareto principle and the A–B–C method are based on the condition that a small percentage of items comprises the greatest value of stock. The Pareto principle

Table 7.3 Stock and debtor ratios for a range of industrial classifications

Median values	Services			Manufacturing			Hotels			Eating establishments			Alcoholic drink establishments		
	1991	1992	1993	1991	1992	1993	1991	1992	1993	1991	1992	1993	1991	1992	1993
Stock turnover	33.4	34.6	36.1	10.4	10.5	10.6	47.7	47.9	51.2	50.2	52.5	53.6	36.1	36	41.8
Debtors days	47	45.1	44.9	63.2	63.3	63.8	17.5	15.5	14.1	9.6	9.7	8.5	4.6	4.3	5.6

Source: The Guide to British Performance, Dun & Bradstreet International, 1995

works on the assumption that 80 per cent of the value of the stock may be held in only 20 per cent of the items. This may well be close to reality in a hotel operation where liquor stocks often have the largest value per item. The A–B–C method of stock control is based on the principle that stock is classified into three groups depending on item value and degree of usage. The distribution of the value of these items may typically be illustrated as follows:

	% Stock volume	% Stock value
Category A	10	50
Category B	30	35
Category C	60	15
	100	100

Category A stocks will be essential items where the probability of a stock out is much higher and therefore levels must be monitored closely. Category B stocks will require less control and Category C stocks almost none. In practice, all stock items can be monitored effectively using computerized inventory systems and in many hospitality organizations these have replaced traditional stock recording systems such as the bin cards used for liquor stocks.

Stock management models

The quantity of stock ordered each time depends on the balance between the costs of holding stock and the costs of a stock shortage. A common model is Economic Order Quantity model (EOQ) which calculates the most efficient order quantity for each item given the costs involved. The calculation is as follows:

$$EOQ = \sqrt{\frac{2CoD}{Ch}}$$

where

EOQ	= Economic Order Quantity
Co	= Cost of ordering
D	= Annual demand
Ch	= Cost of holding stock

The assumptions underlying the model place limits on the use of the model in the hospitality industry. They are that there is a known constant stock-holding cost, a known constant ordering cost, the rates of demand are known and there is a known constant price per unit. The seasonality of the hospitality industry may, in many cases, render the model almost totally useless. However, the model may well have useful applications in the food production industries where production is constant. The following example illustrates how the model is used.

Ingredient X is required on a regular basis throughout the year. It is estimated that the annual demand is 4,095 kg and the cost of holding one kg in terms of refrigeration costs and other costs amounts to £4.00. It is estimated that it costs £4.85 to place and process a purchase order.

The Economic Order Quantity is calculated using the formula:

$$EOQ = \sqrt{\frac{2CoD}{Ch}}$$

Using the given values

$$EOQ = \sqrt{\frac{2 \times 4.85 \times 4095}{4.00}} = 99.65 \text{kg}$$

Assuming that demand is constant over the year purchase orders need to be made

$$\frac{4,095}{99.65} = 41.36 \text{ times per year}$$

which is approximately equivalent to every 8 days.

Stock ratios

Stock control can be improved with the use of ratios. These are most effective when compared with budget, target or forecast figures. The most useful ratio is the stock turnover ratio which is calculated as follows:

$$\text{Stock turnover} = \frac{\text{Cost of sales}}{\text{Average value of stock}}$$

The greater the number of times the stock turns over, the more efficient the stock control. The value can also be expressed in terms of the number of days the commodity has been stored which is calculated as follows:

$$\text{Stock days} = \frac{\text{Value of stock}}{\text{Average cost of sales}} \times 365$$

The ratio may be calculated for stocks in total and also for individual items of stock to highlight slow-moving items.

CASH MANAGEMENT

Cash held by a business will be present in a variety of forms and may well include cash paid by customers, floats, cheques received, cheques paid but not sent and cash held in bank accounts. It is essential therefore, that internal controls are maintained to minimize losses. Such controls include:

- **Separation of duties**. This imposes checks on the individual where tasks are shared and individuals will need to collude in order to misappropriate funds.
- **Management authorization** to raise payment for suppliers invoices, employee expense claims or cash advance requisitions.
- **Surprise checks** where cash is unexpectedly counted.

No system of control can be perfect but internal checks can assist in preventing fraud and can reduce the likelihood of temptation.

Cashflow forecasts

A business needs to have cash available to meet day-to-day expenditure such as payment to suppliers and staff, but it should also not be holding too much cash as this is an inefficient use of funds. Forecasted cashflow statements are essential for identifying peaks and troughs in cash requirements. They may be produced with a simple receipts and payments approach or, alternatively, using a balance sheet approach as recommended by FRS 1 (Financial Reporting Standard 1), an example of which is included in Chapter 3.

CONCLUSIONS

The availability of working capital is essential for business survival. Too little in the form of stocks and cash will mean that the business will literally seize up. Too much will mean that extra costs will be incurred in holding too high a level of stock, cash and debtors. Creditors provide a valuable form of short-term finance and a balance needs to be struck to ensure that creditors are maximized while ensuring that flexibility in supplier relationships remains.

FURTHER READING

Guide to British Business Performance (1995). London: Key Business Ratios, Business Reference Division, Dun & Bradstreet Ltd.
McLaney, E. (1994) *Business Finance for Decision Makers*, London: Pitman Publishing.

8

Performance measurement

INTRODUCTION

The measurement of performance is central to control in both profit-making and non-profit-making service organizations. It is essential for the manager to know *what* has happened, *why* it has happened and *what* can be done now to improve future performance. To be successful, systems for control should support all the organizational objectives as well as the competitive strategies of the business. Yet all too often the focus of performance measurement is centred on easily quantifiable aspects of performance where relationships between measurable quantities are compared with previous performance or standard benchmarks. For many service-orientated businesses, the use of non-financial measures can provide a valuable additional dimension by providing information which attempts to quantify the competitive positioning of the business. As a result, many operations now try to use a mix of financial and non-financial measures where intangibles such as quality and flexibility can be measured along with more traditional measures such as profitability and return on investment. The structure and size of the organization clearly have implications for the scale and range of measures which are appropriate, with particular problems arising as organizations increase in size and change in structure.

Consequently this chapter reviews the different forms of organizational structure in the hospitality industry and provides guidance on current practice in terms of both financial and non-financial performance measures.

STRUCTURE OF THE ORGANIZATION

The role of performance measurement is linked directly to the development of the structure of the organization. A relatively small business, functioning with one or two key members of staff who also happen to be the owners, will still require accurate information in terms of sales and costs. However, much of the information will be carried in the heads of the persons involved, in terms of costs and sales figures, which are easily remembered as each sales order and purchase invoice will have been processed personally. Many businesses start in this way, progressing as tightly focused, owner-managed organizations with a restricted range of products and serving a well-defined market. As the business grows more sophisticated systems for passing information are required and this information may be summarized in the form of performance measures. At this stage of growth a purely functional structure may be considered to be appropriate, with the justification being that by concentrating similar resources in one area of the business, the greatest possible level of economies of scale can be achieved. Evidence suggests that the larger the organization becomes, the more elaborate its structure becomes, requiring the specialization of tasks and the greater need for planning and control to ensure integration. As size increases, individual areas of activity may become larger and increase in number and, in general, the behaviour of the organization becomes more formal. Consequently, within the larger organizations the trend has been to move towards divisionalized structures where individual divisions are given greater autonomy and are responsible for short- and medium-term operating decisions; only strategic decisions are made centrally. Figure 8.1 illustrates the changing structures which can arise as an organization grows in size.

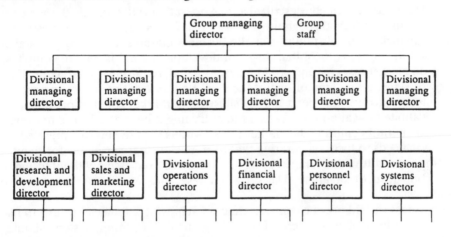

Figure 8.1 Divisionally based organization structure
Source: Keith Ward *Strategic Management Accounting*, 1992.

The functional organization is divided into the key activities of the organization, such as operations and purchasing, along with the support activities, such as marketing, finance and human resource management. The essential feature of this type of organization is that the operating areas share the services of the central support activities. This differs from divisionalized structures where the support activities are dedicated to each operating area. A division should be a natural grouping within the organization such as a group of similar operations which share common operating practices, markets and possibly operate in a common environment. However, the completely divisionalized structure is often unable to achieve the same degree of economies of scale as a functional structure, particularly when each division is made effectively to stand alone. As a result, a combined structure can evolve which tries to obtain the benefits of both formats and this is illustrated in Figure 8.2.

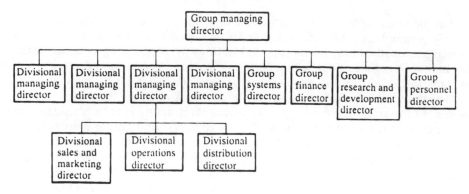

Figure 8.2   Mixed organizational structure
Source: Keith Ward *Strategic Management Accounting*, 1992.

NEEDS OF SINGLE-FOCUS BUSINESSES

A single-focus business can be described as one operating with basically the same range of products and markets throughout. The key issue for single-focus businesses is the changing financial controls required as the business matures. Following the stages of the product life cycle, in the initial stages of development and launch the emphasis is logically on market research and product development, requiring capital spend. During the growth stage, a key area of importance will be the levels of marketing spend. In addition to monitoring this spend and the subsequent market penetration, it is also the time to evaluate how alternative barriers to entry might be erected so as to prevent a flood of competitors entering the market place. At this time the management accounting function needs to focus on ensuring that resource levels are available for significant marketing expenditure and for increasing investment in fixed assets without losing sight of cost control in other areas. The growth phase ends as the market moves into maturity.

The business should now be concentrating on achieving a financial return to justify the earlier periods of investment. The management accounting system should be focusing on cost control and competitor analysis in order to improve and identify opportunities for developing a competitive cost advantage. Once the business is in decline the management accounting process should be evaluating the alternative opportunities for leaving the industry. However, this stage may be avoided if action is taken at the maturity stage to prolong the life of the product through product changes or market expansion or both.

NEEDS OF DIVISIONALIZED STRUCTURES

Systems for performance measurement should be tailored to suit the operational needs of divisionalized structures and may also need to be linked to incentive and reward programmes. As a result, the development of suitable performance measures requires careful planning. Many organizational activities are complex and performance cannot easily be reduced to a single statistic which is meant to serve as a summary of the integrated areas of activity. Additionally, some tasks within the organization are interdependent and require co-operation to exist between divisions, so a performance measure for one division is bound to be inadequate. Some aspects of performance cannot be measured quantitatively while those that can, still require some exercise of judgement where results cannot be clearly predicted. Finally, the process of management can take place in a complex and uncertain environment and, as a result, it may be appropriate to reward effort in addition to achievement. This means that there may need to be a distinction between unit performance and individual performance. There are generally five standards against which performance is normally measured:

- Same unit or department in previous time periods
- Performance of similar units or departments
- Estimates of expected performance
- Estimates of what might have been achieved set after the event
- Performance necessary to achieve desired goals.

The problem with setting standard targets for performance is that the process assumes that the environment remains the same throughout the period. In practice, changes in trading conditions may render the process of comparison useless. As a consequence, a system of this type is often perceived by managers as not being fair. Additionally, the process can fail to take into account what is achievable, especially if standards being set are based on best performance rather than the average performance. This, coupled with the multiple nature of the objectives set, can lead to obsessive behaviour on the part of the manager as he or she attempts to meet all the targets, many of which are in conflict with each other.

To summarize, in order to develop effective processes for performance measurement it is important to consider the following major issues:

- Organizational objectives are complex and cannot easily be reduced to a single, integrated measure of overall performance such as return on capital employed.
- Some tasks and activities within the organization are interdependent and require co-operation between divisions, units or departments and, as a result, performance measurement should be based on the characteristics of the organization.
- Some aspects of performance, such as service levels, are difficult to measure quantitatively.
- It is not always possible to specify the results clearly in advance and as a result the evaluation of performance must also involve the exercise of judgement.
- Management can take place in a complex and uncertain environment and as a result it may be appropriate to reward effort in addition to achievement.

Divisionalized structures based on vertically integrated organizations, that is those that have expanded through the value chain into buyers and suppliers, can also suffer from problems arising from transfer pricing when products and services are sold internally.

The problem of transfer pricing

Transfer pricing situations occur when an organization structures itself into divisions which make independent decisions. A transfer price is needed when profit-making divisions sell products to each other within the organization. The transfer price may be defined as the cost of buying the product or service in the buying division and as sales revenue in the selling division. Consequently, the level of the transfer price will affect the profitability of each division and will therefore, have serious implications for the process of performance measurement. The alternatives available for setting a price are to use cost price, but this will undermine the profitability of the selling division, or to use a marginal cost figure, but this can be difficult to agree, or finally to use a market price. The final option can be achieved easily where there is a highly competitive market outside the organization. The price is set using the outside market and the two divisions can be allowed to deal with each other or not. In either case, total organizational profits will be achieved. The problem becomes far more acute when the outside market is non-existent or non-competitive. In this case, the marginal cost may be used but this means that the selling division is making no profit on the transfer. This is not appropriate for a division classified as a profit centre where performance measurement will be based on profit-related measures.

Additional problems occur with price setting where capacity constraints exist and in this case it might be appropriate to use the opportunity cost, that is the product's value in its next best use, but this is difficult to calculate in practice.

A suggested approach to overcome some of these problems is to set the price using a process of negotiation. If managers are placed in the position where they have to negotiate with each other in order to arrive at acceptable transfer prices, it is felt by behaviourists that they get to understand each other's problems and that this is good for the organization as a whole. The process is less effective, however, where the two parties have unequal power. The remainder of this chapter will focus on the range of performance measures available to the hospitality industry.

NON-FINANCIAL MEASURES OF PERFORMANCE

There is a range of non-financial measures appropriate to service industries, both quantitative and qualitative, which may be used as part of a control process where actual results are compared to plans, budgets, standards and targets. In the last 50 years experts in management have attempted to identify performance criteria to cover all aspects of business performance. Drucker (1953) identified seven generic criteria set by organizations for each performance area and these should be supported by appropriate measures which could be used continually to monitor and control performance against objectives. More recently, Sink (1985) developed Drucker's framework and redefined his own set of performance criteria. These are:

- profitability
- productivity
- quality
- innovation
- effectiveness
- efficiency
- delivery performance
- flexibility

The work of Fitzgerald *et al.* (1991) has focused specifically on service operations, classifying the business along a continuum based on numbers of customers processed per day and the level of services received by those customers. The research is based on operations drawn from this classification and has produced six dimensions against which measurement of business performance can take place. The research also suggests that every service organization will need to develop its own set of performance measures to help it gain and retain competitive advantage. The six criteria are summarized in Table 8.1.

The extent to which this comprehensive range of measures may be used will depend on the nature of the service business. Fitzgerald *et al.* (1991) have reviewed performance measures used in a major international hotel chain with three and four star accommodation. The guidelines illustrated in Table 8.2 have been adapted from their work and others to illustrate how a range of measures may be used to assess performance in a quality hotel operation.

FINANCIAL MEASURES OF PERFORMANCE

Ratio analysis sometimes referred to as univariate analysis, is based on the calculation of individual ratios using data from the trading accounts and the balance sheet. These

Table 8.1 Business performance criteria identified by Fitzgerald *et al.*, *Performance Measurement in Service Businesses* (1991)

Financial performance
  Profitability
  Liquidity
  Capital structure
  Market ratios

Competitiveness
  Relative market share and position
  Sales growth
  Measures of the customer base

Resource utilization
  Productivity (input: output)
  Efficiency (resources planned: consumed)
  Utilization (resources available: consumed)

Quality of service
  Measures of twelve determinants of service quality: reliability, responsiveness, aesthetics, cleanliness, comfort, friendliness, communication, courtesy, competence, access, availability, security

Innovation
  Proportion of new to old products and services
  New products and service sales levels

Flexibility
  Product/service introduction flexibility
  Product/service mix flexibility
  Volume flexibility
  Delivery flexibility

Table 8.2 Measures to assess performance in a quality hotel operation

1. Financial performance

(a) Profit and loss (P/L) account — Weekly/monthly report to management team
Costs and revenue broken down by department/product/market

(b) Average spends — Accommodation, food, beverage

(c) Budget variance analysis — Each month general managers have to submit with their P/L account explanations for the largest variances

(d) Breakdown of pay-roll costs, days absence, overtime, etc. — Reported by each hotel every week

(e) Working capital measures — Debtors, creditors, stock, cash holdings

2. Competitiveness

(a) Market share (number of rooms occupied out of total number of rooms available in the local market) — Weekly/monthly report to management team

(b) Number and percentage of rooms occupied for each of the top six local competitors — Weekly/monthly report to management team

(c) Average room rates charged by top six local competitors — Weekly/monthly report to management team

(d) Number of rooms sold by customer type — Weekly/monthly report to management team

(e) Customer loyalty: number of repeat bookings — Data available from computerized reservations

3. Resource utilization

(a) Percentage of rooms occupied out of total rooms available — Weekly/monthly report to management team

(b) Percentage of beds occupied out of total beds available — Weekly/monthly report to management team

(c) Food and beverage sales per staying guest — Weekly/monthly report to management team

4. Quality of service

(a) Customer satisfaction with overall service levels — Guest questionnaires with data compiled into statistics

(b) Likelihood of repeat custom — Guest questionnaires

(c) Staff turnover by avoidable/unavoidable reasons for transfer — Monthly report to management committee

(d) Number of training days per employee — Occasional report

(e) Complaints per 1,000 customers — Occasional report

5. Innovation

(a) Average age of menus — Occasional report

6. Flexibility

(a) Average time to respond to a customer's request — Relevant in various areas

ratios may then be used for comparison with previous trends, budget or with other similar operations. An alternative and much less widely known technique is that called Multi Discriminant Analysis (MDA) or Z-scoring. This technique has attracted much attention in accounting circles in recent years. Broadly speaking, the methodology is based on a series of traditional ratios such as return on investment and working capital measures, and combines them to produce a single weighted statistic. This statistic may then be used within specific guidelines to assess the potential for success or failure for individual companies. The method was initially devised to overcome the key problem associated with single ratios where some ratios sometimes move in the opposite direction to all the others, thus making interpretation difficult.

Ratios by type

Traditionally financial ratios may be classified into five groups, as follows:

- Profitability and operating ratios
- Asset utilization ratios
- Liquidity (control of cash and other working capital items) ratios
- Capital gearing ratios
- Shareholder investment ratios.

The constituent ratios for each of these groupings are shown in more detail in Table 8.3. Many of these are standard ratios which are used throughout many types of industry where benchmarks and guidelines for ratios are commonly cited. However, care should be taken as the magnitude of the ratios can vary considerably from one industry to another.

The following section aims to provide some guidance for the calculation and interpretation of these ratios when attempting to analyse company performance. It should be remembered that ratio analysis is not an exact science and there are quite often a variety of compositions quoted for one particular ratio.

Profitability and operating ratios

The following ratio is widely used for comparing the return generated with the investment:

Return on net assets (return on capital employed) =

$$\frac{\text{Net profit before long-term interest and tax}}{\text{Total assets less creditors due within one year}} \times 100\%$$

This version of the ratio calculates the return on the fixed and current assets less current liabilities. The usual level of profit to use with this ratio is operating profit or profit before interest and tax, which is the profit available to both lenders and shareholders. By using the profit figure at this level in the profit and loss account the distortive effects of taxation are avoided.

The ratio should produce a value which is as high as possible without undermining the long-term success of the business. A short-term view will mean that earnings are increased through reducing expenditure in a number of areas such as training and maintenance, and capital expenditure is reduced, but both of these policies will adversely affect the long-term viability of the business.

It is important to note that alternative forms are sometimes used, such as return on total assets (fixed assets and current assets), and this will obviously produce a value which is quite different. Consequently, it is important to be clear as to the basis of the ratio being used.

The gross profit margin ratio considers the proportion of sales revenue remaining after the expense of making the product is taken into account. The ratio is calculated as follows:

$$\frac{\text{Gross profit}}{\text{Sales}} \times 100\%$$

The proportion remaining will depend on the pricing strategy of the firm. High volumes may be achieved with lower prices or low volumes may be supported with a high average spend. The other important factor to consider where many products are sold, as in a restaurant, is the sales mix. The next level of profit is described as net margin.

Table 8.3   Financial ratios for measuring performance by category

---

Profitability and operating ratios
   Return on net asset
   Gross profit margin
   Net profit margin

Asset utilization
   Net asset turnover
   Stockholding period
   Debtor collection period
   Creditor payment period

Capital gearing ratios
   Debt to equity ratio
   Number of times interest earned

Liquidity ratios
   Current ratio
   Quick assets ratio

Shareholder investment ratios
   Return on shareholders' funds
   Earnings per share
   Price/Earnings ratio
   Dividend yield
   Dividend cover

$$\text{Net margin} = \frac{\text{Gross profit less salary and wage costs}}{\text{Sales}} \times 100\%$$

Staff costs are a significant expense in the hospitality industry and this ratio reflects the importance of wage costs. The net margin ratio cannot usually be calculated from published figures but can be employed very usefully for internal reporting.

Finally the net profit margin ratio shows what is left of sales revenue after all the expenses of running the business.

$$\text{Net profit margin} = \frac{\text{Net profit before long-term interest and tax}}{\text{Sales}} \times 100\%$$

The value should be as high as possible provided that the business is not earning high profits at the expense of some other aspect. A short-termist attitude to maximizing profit may mean that expenditure on maintenance and replacements is cut, undermining the future potential of the business. The expected value of this ratio will differ quite considerably from one business to the next.

Asset utilization ratios

These ratios are used to assess the effectiveness of the business in using its assets. This includes both long- and short-term assets. The first of these is the net asset turnover ratio which focuses on net assets in total.

$$\text{Net asset turnover} = \frac{\text{Sales}}{\text{Total assets less current liabilities}} \times 100\%$$

The net asset turnover ratio enables judgement to be made on the extent to which the business has generated sales. The size of the ratio will be dependent on the nature of the business and a high ratio does not necessarily indicate profitability, but generally speaking the higher the better. The following ratios focus on short-term assets.

The stock ratio can be calculated in a number of ways which is dependent on the information available. When internal information is available it is possible to calculate a stock-holding days value for every individual product line.

$$\text{Stock holding period} = \frac{\text{Stock held}}{\text{Stock used}} \times 365 \text{ days}$$

The ratio indicates the average number of days which stock remains in the business before it is sold. The stock turnover ratio is the reciprocal of this, that is stock used divided by stock held. It is not possible to provide a standard figure as the days held will depend on the nature of the stock and the mix between fresh and dry goods. However, to maximize the use of working capital, the figure should be as low as possible without a shortage arising.

Another current asset warranting control is debtors, that is those customers who have yet to pay for goods and services received. Ideally, the debtors ratio should be calculated using credit sales, but for analysis using published figures, normally only the total sales are disclosed.

$$\text{Debtor collection period} = \frac{\text{Trade debtors}}{\text{Credit sales}} \times 365 \text{ days}$$

This ratio tells us how long, on average, trade debtors take to pay. The figure should be low as possible and, ideally, it would be better to allow no credit sales. However, the provision of credit is a necessity for many business operations in the hospitality industry, but every effort should be made to ensure the bills are paid up promptly and in full.

$$\text{Creditor payment period} = \frac{\text{Trade creditors}}{\text{Credit purchases}} \times 365 \text{ days}$$

The creditor payment period ratio tells us, on average, after a purchase on credit, the length of time the business takes to pay its debts. A good credit policy will ensure that the business will take as much 'free credit' as possible without losing the goodwill of suppliers.

Liquidity ratios

These ratios are used to assess how well a business is using its working capital. The following ratio provides a measure of the firm's ability to meet its short-term liabilities by matching short-term assets with short-term liabilities.

$$\text{Current ratio} = \frac{\text{Current assets}}{\text{Creditors falling due within one year}}$$

A standard for the current ratio is often quoted as 1.5 to 1, that is ensuring that current liabilities are covered at least 1.5 times by current assets. However, companies in the hospitality sector have survived with ratios which are considerably less than 1, where current liabilities have exceeded current assets. The leisure sector in particular is typical. Where sales are predominantly made for cash, stocks and cash holdings are kept at minimal levels and purchases are bought on credit. Consequently, a consistent ratio of 0.5 to 1 can be expected. This ratio can be adapted to highlight liquid current assets.

$$\text{Quick assets or acid test ratio} = \frac{\text{Liquid assets}}{\text{Creditors falling due within one year}}$$

Liquid assets are normally taken to be cash and debtors excluding stock. However, in some cases the stock may be more liquid than the debtors. Again, the often quoted benchmark is 1 to 1 but the value very much depends on the nature of the business.

Capital gearing ratios

Capital gearing is concerned with the level of funding provided by shareholders and loan providers. Loan financing in practice tends to be cheaper than equity, but loan funding exposes the shareholders to greater risk through the obligation to pay interest and the possibility of changing rates. The recommended value for this ratio changes from industry to industry and the assessment as to whether the value is high or low should be made in relation to industry values.

$$\text{Debt to equity} = \frac{\text{Borrowings (long-term and short-term)}}{\text{Total equity (shares plus reserves)}} \times 100\%$$

A measure of what is considered to be high risk should be based within the context of the nature of the industry. Typically, hotel ventures, for example, require substantial investment and a new operation is likely to be highly geared, with possibly debt exceeding equity in the early stages. As retained earnings increase the ratio is likely to change, with equity becoming the dominant form of finance. The gearing ratio is usually quoted with the following ratio which measures the ability to service the loan finance.

$$\text{Number of times interest earned} = \frac{\text{Net profit before long-term interest and tax}}{\text{Interest payable}}$$

This ratio considers the profitability of the company from the viewpoint of the lender and assesses the ease with which interest is payable. A multiple factor of four times profit to interest is often suggested as a 'safe' value, although there is little evidence to support this.

Shareholder investment ratios

These ratios consider the performance of the business from the viewpoint of the shareholder. Shareholders purchase shares in order to receive a regular income in the form of dividends and to achieve capital growth when the share price increases.

$$\text{Return on equity (return on shareholders' funds)} =$$

$$\frac{\text{Net profit after long-term interest and tax}}{\text{Share capital and reserves}} \times 100\%$$

The return on equity ratio considers return on capital specifically from the shareholders' point of view by considering the relationship between those profits which are attributable to the shareholder and their total funds invested. The following ratio, the earnings per share, is considered to be an important measure of corporate performance.

$$\text{Earnings per share} = \frac{\text{Profit after interest and tax}}{\text{Number of ordinary shares in issue}}$$

This is the profit attributable to each share. The profit generated by the firm belongs to the shareholders whether it is paid out as a dividend or not. The more equity increases, the greater the dilution of the earnings per share. This would indicate that funding from loan sources would serve to improve the resulting value. Although this is true, it should be remembered that loan finance carries its own risks, associated with the commitment to pay interest and repay the capital sum. Earnings per share is normally linked with the following ratio, the price/earnings ratio.

$$\text{Price/Earnings} = \frac{\text{Current market price per share}}{\text{Earnings per share}}$$

This ratio can be seen as the number of years that it would take, at the current share price and rate of earnings, for the earnings from the share to cover the price of the share. The ratio indicates how much an investor is prepared to pay for the business earnings. The value of the ratio depends not only on the business itself, but also on the industry in general.

The following ratio is a measure of the return the investor is receiving on the current value of the investment.

$$\text{Dividend yield} = \frac{\text{Dividend per share (grossed up for tax)}}{\text{Current market price per share}} \times 100\%$$

This measure enables investments to be compared with each other and enables the investor to seek out those investments which out-perform the market in general.

The ability to pay the dividend is measured by the following ratio, dividend cover.

$$\text{Dividend cover} = \frac{\text{Earnings per share}}{\text{Dividend per share}}$$

This ratio indicates how comfortably the firm can meet the dividend out of current profits. A public limited company is under some pressure to provide a consistent dividend in order to maintain share price. However, failure to reinvest in the business can undermine the long-term viability of the operations.

To conclude, shareholder investment ratios are important for the manager of a business because of the power of the market in determining the fortunes of the business in the long term.

Operating statistics

Ratios need not be derived exclusively from the accounting reports. Specific operating statistics, focusing on resource utilization, are well used in the hospitality industry and these may be classified into two categories: those that focus on sales activity and those that focus on cost reduction. Table 8.4 includes several key ratios highlighted in the Uniform System of Accounts for Hotels.

A cost reduction approach may bring increases in profitability but only increases in revenue can bring about an increase of cashflows into the business, and for high fixed-cost industries increases in sales brings about substantial increases in profitability.

Table 8.4 Sales-related and cost-related ratios

Sales-related ratios	Cost-related ratios
Rooms division	
Room occupancy percentage	Wages in relation to sales
Double room occupancy percentage	Laundry costs in relation to sales
Bed occupancy percentage	Servicing cost per room
Maximum rooms revenue	
Average room rate per room occupied	
Average room rate per guest	
Room sales per front desk clerk	
Total average spend of each guest	
Food and beverage operations	
Restaurant occupancy by meal or by day	Wages in relation to sales
Average spend per cover	Material costs in relation to sales
Sales revenue per employee	Stock turnover
Percentage of beverage to food revenue	
Percentage of food/beverage to rooms revenue	

Problems with using ratios

The use of ratios can be confusing where differing advice is offered as to how the ratios can be calculated. The choice of ratios used, the exact definition of the ratio and the conclusions drawn are very much based on personal judgement. Weaknesses in the use of ratios can also stem from the nature of the accounting information used in the analysis. There is a tendency for the profit and loss account to overstate the profit levels and for the balance sheet to mis-state the value of capital tied up in the business.

The balance sheet figures represent the position at a single point in time and the figures may not be representative of the business in general. This creates problems for the interpretation of ratios particularly where ratios are calculated using profit statement and balance sheet figures combined. Figures from the profit and loss account represent a series of transactions over a period of time whereas balance sheet figures do not. Finally, the process of dividing one figure by another means that information is lost. Therefore, the most useful way to analyse performance is to use the ratios with the original statements and to adopt an enquiring and critical approach.

Problems with specific ratios and performance measurement

The most common form of measuring business performance is to use some form of profit in the context of the investment needed to generate that profit, that is the return on capital employed or return on net assets. One particular problem with this ratio, when it is used to compare managers' performance, arises where managers attempt to 'manage' the ratio by reducing the level of investment rather than attempting to increase profit. Consequently, it may be useful to use a related concept called Residual

Income (RI). In this case the group makes a notional charge for interest to the divisions for the funds used. The level of interest may be varied from division to division to reflect the perceived risk associated with the division and its related assets. The notional interest charge is subtracted from the profit figure and the remaining figure is known as residual income and performance is measured using this absolute figure.

Using accounting ratios to predict failure

The calculation of a series of individual ratios using data taken from the company accounts for performance measurement was first used in the 1930s. The technique is now widely used as a monitoring device but there are, as already described, serious problems associated with using ratios. This is based on the fact that published accounts are historical and by the time the results have been published it may be too late to take evasive action. The practice of 'creative accounting', often introduced by failing companies, may also serve to render the process of ratio analysis useless where values in the accounts have been manipulated to mask poor results. Finally, there is the problem of interpretation. One ratio on its own is virtually useless. Instead, a group of ratios should be calculated to obtain the overall picture.

Much research has been carried out to establish if ratios are capable of predicting failure. Ratios focusing on cashflow are generally recognized as being important indicators of performance and Beaver (1968), in a general study, determined that the ratio measuring cashflow to total debt correctly classified firms as failed or non-failed at least 76 per cent of the time, with the ratio profit to capital employed being the next best indicator. In each of the cases the predictions were for one to five years prior to failure.

In a study specifically on restaurant failure in America, Olsen *et al.* (1983) found the ratios in Table 8.5 to be the best indicators of impending failure over the time spans indicated.

To use single ratio analysis effectively as a monitoring device, a variety of ratios should be calculated regularly, taking care to ensure that a standard formula is always used with similar data from the trading accounts to ensure comparability. The predictive power is derived by the process of comparison, where ratios are compared over time for the same business to establish whether the situation is improving or declining and between similar businesses to see whether the company in question is performing better or worse than the average industry result.

Intra-firm comparison, although useful to potential investors, industry observers and participants, does have several inherent dangers, the most significant being the validity

Table 8.5   Ratios used to predict failure in restaurant businesses

Ratio	Months prior
Current assets/Current liabilities	5–9
Working capital/Total assets	6–9
Earnings before interest and taxes/Total assets	16–18
Earnings before interest and taxes/Revenue	12–18
Total assets/Revenue	11–19
Working capital/Revenue	7–11

Source: Olsen *et al.* Improving the prediction of restaurant failure through ratio analysis, 1983.

of the resulting averages calculated by leading industry consultants using a diverse sample of companies from the hospitality industry. The details of the individual companies within the sample are withheld by the consultants to protect the individual organizations but the observer is unable to ensure that the comparability is valid.

Multi Discriminant Analysis

The volume of information provided from traditional ratio analysis methods has led many writers and analysts to be critical of accounting ratios as a sound monitoring device. It can be argued that traditional ratios do not work because they fail to change and adapt to changes in the business environment, and, in reality, businesses have continued to fail despite the use of the technique as a monitoring device. In 1968, an American named Altman proposed, in a leading journal, that the prediction of corporate solvency or failure could be measured by a single value or Z-score. The Z-score model was refined by Altman and subsequent predictive models in use in the UK and USA are all based on the statistical technique, Multi Discriminant Analysis (MDA). Generally, MDA models contain a number of predetermined ratios (five in Altman's version), each with its own weighting, such that the sum of the products of the individual ratios and individual weights yield a Z-score. Guidelines are then provided from research for the interpretation of the score. A number of models has been produced by different researchers following Altman's first publication. Altman himself has revised his model, publishing a later Zeta model, but details for this are not available for the outside user. In the UK, Taffler's model is perhaps the most well known but the full details for the model structure and coefficients are not publicly available. Examples of the models used by Altman and Taffler are illustrated in Figure 8.3.

Problems in the usage of multi discriminant models

Controversy has continually surrounded the use of such models and leading writers in the field of accounting continue to disagree on the effectiveness of the models as a means for predicting corporate failure. However, what is certain is that the models cannot, in their present form, be considered to be 100 per cent successful. In addition, the authors themselves have issued different and conflicting guidelines for the use of these models over the period since their initial publication. The essential criticisms are that almost all models handle failing companies successfully but are less accurate in respect of surviving companies. Inaccuracies may be due to the difficulty in establishing whether the model may be used to transcend industry groups, and particularly whether a model developed for the manufacturing industry may legitimately be used for service industries. Although there is no clear evidence to indicate the importance of industry type, common sense would indicate that specific industries have specific requirements in terms of prediction models and that the ideal solution would be for each industry type to have its own model. Secondly, the methodology in developing the original model is complex and, consequently, a model cannot be easily altered in terms of constituents or cut-off points to meet different needs. For example, Altman's original model included a ratio based on the market value of equity and many researchers

Altman's model:

$$Z = 1.2 \times 1 + 1.4 \times 2 + 3.3 \times 3 + 0.6 \times 4 + 1.0 \times 5$$

where

$X1$ = working capital/total assets
$X2$ = retained earning since inception/total assets
$X3$ = earnings before taxes and interest/total assets
$X4$ = market value of equity/book value of debt
$X5$ = sales/total assets

Altman's revised model (1983):

$$Z = 0.717 \times 1 + 0.847 \times 2 + 3.107 \times 3 + 0.420 \times 4 + 0.998 \times 5$$

where

$X4$ = book value of equity/book value of debt

Taffler's model:

$$Z = 0.53 \times 1 + 0.13 \times 2 + 0.18 \times 3 + 0.16 \times 4$$

where

$X1$ = profit before taxation/current liabilities
$X2$ = current assets/total liabilities, i.e. total debt
$X3$ = current liabilities/total assets
$X4$ = the 'no credit interval'

The 'no-credit interval' is defined as:

$$\frac{\text{Immediate assets} - \text{Current liabilities}}{\text{Operating costs} - \text{Depreciation}}$$

Figure 8.3 Z-score models developed by Altman (1968, 1983) and Taffler and Tisshaw (1977)

assumed, including Altman himself, that the book value could be substituted. This has since been shown to produce spurious results and Altman had to revise the model.

CONCLUSIONS

This chapter has reviewed a variety of performance measures and, where possible, has attempted to use the measures to assess company performance. Single ratio analysis continues to be the most widely used technique for monitoring company performance but many companies in the service sector are supplementing these with operational measures based on non-financial criteria. In order to be effective, ratio analysis requires standardization of the definitions used in the process and consequently, the alternative approaches to items such as the revaluation of assets, the capitalization of interest and the misuse of extraordinary items, can seriously undermine the effectiveness of the technique for monitoring performance.

REFERENCES

Altman, E.I. (1968) Financial ratios, discriminant analysis and the prediction of corporate bankruptcy, *Journal of Finance*, 23 (September): 589–609.

Altman, E.I., Haldeman, R.G. and Narayanan, P. (1977) Zeta analysis: a new model to identify bankruptcy risk of corporations, *Journal of Banking and Finance*, 1: 29–54.

Beaver, W.H. (1968) Alternative accounting measures as predictions of failure, *Accounting Review*, 43: 113–22.

Drucker, P. (1953) *The Practice of Management*, New York: Harper Brothers.

Fitzgerald, L., Johnston, R., Brignall, T.J., Silvestro, R. and Voss, C. (1991) *Performance Measurement in Service Businesses*, London: Chartered Institute of Management Accountants.

Olsen, M., Bellas, C. and Kish, L.V. (1983) Improving the prediction of restaurant failure through ratio analysis, *International Journal of Hospitality Management*, 2(4): 187–93.

Sink, D.S. (1985) *Productivity Management: Planning Measurement and Evaluation, Control and Improvement*, Chichester: J. Wiley.

Taffler, R. (1982) Forecasting company failure in the UK using discriminant analysis and financial ratio data, *Journal of the Royal Statistical Society*, 145 (part 3): 342–58.

Taffler, R. and Tisshaw, H. (1977) Going, going, gone – four factors which predict?, *Accountancy*, 88: 50–4.

Ward, K. (1992) *Strategic Management Accounting*, Oxford: Butterworth Heinemann.

Data for analysis supplied by EXTEL Financial Ltd, Fitzroy House, 13–17 Epworth Street, London, EC2A 4DL.

PART 4
STRATEGIC OPTIONS

INTRODUCTION

Developing the future strategy for an organization is often the most important part of the strategic planning process because it is at this stage that the long-term future operations for the business are determined. The strategic direction taken will depend on the existing position of the organization and the current level of success at meeting the organizational key goals. Having established where the organization is currently placed in terms of resources, efficiency and competitiveness the process of formulating the future strategy can follow. The first step is normally to decide upon a fundamental strategy for the organization and the nature of this can be summarized by the following five simple terms: conservative growth, high growth, neutral, recovery and reduction. Each of these terms is developed in more detail in the following table.

FUNDAMENTAL STRATEGY GOALS AND APPROACH

Conservative growth	An approach to increase sales, profits etc, through the same or related businesses. This is achieved through the development of new products and/or new markets in the existing business.
High growth	An approach to significantly increase sales by acquiring further existing or new products to be sold in existing or new markets. This approach is typified by a strategy of acquisition of companies with similar or unrelated products or by buying 'supplying' or 'buying' companies.
Neutral	An approach to maintain the status quo holding sales and profit at historical levels of performance.
Recovery	The purpose of this strategy is to simply survive. This may involve reducing assets, reducing costs and attempting to increase sales.

Reduction	This approach is to maximize the value of a declining business by salvaging remaining assets and liquidating the business. Alternative approaches might be to sell, negotiate management buyouts or franchise.

A business can grow through either internal expansion by increasing sales or by external acquisition by operating at more and more sites. One of the tasks of senior managers is to identify and evaluate potential investment opportunities and to proceed with those that should be successful. In this section the chapters are devoted considering the sources of long-term funds, the financial tools available to help evaluate projects and a consideration of the merits, disadvantages and practicalities of each. The first step in evaluating a strategic decision is to perform a feasibility study.

Feasibility studies

A decision involving capital investment will require supporting information in the form of an in depth analysis of the financial feasibility of the project. The nature of the investment may range from a decision to purchase new equipment through to a major new property development. Research by Collier and Gregory (1995) identified the following types of decision as being typical for major hotel companies.

- New builds – to include new hotels, extensions to existing hotels and facility additions
- Acquisition of existing hotels
- Disposals of existing hotels
- Equity stakes in new hotels, existing hotels and projects involving management contracts
- Refurbishment and replacement programmes.

Typically a feasibility study for a new operation should include an economic overview of the location, a site evaluation, an assessment of the competition and market research to estimate the demand for the facilities offered. Obviously the financial content of the feasibility study is of paramount importance and should address the following issues.

- Calculation of capital investment required and financing plan. This will include fixed assets, preopening expenses and working capital requirements.
- The expected useful economic life and an estimate of the residual value. A complication arises with investment decisions relating to businesses such as hotels and restaurants and that is that the project does not have a finite life. Unlike a piece of equipment which may be depreciated to zero book value a business operation will be at least holding its value. The problem can be solved by attempting to place a valuation on the business at a point in time when the business can be realistically assessed to be stable. This typically involves considering a five year or ten year time horizon.
- Preparation of forecasted trading statements for a five year period based on expected revenues and costs.

- Preparation of cash flows to show income from trading, capital spend and repayments of debt. In the case of an hotel, this involves an assessment of room occupancy, room rates, food, beverage and other sales, wage costs and other cash expenses. From these cash flows are deducted management fees, property taxes and insurance.
- Sensitivity analysis to show the likely effect of price level changes for each cost and revenue component.
- Taxation effects.
- The anticipated cost of capital associated with the financing of the project.
- Evaluation of the project using capital budgeting methods.

Several of the aspects described above are now given detailed consideration in the following chapters.

9

Funding growth

INTRODUCTION

A business selecting a strategy based on expansion will certainly need to consider additional sources of long-term finance. There are numerous sources of finance that a business may wish to consider and the choice very much depends on a range of factors. These include:

- The cost of raising the finance
- The cost of servicing the finance
- The obligation to pay a return on the capital
- The obligation to repay the finance
- The tax effects
- The effect on the levels of control.

This chapter reviews the alternative forms of finance available to expanding businesses from either equity sources or from borrowing, and considers the advantages and disadvantages of each in terms of the criteria listed above. The hospitality industry often takes advantage of less traditional routes to funding expansion, such as franchising and management contracts and leases, and the merits and the implications of these will also be considered.

RISK AND RETURN

For many new businesses a variety of sources of investment are required in order to raise the necessary funds to purchase the required fixed assets and provide for working capital. The hospitality industry is traditionally heavily fixed-asset-based and often considerable sums of investment are required just to get started. Each of the possible source of funds will have its own cost, that is the return required by the provider of the source of funds, and the size of cost is normally related to the size of the risk as perceived by the lender. Generally, research in this area has indicated that investors expect and normally get higher returns in exchange for accepting increased risk.

For the small business just starting out, the proportions of borrowings to equity can be crucial to survival in the early years of trading. In the past it has been relatively easy to borrow 70 per cent or even 80 per cent against assets from the banks, but this presents the business with enormous debt servicing costs in the form of interest payments. Experience has indicated that levels of 50 per cent to 60 per cent borrowing against assets can provide a workable level of debt without causing cashflow problems later.

The other crucial factor to consider when raising finance is the maximum cost of the finance. In the case of long-term borrowings, such as loans, the cost of servicing the finance is determined by interest rates and the amount of interest to be paid. Alternatively, equity funds are serviced by the payment of dividends which are often flexible in payment and size. However, despite this flexibility, experience indicates that equity investors, that is company shareholders, expect the highest returns in return for being subject to the highest risk. The relationship between risk and return is summarized in Figure 9.1.

The merits and disadvantages of each type of finance will now be considered in detail.

EQUITY CAPITAL

Financing from equity is principally the most important source of finance in the UK, being the largest source of capital and attracting both private and institutional investors. The ordinary shareholders are principally the owners of the business who, through their voting rights, have control over the business. As owners they carry the greatest risk, being the first to suffer if the firm collapses. However, in a successful business the

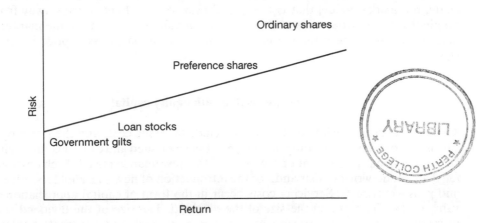

Figure 9.1 The relationship between risk and return

shareholders are the principal beneficiaries, as their return in the form of dividends and capital growth is directly related to the firm's success.

Raising equity funds

There are three main markets for raising equity, and these are:

- Primary capital market
- Secondary capital market
- Alternative Investment Market (AIM).

The primary market is used for providing new finance in the form of new equity issues to the public at large. There are numerous Stock Exchanges around the world, including the International Stock Exchange, and normally a business will choose to raise funds in the country in which it predominantly operates. The secondary market is used for the buying and selling of existing shares and the Alternative Investment Market, which opened in 1995, has been especially created to meet the needs of smaller and growing companies. It replaces the Unlisted Securities Market. The benefits offered by this market are targeted at the ease of access. There are no qualifying restrictions in terms of capital value, length of trading record or percentage of shares in public hands. There are, however, a number of conditions to be met and advice should be sought on meeting these.

Nominal value

When a business undertakes a listing on the Stock Exchange, a decision is made to establish how much equity finance can be raised and the number of shares available to do this. It requires setting a price per share, by which the total number of shares can be multiplied to calculate the total capital to be raised. This initial value for the share is known as the nominal value and is usually about £1 in value. Once the business starts to trade, the market value, that is the traded price of the shares moves away from the nominal value. Further sales of shares will be at values representing the market value and the difference between the nominal value and the latest issue price is called the share premium.

Costs associated with equity capital

The costs associated with equity capital include the issue costs and the servicing costs. The issue costs vary depending on the type of shares issued and can range from virtually zero up to about 15 per cent of the value of the new finance raised. Such costs include legal and underwriting costs and, for the introduction of new shareholders, advertising and prospectus costs. Servicing costs occur in the form of capital appreciation of the value of the share and in the size of the dividend. The size of the dividend is at the discretion of the directors who have the right to withhold payment if they wish. However, this is often not the case as shareholders will soon display their displeasure by selling shares, causing the market price per share to drop which in the majority of cases is undesirable. A drop in share price downvalues the company and creates opportunities for predator companies to engineer a takeover bid while the price is lower.

Equity finance offers the benefit of no obligation to repay the investment unless, of course, the firm is to be liquidated. However, a disadvantage lies in the fact that dividend payments are not deductible for corporation tax. This tends to make dividend payments more expensive than loan interest repayments which fall above taxation in the profit and loss account and are, therefore, tax deductible.

Forms of equity capital

There are three approaches to raising equity finance. These are:

- retained earnings which are past profits held by the firm for investment purposes
- new issues of shares made to existing shareholders
- new issues of shares made to the general public.

Retained profit is obviously an effective source of funds as there are no issue costs. However, it is not true to say that this is a free source of finance. Retained earnings are the property of the shareholders and, as a consequence, there is an opportunity cost incurred by reinvesting in the existing business. The business has, therefore, an obligation to ensure that the retained earnings produce a satisfactory return for the shareholders. Retained earnings represent the most effective method for funding expansion for most companies in terms of cost and the distribution of control remains unaffected. However, projects which require an injection of finance over a period of years face uncertainty using this method of finance as the level of retained profits from year to year depends on the trading success of the business.

A rights issue is one where existing shareholders are given the opportunity to purchase additional shares often at favourable rates. The number of new shares available to each shareholder is usually dependent on their current level of ownership and does not therefore dilute their current level of control. The price is often set at about 20 per cent below the market price for the period just prior to the issue. This ensures that the shareholder takes up the offer or sells the offer to avoid being disadvantaged in the future. The effect of the share issue will be to dilute the value of the share as more shares come into circulation. The price immediately after the share issue is called the *ex-rights price*. The effect is demonstrated by the following example.

Given a balance sheet extract (£000s)		
Total net assets	5,000	
Funded by:		
Share capital	Authorized	Issued
Ordinary shares of £1 each	6,000	3,000

Reserves
Retained profit   2,000
                                                                        5,000

When the market price of the share is 150p the company is said to have a capital value of

3,000 shares at 150p = £4,500,(000)

If a rights issue is made on a 1 for 3 basis at a price of 120p when the market price is 150p, a 20% discount on market price has been given. The effect is that 1,000,000 new shares are issued raising £1,200,000 in cash if all the shares are taken up. This is shown in the balance sheet as £1,000,000 at nominal value and £200,000 as share premium.

The likely new share price after the share issue is theoretically

$$\frac{£4,500,000 \ + \ £1,200,000}{4,000,000} \ = \ 142.5p$$

The value of the rights is calculated as being 142.5p less 120p, that is 22.5p per share. The effect on the balance sheet is as follows:

		£000s
Total net assets		6,200
Funded by:	Authorized	Issued
Share capital		
Ordinary shares of £1 each	6,000	4,000
Reserves		
Share premium account	200	
Retained profit	2,000	
		2,200
		6,200

If a shareholder does not wish to take up the entitlement to purchase shares at a discount, the rights may then be sold to someone else irrespective of whether the person is an existing shareholder or not. However, for the majority of existing shareholders it is not financially viable to ignore the share offer, even if this means buying the rights to sell on immediately. This ensures that most rights issues are successful in terms of all the shares being sold and the required amount of capital is subsequently raised.

Equity issues to the public are much less common and are normally only used for major issues, when a firm is new to the Stock Exchange for example. There are two approaches to issuing the shares. The first is through a third party, normally an issuing house, and is known as an offer for sale. The second is by selling the shares directly to the public via a prospectus, and this is known as an offer by prospectus. The issue costs are much higher compared to a rights issue because of the volume of information which needs to be prepared regardless of which approach is used. The issue price is crucial to ensure that the maximum number of shares is sold for the maximum price. There are two ways in which the problem of price-setting can be reduced. The first is to have the shares underwritten by a broker but this process incurs additional costs. The second is to offer the shares for sale by tender. This is demonstrated by the following example.

A business wishes to issue 5 million shares by tender. After publishing an advertisement to attract potential buyers the following offers are received:

1m shares at £5.00 each
1m shares at £4.50 each
1m shares at £4.00 each
2m shares at £3.00 each
2m shares at £2.00 each
5m shares at £1.00 each

The share issue will be successful if priced at £3.00 per share as there are offers for £5 million shares at £3.00 and above. All the shares will be offered at this price.

The final consideration is the change in control which is likely to occur by inviting further parties to purchase shares.

Preference shares

Shares can be categorized into two types, ordinary shares and preference shares. Preference shares confer preferential rights to the shareholder in the event of liquidation and provide a fixed rate of return. The issue costs are similar to those to be incurred when issuing new shares whereas the servicing costs tend to be lower than for ordinary shares and are directly related to the nominal value of the share. There is no obligation to pay preference dividends but where a dividend is to be paid the preference shareholders have priority over ordinary shareholders. Some preference shares are redeemable and this fact needs to be built into the cashflow. Generally, preference shareholders have no voting rights so the balance of control within the business remains unaltered. In practice, the issue of ordinary shares remains by far the most common form of raising equity finance.

LONG-TERM BORROWINGS

There are basically two types of long-term borrowing:

- Loan stocks or debentures
- Term loans.

The first of these are described as securities and are issued through the capital markets with a fixed interest rate and a pre-stated repayment date to individual investors. When the securities are raised the loan may be secured on the assets of the business or be simply based on a contract. The issue costs tend to be relatively low and the service costs in the form of interest are lower than those returns often expected by shareholders. Holders of loan stocks have the right to enforce payment of interest and also the repayment of the loan itself and this can present a sizeable commitment to the business, particularly during periods of poor trading.

Convertible loan stocks bridge the gap between loan stocks and ordinary shares, being securities which are essentially loan stocks. At a pre-stated date they may be converted by the holders into ordinary shares. This can represent a cheap way to issue shares as the costs of issuing loan stock is lower than for shares. From the investors' point of view it represents a simple way of diversifying risk in that loan stocks may be purchased during the early life of the company, minimizing risk, and these then convert to ordinary shares later with the potential for higher return when the company has become more established.

A term loan is a single loan negotiated from a bank or financial institution. These differ from loan stocks in that a single sum is received from one lender and is not passed from lender to lender, nor may it normally be traded in the capital markets. The usual source of this type of finance is a recognized financial institution and investment seekers should beware of non-legitimate sources of borrowings. Offers of finance advertised in a quality newspaper are no guarantee that the finance is genuine. The fund should be checked out with associations such as the National Association of Commercial Finance Brokers as early as possible. Funds offered below existing market rates should be avoided as these are often not viable.

The remaining part of this chapter will look at what might be considered as less traditional sources of funds but in practice represent effective routes to securing funds for expansion.

FRANCHISING

Franchising is an alternative approach to growth strategy in that it enables a business to expand by forming strategic alliances. The process may be defined as an arrangement whereby a producer or marketeer of a product or service grants exclusive rights to local, independent entrepreneurs to conduct business in a prescribed manner in a certain place over a specified period of time.

The origins of franchising can be traced back to the middle ages when King John of England granted franchises to tax collectors. However, the use of franchising as a business strategy gained prominence in the early 1900s when manufacturers attempted to establish links with retailers. Today franchising is used in many different business sectors as a means of achieving rapid expansion.

Franchising in the hospitality industry has long been associated with high street restaurant chains and hotel operators where it has, for the most part, been highly successful. The restaurant chain probably most often associated with franchising is McDonald's, where the majority of outlets worldwide are franchised rather than company-owned. In the early 1990s it was estimated that as many as 20 per cent of all hotel and restaurant units were operating under franchise arrangements and this figure continues to increase.

Types of franchise strategy

Franchising is a form of strategic alliance and, compared to other forms of alliances, it is low in risk. In terms of cost, it has been found to be more expensive than licensing but cheaper than operating a joint venture. Franchises appear in three general forms:

- Product trade name
- Business format
- Conversion.

Product trade name franchising refers to alliances where the franchisee distributes a franchisor's products, such as The Body Shop stores.

Business format franchising, also known as package franchising, provides the franchisee possibly with a product or service, but certainly with trade name, methods of operation and continuous guidance for aspects such as marketing, administration and staff training in return for a fee. This type of franchising is used most regularly in the hospitality industry. Hotel groups that successfully utilize this strategy for growth include Bass with Holiday Inns, Manor Care with Choice Hotels and Accor with the Mecure brand. In addition to the benefits arising from the support activities already described, the franchisor may well offer access to centralized reservation systems, yield management systems and property management systems.

Conversion franchising describes the development of a network of operations by attracting independent operators and persuading them to work together under a brand name, to attract customers and achieve cost savings through bulk purchasing power. This arrangement is best illustrated by consortia arrangements such as Best Western Hotels. Often membership requires meeting strict targets in terms of quality, as illustrated by the Leading Hotels of the World brand.

Advantages of franchising

For the corporate franchisor, the franchising arrangement offers considerable advantages, primarily allowing a company to expand without using its own capital and therefore incurring relatively lower costs than with other methods of expansion. There are also less administrative problems as the individual franchisee takes over the workload. Finally, the franchisor can obtain greater purchase discounts from suppliers when individual outlets are tied to one supplier as part of the franchise agreement. There are, however, drawbacks for franchisors. The loss of control over franchisees can sometimes harm the overall company image if standards start to drop.

Benefits to the franchisees include the advantage of starting up with a proven name and a tried and tested concept. The franchisor often provides management assistance in the areas of business location, facilities design, operating procedures, purchasing and promotion. Research has shown that the failure rate among new franchised businesses is much lower than among new small independent businesses. In return, the franchisee pays a fee and often an on-going royalty. They may also be tied to the company's nominated suppliers.

Where franchise relationships fail, a deteriorating relationship between franchisor and franchisee is usually cited as the key cause. Often the franchisee resents the royalty imposed by the franchisor and finds it difficult to assess the benefits being received in return. One way to overcome such problems is to expand with some partly franchised units and some wholly owned units. Wimpy have successfully adopted this approach. It enables new products, equipment and management techniques to be evaluated and provides an example of 'best practice' for the franchisees.

Managing and controlling franchises

It is commonly believed that the average length of period for a franchise is about twenty years. During this time the link between franchisor and franchisee can be highly intensive with continual flows of information, funds, products and services, supplies, operations technology and administrative activity. Links between franchisees are also encouraged in some organizations, such as McDonald's, Wendy's and Best Western Hotels where franchisees face similar market conditions and can then co-operate on promotions and share costs. The co-ordination between franchisee and franchisor is based on legal documentation but also on trust. The franchisor can foster trust by offering, in addition to start-up training, ongoing programmes to encourage the development of a culture of trust and shared values. This activity also ensures that standardization is maintained throughout the organization.

Franchise fees

These vary from group to group depending on the nature of the contract. In the case of hotels the basic fee is often around four to six per cent of rooms revenue. In addition, there may also be a requirement for the franchisee to pay joining fees, royalties, reservation commissions and specific fees for other services provided by the franchisor. As a result, Kleinwort Benson Securities (1995) estimate that a typical franchise fee for a 150-room, city, mid-market hotel with a full complement of facilities would be calculated as follows:

Total number of rooms	150
Room nights available per year	54,750
Average room occupancy (%)	65.0
Room nights sold	35,588
Achieved room rate (£)	45.00
Room turnover (£m)	1.60
Franchise fee @ 5%	£80,000

Source: Kleinwort Benson Securities (1995)

Clearly, franchisors need to be fairly large in order to generate significant profits, but with careful planning the process of franchising can provide the route for considerable expansion. Economies of scale ensure that for the larger franchisor the conversion of franchise revenue into profit may be as high as 95 per cent.

MANAGEMENT CONTRACTS

This method of hotel operation separates ownership from management. The management contractor is responsible for the day-to-day running of the operation and its performance. Many international hotel chains now include a number of managed hotels in their portfolio of total operations, including Bass, Forte, Four Seasons, Hilton Hotels Corporation, Intercontinental, Ladbroke and Marriott. The providers of equity for the investment range from individuals, governments, financial institutions and property developers.

The nature of management contracts

Research by Kleinwort Benson Securities indicates that the arrangement between owner and management contractor is typically based on a two-part fee structure. The base fee is approximately three per cent of hotel turnover for a 300-bedroom city-centre operation with high demand and a full complement of facilities, with an additional fee of around ten per cent of gross operating profit. Typical calculations are shown in the example below.

Total number of rooms	300
Room nights available	109,500
Room occupancy (%)	65.0
Room nights sold	71,175
Achieved room rate (£)	70.00
Room turnover (£m)	4.98
Room turnover (%)	60.0
Non-room turnover (£m)	3.32
Hotel turnover (£m)	8.30
Trading margin (%)	30.0
GOP (£m)	2.50

The management contract fee would be calculated as follows:

3% of hotel turnover, £8.3 million	=	£0.25m
10% of GOP, £2.5 million	=	£0.25m
Total management fee	=	£0.5m

Source: Kleinwort Benson Securities (1995)

LEASES ON HOTELS

This is another approach to expansion, again based on the separation of ownership and control. The key difference between a management contract and a leasing arrangement is that whereas with a management contract a fee is made to the managing company, with a lease the managing company pays a rent to the owners and the remainder of the profits remain with the managing company. The most effective form of lease arrangement is a rental charge based on a proportion of turnover. Fixed rental payments tend to be based on providing the owner with a target return on capital and could, in periods of recession, be more than the profit made for the period.

Sale and leaseback

This approach to funding, based on the sale of assets which are then leased back, was popular during periods of high asset values and interest rates. At one time it could also be used as a form of off balance sheet financing whereby the asset itself was not required by accounting convention to be shown on the balance sheet. This served to improve return on capital calculations and reduce gearing ratios. Accounting conventions have now changed, following the requirements of Financial Reporting Standard 5 where assets sold and leased back are now required to be shown on the balance sheet as an asset and as a liability. This serves to increase gearing and reduce the size of rental charges showing in the profit and loss account which gave certain tax advantages. As a result, this form of funding is now considered to be much less attractive.

ALTERNATIVES TO PURCHASING EQUIPMENT

If the resources are available, buying a piece of equipment outright is often the most cost-effective method to adopt as it gives the purchaser the freedom to buy from a wide range of choices. However, if cashflow does not permit immediate purchase, or uncertainty exists over the purchasing decision, then other alternatives may be more suitable.

The principle of free-on-loan is widely used in the hot beverages market. Dispensers are provided free of charge but need to be filled with ingredients from the supplier of the machine. This may mean that a business is able to have access to equipment of a standard that it could not normally afford and be able to benefit from free up-grades as well.

Renting equipment presents an alternative option. Renting agreements are often fixed and are therefore unchanged by fluctuations in interest rates, for example. They are fully deductible for tax purposes.

Leasing arrangements can be confusing when it comes to ownership and tax implications. With lease rental agreements, where the leasing company retains ownership at the end of the lease, all payments are fully tax deductible. However, with any financing agreement there is usually a premium to pay for saving money now and paying later.

Leasing equipment

Leases may be divided into two types:

- Operating leases
- Financial leases.

Operating leases equate to simply hiring the use of an asset and the ownership remains with the lessor who carries out any necessary maintenance. Financial leases are effectively loans with the capital repayable in instalments. As described earlier, these used to be popular because although the effect is basically a loan, neither the asset or the obligation needed to appear on the balance sheet. Changes in accounting practice now ensure that both the asset and the obligation appear on the balance sheet, ending the practice of off balance sheet financing. Another important feature of leasing is the tax efficiency which may arise. Lease payments are shown as an expense in the profit and loss account and are therefore fully deductible for corporation tax.

Despite accounting changes in the approach to leasing, it remains a popular method of funding as the implied interest rate in the leasing contract is often lower than that which the business would have to pay if it bought the asset itself.

The leasing decision

When the business is considering the purchase of an asset the usual procedure is to assess the net benefit of owning the asset in terms of incoming cashflows and to then discount those cashflows using an appropriate discount rate which reflects the level of risk in the project. When the resulting net present value is positive the project is worth pursuing. The decision to invest or not is a completely different decision from that regarding the source of finance. This is illustrated by the following example:

A hotel has decided to purchase new equipment at a cost of £100,000. The decision to make the purchase has already been made on the basis of the expected savings to be gained, but the method of funding the purchase has still to be decided. The asset may either be purchased outright with a loan costing 12% per annum or, alternatively, the company could enter into a lease agreement. The terms of the lease are £20,000, to be paid from the date of the acquisition and for the next four years. After that date the lease may be extended by paying a nominal charge of £100 per year for a further five years. The differences in the financing should be assessed based on the fact that leasing incurs a timing difference in the cash outflows. The timing difference is assessed using discounted cashflow tables. (The principle of discounted cashflows are explained in more detail in Chapter 10.) The future payments on the lease should be discounted using the cost of borrowing as a discount rate.

The net present value of the lease is calculated as follows:

Year	£000	Discount factor	Present value £000
0	20.0	1.00	20.00
1	20.0	0.89	17.80
2	20.0	0.80	16.00
3	20.0	0.71	14.20
4	20.0	0.64	12.80
5	0.1	0.57	0.057
6	0.1	0.51	0.051
7	0.1	0.45	0.045
8	0.1	0.40	0.040
9	0.1	0.36	0.036
Net present value			81.029

The lease option is worth pursuing as the net present value of the payments equates to £81,029 which is less than paying £100,000 now.

TAXATION ISSUES

Cashflows associated with taxation also need to be included in the project analysis and these will vary depending on the project and the nature of the taxation relief attracted. Capital allowances are forms of relief set against taxable profit based on the type of asset purchased. It is beyond the scope of this book to go into further detail apart from noting that there are generally two types of capital allowance available for hotels. These are Industrial Building Allowances and Plant and Machinery Allowances. Further details should be sought from specialized sources.

GRANTS FOR THE UK HOSPITALITY INDUSTRY

In the UK there are numerous grants available at little or no cost that are designed to encourage investment in particular industry sectors or different geographical locations. Obviously, the nature of these grants tends to change on a regular basis and up-to-date information would need to be sought if a business is considering this approach as a form of funding. However, as an example, it is useful to consider the current forms of grant available.

CONCLUSIONS

The purpose of this chapter has been to review the various forms of long-term finance available for expansion and to consider the merits and disadvantages of each. Equity capital provides the vast majority of finance used by hospitality organizations and offers the benefits of low gearing. However, it should be remembered that the cost of servicing equity finance is often higher than that required for loan finance.

FURTHER READING

Field, H. (1995) Financial management implications of hotel management contracts: a UK perspective, in *Accounting and Finance for the International Hospitality Industry*, ed. P. Harris. Oxford: Butterworth Heinemann.
Hoffman, R. and Preble, J. (1991) Franchising: selecting a strategy for rapid growth, *Long Range Planning*, 24(4): 74–85.
McLaney, E. (1995) *Business Finance for Decision Makers*, London: Pitman Publishing. 197–225.
Seltz, D. (1982) *The Complete Handbook of Franchising*, Reading: Addison Wesley.

REFERENCES

Kleinwort Benson Research quoted hotel companies: the world's markets, *9th Annual Review* (1995), *UK Research – Leisure and Hotels*, March: pp. 85–90.

10

Capital budgeting

INTRODUCTION

Capital budgeting is a process concerned with long-term decision-making based on major investments which will affect the strategic direction of the organization. The process includes planning the capital expenditure, evaluating and selecting projects and finally controlling capital expenditures. Planning capital expenditure involves ensuring that the projects selected by the organization yield maximum returns with a minimum level of risk. Generally, the basis for selecting the potential investment should be that only those projects which meet the objectives of the business should be considered and the expected rate of return should exceed the financing cost for the project to be worthwhile. Selecting which investment proposal to pursue and which to avoid is crucial to the business because of the large sums of finance that are often involved and the long-term nature of the commitment. Therefore, a long-term financial investment decision needs to be financially justified by evaluating all the relevant costs and resulting inflows associated with the project. A number of factors needs to be taken into account including:

- The size of the investment
- The economic life of the project
- The certainty of the returns
- The strategic importance to the company.

There are several standard approaches to capital investment appraisal and these will be considered in detail. They include:

- The accounting rate of return (ARR)
- The payback method (which may also be discounted)
- The net present value
- The internal rate of return (IRR).

ACCOUNTING RATE OF RETURN (ARR)

This method, also known as the return on investment (ROI) method, compares the average annual profits over the life of the project with the initial investment, expressing the outcome as a percentage. This is the only method to be considered that uses profits rather than cashflows as the basis of the calculation. The profit, after depreciation, is averaged for the estimated life of the project and the resulting percentage is then compared to some predetermined rate. Competing projects can then be compared with each other. The project with the higher accounting rate of return is the more worthwhile, as the following example demonstrates.

Two investment projects are being considered, both with a six-year life and both with an original investment of £60,000. This value is to be depreciated in full over the life of the project using straight-line depreciation. The anticipated profits for the projects are as follows:

	Project A £	Project B £
Year 1	20,000	4,000
2	16,000	6,000
3	10,000	8,000
4	6,000	10,000
5	4,000	16,000
6	2,000	18,000
Total	58,000	62,000

The average net profit over the life of each project is £9,667 for Project A and £10,333 for Project B. The return on the original investment is:

$$\text{Project A} \quad \frac{9,667}{60,000} \times 100\% = 16.1\%$$

$$\text{Project B} \quad \frac{10,333}{60,000} \times 100\% = 17.2\%$$

The ROI method marginally favours Project B.

The benefits of accounting rate of return can be summarized as follows:

- The result is easy to understand by non-financial managers
- The principle is based on a widely used performance statistic, the return on capital employed.

The principal disadvantage of ARR is that the method is based on profit rather than cashflows, the latter now being recognized as a clearer indicator of company health. As a result, the method ignores the timing of the cashflows and hence the financing cost. Returning to the above example where the timing of the profits are quite different for each project, Project B is favoured despite the fact that the majority of the profits are forecast to occur at the end of the six-year period and are subject to far greater uncertainty.

Where just one project is to be evaluated, the decision is made on the basis of a comparison of the resulting ARR with the prevailing cost of borrowing. Targets are often set at five to ten per cent in excess of these rates. Some organizations use the average capital outlay rather than the total outlay as the basis of the calculation and this will obviously lead to higher percentage returns. The ARR approach is acceptable as long as the meaning of the result is understood throughout.

PAYBACK METHOD

This technique is based on an assessment of how long it will take for the investment to pay for itself out of the cash inflows generated by the project. A project will only be selected if it pays for itself within a certain time period or, alternatively, competing projects will be selected on the basis of the project which pays for itself first.

The payback method is very easy to use and interpret, although the basis of the decision is fairly simplistic. Setting suitable payback periods is a somewhat arbitrary decision and too much emphasis on this aspect will ensure that only short-term decisions are made. However, the acceptability of the payback approach can be improved by discounting the cashflows to take account of the changing value of the inflows over time, although this still tends to emphasize cashflows prior to payback rather than those occurring in the long term. The method is illustrated below using data from the previous example.

The anticipated profits for the projects are as follows:

	Project A £	Project B £
Year 1	20,000	4,000
2	16,000	6,000
3	10,000	8,000
4	6,000	10,000
5	4,000	16,000
6	2,000	18,000
Total	58,000	62,000

The depreciation based on £60,000 over 6 years is £10,000 per year on a straight line basis.

Therefore the anticipated cashflows are:

	Project A £	Project B £
Year 1	30,000	14,000
2	26,000	16,000
3	20,000	18,000
4	16,000	20,000
5	14,000	26,000
6	12,000	28,000
Total	118,000	122,000

These cashflows can be used to identify the point when the original investment will be repaid. For Project A the payback period will fall between Year 2 and Year 3 and for Project B at some point between Year 3 and Year 4. On this basis, Project A would be favoured despite the fact that Project B provides the greater cash inflow.

Despite the disadvantages of the method it is widely used in the hospitality industry to assess both refurbishment and new investment decisions.

DISCOUNTED CASHFLOWS

Capital investment appraisal is based on an assessment of future returns forecasted to be generated by a project. The earlier the funds are made available, the sooner they can be used to make a further contribution to profit. The discounted cashflow attempts to analyse the timing and size of future cashflows. However, the difficulty lies in comparing a £1 of cash inflows received today with £1 received in the future as the two cannot be equal to each other. There are three reasons for this:

- The interest lost
- The effects of inflation
- Risk.

First, there is the interest foregone if the £1 were to be invested over the time period. This represents an opportunity cost. So £1 invested for one year at 10% will be worth £1.10 at the end of this period. Second, inflation undermines the purchasing power of the £1 so that the same amount will not buy the equivalent value of goods and services in one year's time. Finally, risk needs to be considered because £1 received today has more certainty attached to it than the possibility of £1 being received in one year's time.

The process of discounting the cashflows aims to take into account the timing of the cashflows based on the interest foregone. Levels of inflation and anticipated risk are less easy to determine, although a premium may be built into the discount rate in order to compensate for this. Issues surrounding these aspects will be discussed in Chapter 11.

DISCOUNTED PAYBACK

This is a variation of the technique described earlier and is based on an assessment of how long it will take for the investment to pay for itself using discounted cashflows. The example below uses data from the earlier example.

Two projects are being considered, both with a six-year life and both with an original investment of £60,000. The anticipated cashflows are discounted at 10% to give the present values (PV)

	Discount rate	Project A £	PV £	Project B £	PV £
Year 1	0.909	30,000	27,270	14,000	12,726
2	0.826	26,000	21,476	16,000	13,216
3	0.751	20,000	15,020	18,000	13,518
4	0.683	16,000	10,928	20,000	13,660
5	0.621	14,000	8,694	26,000	16,146
6	0.564	12,000	6,768	28,000	15,792
Total		118,000	90,156	122,000	85,058

Project A pays back between Years 2 and 3 and Project B pays back between Years 4 and 5. Therefore, Project A would be preferred.

NET PRESENT VALUE

This technique for assessing capital projects is based on an assessment of future cashflows that have been discounted to take account of the opportunity cost of the interest foregone. If we were to compare investing £10m held today at 10 per cent for one year with an investment which is expected to be worth £12m to be received in one year's time, this would mean that the future cash inflow represents a better return than could be achieved with the present £10m invested at 10 per cent. Alternatively, we could compare how much would need to be invested now (I) to achieve a return of £12m in one year's time at an interest rate of 10 per cent.

$$£12m = I \times 1.10$$

I can be deduced to equal £10.9m and is called the present value. The present value of the future cashflows forms the basis of the capital appraisal technique known as net present value. Where the sum of the future discounted cashflows exceeds the initial investment, the project is deemed to be acceptable and is described as having a positive net present value. Where more than one project is to be assessed, the one with the highest NPV is deemed to be the most acceptable. The discount factor is calculated from the interest rate, where it is assumed that the cost of borrowing equals the cost of lending.

After one year the discount factor at 10% will be 1/1.10, that is 0.909.

To take account of several years the discount rate needs to be compounded and although this can be done arithmetically it is usual practice to make use of published tables giving discount factors for a range of interest rates over a number of years. These are published as an appendix in most accounting textbooks and can be found in Appendix 1 of this text. The following example demonstrates the net present value principle.

A hotel owner decides to invest in renting an adjacent building to run as a restaurant. His initial feasibility study shows that it will cost £200,000 to prepare and equip the site for trading. The projected cashflows derived from net profit after tax, with depreciation added back, for the next five years are as follows:

	£
Year 1	30,000
Year 2	35,000
Year 3	40,000
Year 4	50,000
Year 5	55,000
Total	210,000

The depreciated value of the furnishings at the end of this period is anticipated to be £20,000. Given these values, the hotel owner appears to be gaining by investing in the new site. However, a more accurate picture emerges when the time value of money is taken into account. The future cashflows discounted at 12% are as follows:

Year 1	30,000 × 0.893 = 26,790
Year 2	35,000 × 0.797 = 27,895
Year 3	40,000 × 0.712 = 28,480
Year 4	50,000 × 0.636 = 31,800
Year 5	55,000 × 0.567 = 31,185

Plus residual value of the investment

  20,000 × 0.567 = 11,340

Total value of cash inflows = 157,520

The cash inflows are less than the initial cash outflow and this creates a negative net present value to the value of £42,480. On this basis, the project should be rejected because the investment is failing to achieve a 12% return.

With the use of discounted cashflows it is possible to identify for any project the present value for all future cashflows over the life of the project. The present value of the investment, when taken away from the present value of the cash inflows, produces the net present value which indicates the financial benefit of going into the project in today's cash terms. The higher the present value, the more attractive the project. The NPV approach is a logical method for assessing potential investments because the calculation takes into account the timing of the cashflows and the cost of financing the project, as well as being practical and easy to use. Despite these benefits, the method is not always widely used as many businesses prefer to use the other approaches.

The discount factor

The discount value applied to the calculations is obviously of critical importance. The higher the discount factor, the lower the resulting net present value. If the factor chosen is too high, there is the danger that profitable projects will be rejected, while using a factor which is too low will result in loss-making projects being pursued. Normally, the factor is chosen by considering the cost of the funds being used for the project with additional premiums built in for risk, as required. The calculation of the discount factor is considered in further detail in Chapter 12.

Cashflows

When discounting cashflows a number of assumptions are made. The first is based on when the cashflows actually occur. The discount tables assume that the cashflow is received in its entirety on the last day of the year. Obviously, this is not likely to be the case but in order to simplify the workings the last day principle is used. This means that the cashflows are always slightly understated in terms of value. Selecting which cashflows to put into a forecast can cause difficulty, particularly when the project is based on existing assets. Generally, it is essential to determine the relevant cashflows, that is the future likely cashflows, and ignore past or sunk costs. Opportunity cost cashflows are cashflows which are not actually paid out but instead represent the benefit foregone by taking one particular course of action.

INTERNAL RATE OF RETURN (IRR)

This approach assesses the rate of return required by the project to balance cash inflows and outflows. This is a development from the NPV method where IRR is the rate which, if applied to a project, yields a zero NPV. Solving the value of IRR is not easy and a process of trial and error is required. To assess a project only those with an IRR above a predetermined level are accepted or, if competing projects are being assessed, the one with the higher value is the one to be accepted. Using the data given for the NPV calculation, the following workings demonstrate the IRR method.

The future cashflows were discounted at 12% as follows:

Year 1   30,000 × 0.893 = 26,790
Year 2   35,000 × 0.797 = 27,895
Year 3   40,000 × 0.712 = 28,480
Year 4   50,000 × 0.636 = 31,800
Year 5   55,000 × 0.567 = 31,185

Plus residual value of the investment

  20,000 × 0.567 = 11,340

Total value of cash inflows = 157,520

The cash inflows are less than the initial cash outflow and this creates a negative net present value to the value of £42,480. On this basis, the project should be rejected because the investment is failing to achieve a 12% return. In order to find the IRR it is necessary to discount the cashflows a second time to provide the basis for finding the discounted rate. This will give a net present value of zero.

The future cashflows are now discounted at 4%, as follows:

Year 1   30,000 × 0.962 = 28,860
Year 2   35,000 × 0.925 = 32,375
Year 3   40,000 × 0.889 = 35,560
Year 4   50,000 × 0.855 = 42,750
Year 5   55,000 × 0.822 = 45,210

Plus residual value of the investment

  20,000 × 0.822 = 16,440

Total value of cash inflows = 201,195
Net present value 201,195 − 200,000 = 1,195

Therefore the IRR must fall between 4% and 12%, but fairly close to 4%. The exact value can be pin-pointed as follows. A factor of 12% represents negative 42,480 present value whereas 4% represents positive 1,195. Therefore a NPV of zero will fall between the two positions.

(42,480) - - - - - - -   0   - - - - - - - - - +1195
12%   ?%   4%

A change of 8% represents net present value of 43,675. The distance from 1,195 to 0 is

$$\frac{1,195}{43,675} \times 8\% = 0.219\%$$

Therefore the IRR is 4% + 0.219% = 4.219%

To identify the IRR it is necessary to apply alternative rates of discount to pin-point the exact value and this can be time-consuming. However, the disadvantage can be easily overcome with the use of computer software, and most electronic spreadsheets now contain the facility to calculate IRR.

More importantly, however, there are a number of conceptual shortcomings associated with the IRR method. First, it is possible for there to be more than one IRR associated with a project. This occurs when the cashflows are a combination of positive and negative values throughout the life of the project. Under these circumstances it is not easy to identify the real internal rate of return and the method should be avoided. Secondly, although IRR is closely related to the NPV approach, the two methods can sometimes give conflicting signals. This occurs when the two projects have different levels of investment because IRR is based solely on percentage returns rather than the cash value of the return. As a result, when considering a project one may have a return of say 10 per cent, another of say 13 per cent, but the 10 per cent project may yield the higher NPV in cash terms and would therefore be preferable.

Finally, IRR cannot cope with differing required rates of return. With NPV calculations it is possible to use different discount factors throughout the life of the project as the cost of capital changes, whereas IRR can only provide an average rate of return.

Despite these major shortcomings, IRR continues to be a popular approach to capital investment appraisal. Managers seem to prefer the calculation of a percentage value, which can then be compared to a hurdle rate, rather than the comparison of cash values for choosing between projects.

APPRAISAL METHODS AND HOSPITALITY ORGANIZATIONS

All of the methods discussed here, along with hybrid versions, are successfully used in the hospitality industry. It is not unusual to see capital expenditure decisions in larger groups being split into two types: those associated with refurbishment, which are assessed locally and are not subject to formal analysis, and those associated with development, where considerably larger sums of investment are required and a range of capital investment appraisal techniques may feature in the feasibility study. Table 10.1 is a summary of the relative benefits of the four investment techniques.

Research based on the hotel industry carried out by Collier and Gregory (1994) suggests that a range of methods are used for capital investment appraisal with the NPV approach being the least popular, although a number of businesses use the internal rate of return.

Table 10.1 Summary of the relative benefits of the appraisal techniques

	ARR	PBP	NPV	IRR
Directly related to wealth maximization	No	No	Yes	No
Accounts for timing of cashflows	No	No	Yes	Yes
Uses all relevant information	Yes	No	Yes	Yes
Easy to use and understand	Yes	Yes	Yes	No
Comparison to weighted average cost of capital	Yes	No	Yes	Yes
Takes account of risk	Yes	Yes	Yes	Yes

CAPITAL INVESTMENT CONTROL

The control and evaluation of capital investment projects is essentially concerned with ensuring that the achieved cashflows match the forecasted values and that the anticipated level of net present value will be achieved. Failure to achieve the forecasted NPV is primarily due to actual cashflows falling short of target and/or the discount rate that is used for discounting the cashflows being lower than that actually required. A shortfall in cashflows may be due to the trading environment being less favourable than was originally forecast, or the organization's internal costs associated with the project being higher than originally anticipated. An increase in the required discount rate can come about following either an increase in prevailing interest rates or an increase in the company's own cost of capital percentage. Finally, the initial spend on the investment may be considerably more than first anticipated and this will also reduce the forecasted net present value.

Consequently, the monitoring and control of capital projects is as important as the initial evaluation. The process of monitoring occasionally identifies that a project is no longer worth continuing with, and a decision needs to be taken as to whether the project should be abandoned or not. The final decision should be based on an NPV analysis of the relevant costs and the benefits of continuation relative to those associated with abandonment. Post-completion auditing is the process of reviewing the project once it has reached its conclusion in order to ensure that any errors in the investment decision process are not repeated. This process is less appropriate in the hospitality industry where investments tend to have a long life.

CONCLUSIONS

This chapter describes the various theoretical approaches to assessing investment opportunities. Academically the net present value approach is considered to be the most accurate as it takes account of a range of factors including the changing value of money, future cash flow expectations and risk. Despite this a range of methods are used in practice and it is not uncommon in the hospitality industry for emphasis to be placed on the accounting rate of return and the payback period. In order to use investment appraisal techniques successfully it is essential that other practical considerations are addressed such as taxation, inflation, risk and sensitivity analysis and these will be discussed in the following chapter.

FURTHER READING

McLaney, E. (1994) *Business Finance for Decision Makers*, London: Pitman Publishing.

REFERENCES

Collier, P. and Gregory, A. (1994) Strategic management accounting: a UK hotel sector case study, *International Journal of Contemporary Hospitality Management*, 7(1): 18–23.

11

The practical aspects of capital investment appraisal

INTRODUCTION

The purpose of this chapter is to consider how capital investment appraisal techniques can actually be put into practice as part of the process for evaluating strategic options. A range of important issues are considered, including the practicalities for:

- Forecasting accurate cashflows
- Assessing the life span of projects
- Calculating the residual value
- Allowing for working capital requirements
- The effects of taxation and inflation
- Measuring risk.

Sensitivity analysis and probability are also discussed.

WHICH METHODS ARE PREFERRED?

Several studies on the use of capital investment appraisal methods in organizations from the manufacturing sector conclude that the most frequently used method for capital investment appraisal is the payback method, although this is often used alongside the other methods. Where discounted cashflow is used, the preferred method appears to be the internal rate of return (IRR) rather than the theoretically preferred net present value (NPV) method. The rate of return is also often used despite the problems associated with it. Many organizations also attempt to analyse risk formally through the use of sensitivity analysis, and incorporate estimates for inflation into the calculation. Research carried out in the hotel industry by Collier and Gregory (1994) indicates similar conclusions. Table 11.1 is a summary of their findings in this area.

In view of the arguments against the use of the IRR approach, described in the previous chapter, it is perhaps surprising that the use of the method is so widespread.

Table 11.1 Nature of capital investment appraisal in the hospitality industry

Nature of industry	Management style	Investment technique?	IRR	Cost of capital
Hotel & Leisure	Centralized	Profit payback	No	na
Hotel & Leisure	Centralized	ARR/payback	Partly	Loan rate
Travel	Decentralized	IRR	Yes	1.5 x loan rate
Conglomerate	Decentralized	Cover interest (yr 1)	No	na
Brewing	Decentralized	ARR/IRR	Yes	Business specific rate
Brewing	Decentralized	IRR	Yes	Corporate weighted average cost of capital

Source: P. Collier and A. Gregory *Management Accounting in Hotel Groups*, 1994.

This may be due to the fact that the workings provide a percentage result which is easier to interpret than the NPV result. IRR also provides a ranking of projects of different size and time scale without the need for a predetermined discount rate, as is required by the NPV method. The availability of computer software in the form of a simple spreadsheet greatly assists in the calculation of this method and this has also probably lead to an increase in usage.

VALUE OF ACCURATE FORECASTING

In order for capital investment appraisal to be successfully carried out it is essential that the forecast data be as accurate as possible. In practice this means reliance on management experience and standard relationships unique to the hospitality industry. Collier and Gregory (1994) support this view, commenting that the considerable bank of past experience that is available to many hospitality organizations enables the investment decision to be fairly standard, with rules of thumb such as *build cost per room* for a given star rating often being quoted along with expected room occupancy figures. This information can then be supported with data drawn from sensitivity analysis and computer simulations. The fundamental factor in investment appraisal is the accurate estimate of the annual cashflows from the project. Mills and Stiles (1994) provide three key groupings for analysing all the relevant factors likely to affect the cashflow forecast. These are:

● Financial factors
● Marketing factors
● Operating factors.

Within these headings are included a number of relevant factors. These are shown in Table 11.2

It should also be noted that capital investment techniques assume that cashflows will occur at the year end for discounting purposes. Discount tables can be produced on a

Table 11.2 Factors likely to affect cashflow forecasts

Financial factors	Marketing factors	Operating factors
Inflation	Sales forecast	Operating costs
Risk	Product life	Material and supply costs
Taxation	Discount policy	Start-up costs
Residual value	Promotional policy	Shut-down costs
Working capital	Selling costs	Maintenance costs

Adapted from R. Mills and J. Stiles *Finance for the General Manager*, 1994.

month-by-month basis but the use of these would considerably increase the nature of the workings. As a result, the year end assumption means that cashflows are marginally over discounted and are, therefore, included in the calculation at a slightly lower value than would be the case in reality. The effect of this is marginally to increase the payback period and to understate the net present value and internal rate of return.

ASSESSING THE LIFE SPAN OF THE PROJECT

The determination of life span for a project can prove awkward to forecast in the hospitality industry where investments are considered to have an indeterminant life. A piece of equipment is normally considered to have a certain working life, and on this basis it is then depreciated. This type of investment is, therefore, simple to analyse in terms of initial spend, cash savings and residual value. Projects involving long-term investments obviously cannot be evaluated over an indefinite period as the value of the forecasted cashflows becomes virtually meaningless. As a result, hospitality projects are normally evaluated over a five to ten year period and the accuracy of the residual value at this point is of prime importance. The residual value may well be in excess of the initial spend and the determination of this figure will require an understanding of valuation techniques.

CALCULATING THE RESIDUAL VALUE

Residual value or exit value is the value of the project at the end of the evaluation period. A simple method of arriving at a valuation figure would be to revise the purchase or construction cost in line with the Retail Price Index (RPI). Other valuation methods may be appropriate, such as the current market price or the depreciated replacement cost. However, considerable controversy surrounded the valuation of hotel assets in the early 1990s and several major groups faced a substantial devaluation of fixed assets. As a result, the British Association of Hotel Accountants (1993) have produced a guide to recommended practice and advise that:

> hotels should be valued by reference to their recent/current performance and future trading potential. This is achieved by the 'Income Capitalisation' approach which seeks to assess value by reference to projected net cash flows.

The 'income capitalization' approach is achieved by using either discounted cashflows or a method called the 'earnings multiple'. The discounted cashflow approach is based on the capitalization of the anticipated net cashflows for an operation by discounting at the appropriate discount rate. The earnings multiple approach requires the application of a multiplier to the maintainable earnings which are defined as the adjusted cashflows, expressed in present values, which can be sustained over the foreseeable future.

ALLOWING FOR WORKING CAPITAL

In addition to the capital investment, most projects will require an injection of working capital. This will normally be required throughout the life of the project to fund and maintain stock levels and to allow for credit sales while enabling the suppliers to be paid. It is fair to suppose that this part of the investment will be substantially released at the end of the project and should therefore be shown as a cash inflow in the final year. However, at the end of the project, its value will be considerably reduced due to the changing value of money over time. Consequently, it is normal practice to discount the working capital released with the discount factor rate prevailing at the conclusion of the project.

EFFECTS OF TAXATION

The complexities surrounding taxation and capital appraisal are beyond the scope of this book. However, the basic principles will be discussed briefly. Capital expenditure may attract tax relief for a business in the form of what is known as capital allowances and this should be reflected in the forecasted cashflows. The capital allowance amounts to a reduction in the taxable profit in order to relieve expenditure on fixed assets, and acts as an incentive to industry to encourage investment. There are several categories of fixed asset, each with its own rules and level of capital allowance. However, the two most widely used categories are plant and machinery and industrial buildings.

The first of these, plant and machinery includes a wide range of assets and a business may deduct 25 per cent of the cost of the asset from the profit for the period during which the asset was acquired. In each subsequent year of ownership, 25 per cent of the balance may be deducted.

The second group, industrial buildings, includes buildings used directly or indirectly in manufacturing, the transport industry and other restricted purposes excluding shops and offices. Relief is given by allowing a business to deduct 4 per cent of the cost from the taxable profit for each year the asset is in use. Other types of asset attract capital allowances and these include, in particular, hotels. The important aspects of taxation for the hospitality industry include ensuring that all allowances are claimed for, particularly for plant and machinery, as this represents an important resource, assessing the effect of taxation on the investment decision, and assessing the benefits to be derived from alternative methods of funding, for example, outright purchase versus rental.

Plant and machinery allowances

Plant and machinery allowances can be important to the hospitality industry where there is substantial investment in this form of asset and yet this is often an under utilized resource. The difficulty in gaining the maximum benefit from these allowances lies in the complexities of separating out those items which are allowable from those which are not. This is particularly difficult to achieve where contractors are involved to complete work, the value of which includes equipment costs as well as installation costs. The contractor may be unwilling to reveal the plant and machinery figures within the total cost and a separate valuation may be required. The definitions for plant and machinery that are eligible for capital allowances are often quite complex and specialist advice will ensure that the maximum benefit is achieved. The following example illustrates the calculation of capital allowances.

A restaurant purchases a delivery van for £15,000. The capital allowances would be calculated as follows:

Year	Balance (£)	Capital allowance
1993	16,000	4,000 25% of £16,000
1994	12,000	3,000 25% of £12,000
1995	9,000	2,250 25% of £9,000
1996	6,750	1,688 25% of £6,750

This pattern is continued until the asset is scrapped or sold.

The effects of taxation on the investment decision

A serious implication for capital investment appraisal occurs when taxation distorts the investment decision by converting a viable investment into a non-viable investment. This can occur when profits are different from cashflows generated by the project and may be the case when equipment is purchased and capital allowances are set against the profit and loss account.

The level of distortion depends on the level of sophistication of the tax system. It is important to realize that tax rules change so specialist advice should be sought to ensure that the current rates and benefits are being fully utilized.

EFFECTS OF INFLATION

The term inflation means the erosion of the purchasing power of currency due to the increase in price of goods and services and is a condition which affects most economies of the world at some time. Even relatively low levels of inflation can affect purchasing power over long periods and therefore the implications need to be assessed in the capital investment appraisal workings. The use of discounted cashflows is not sufficient to take account of the full effect of inflation. The general principle is that cashflows stated in real terms, that is without adjusting for inflation, should be discounted with a rate which also excludes inflation in order for like to be compared with like. Where sales and costs and have been adjusted for inflation, then a rate incorporating an adjustment for inflation should be used.

The difficulty in forecasting for inflation lies in the fact that, in reality, the individual cashflow elements, such as sales, material costs, labour costs and others, may not all be subject to the same degree of inflation.

MEASURING RISK IN INVESTMENT APPRAISAL

Any project which is to be assessed over the long term must be subject to some risk or uncertainty. Risk describes the situation where it is possible to identify all the likely outcomes and possibly their likelihood of occurring without being absolutely sure what will actually occur. Uncertainty describes the situation where it is not possible to be sure of all the likely outcomes. All business decisions are subject to some uncertainty and risk but it is really only the latter which can be identified and subsequently assessed.

There are many possible sources of risk which may cause actual revenues and costs to be different from those initially forecast and these may be classified as:

- Business risk
- Operating risk
- Financial risk.

The first of these, business risk, occurs as the result of changes in the economic and business environment and all businesses will be subject to this. It can arise from a variety of sources such as changes in the nature of the competition, technological changes and innovation, and from fluctuations in the national or world economy.

Operating risk arises from the cost structure of the operation and occurs when variable costs are substituted by fixed costs. Substantial fixed costs mean that a certain level of revenue is required simply to cover those costs. In times of good business conditions this can be an advantage, but losses will soon be incurred during periods of recession.

Financial risk arises from the method of financing used by the business and is reliant on the cost of servicing the debt. Sources of funds derived from borrowings incur an interest charge which must be paid regardless of the level of profit. The relationship between equity funds and interest-bearing funds is called gearing and is described in greater detail in Chapter 12. During periods of good trading conditions, high gearing; that is where the majority of funds are provided from borrowings, can be beneficial. The interest charge is fixed and once this has been paid the remainder of the profits can be used for dividend payments or reinvestment. However, during periods of recession the fixed interest charge must be met regardless of the level of trading, which means possibly incurring an even greater loss as a result of paying interest.

It is important to take account of risk, whatever the form, and this should be done on a formal basis for each investment project.

SENSITIVITY ANALYSIS

Sensitivity analysis is used to evaluate the effect of a change on each of the factors contained in the forecast. In the capital investment appraisal calculation a variety of factors will need to be forecast. These include:

- The value of the initial investment
- The length of the project
- The sales projections based on volume
- The selling price and sales mix
- The cost projections
- The predicted discount rate.

All of the values are subject to change either individually or as a result of dependence on another variable. Simple calculations can easily be performed where just one variable changes to determine the likely effect on the project. More complex relationships may require the use of computer simulations and even a basic spreadsheet can be of assistance for modelling 'what if' situations. The following example illustrates a basic approach to sensitivity analysis where each variable changes independently of the others.

The Riverside Hotel plc has the opportunity to invest in a new restaurant to support its existing activities. The demand is estimated to be 10,000 covers per year for a minimum of five years. The following data relate to the decision:

- The restaurant is estimated to have no residual value and will cost £140,000 payable immediately.
- The average spend per cover is estimated to be £10.
- The variable costs are estimated to be £6 per cover (£3 for labour and £3 for materials).
- Overheads are not expected to be affected by the decision.
- The firm's cost of finance for such a project is estimated to be 10%.
- The project is not expected to require any additional working capital.
- The effects of taxation are to be ignored.
- All cashflows occur at the year end.

The annual cashflows will be:

$$10,000 \times £(10 - (3 + 3)) = £40,000 \text{ each year.}$$

Thus the project's cashflows are forecasted to be:

	£
Year 0	(140,000)
1	40,000
2	40,000
3	40,000
4	40,000
5	40,000

The discount factor is 10% and this can now be used to calculate the net present value of the project.

Year	Cashflows (£)	Discount factor	Present value (£)
0	(140,000)	0	(140,000)
1	40,000	0.909	36,360
2	40,000	0.826	33,040
3	40,000	0.751	30,040
4	40,000	0.683	27,320
5	40,000	0.621	24,840
		3.791	11,600

The annuity factor for five years at 10% is 3.791 (see Appendix 2). The NPV is therefore:

$$- 140,000 + (40,000 \times 3.791) = 11,600$$

The project has a positive NPV and is therefore, favourable. The aim of sensitivity analysis is to assess the effect of a change in the input factor on the overall acceptability of the project. The factors used in the above example to calculate NPV are:

Original investment	I
Annual sales volume	V
Selling price per unit	S
Labour cost per unit	L
Material cost per unit	M
Cost of capital	C
Life of the project	n
Annuity factor	A

The workings above can be represented by a single equation:

$$- I + (V \times (S - (L + M))) A = NPV$$

To carry out the sensitivity analysis, each factor will be considered in terms of what change is required to reduce the NPV to zero which is the point when the project would no longer be acceptable.

1. Original investment
$$- I + (10,000 \times £(10 - (3 + 3))) \, 3.791 = 0$$
$$I = 151,640$$

2. Annual sales volume
$$- 140,000 + (V \times £(10 - (3 + 3))) \, 3.791 = 0$$
$$V = 9232$$

3. Selling price per unit
$$- 140,000 + (10,000 \times £(S - (3 + 3))) \, 3.791 = 0$$
$$S = £9.69$$

4. Labour cost per unit
   $- 140{,}000 + (10{,}000 \times £(10 - (L + 3))) \; 3.791 = 0$
   $$L = £3.30$$

5. Material cost per unit
   $- 140{,}000 + (10{,}000 \times £(10 - (3 + M))) \; 3.791 = 0$
   $$M = £3.30$$

6. Cost of capital
   $- 140{,}000 + (10{,}000 \times £(10 - (3 + 3))) \; A = 0$
   $$A = 3.5$$

Looking at tables, the annuity factor is closest to 13% for a project 5 years in length

7. Life of the project
   $- 140{,}000 + (10{,}000 \times £(10 - (3 + 3))) \; A = 0$
   $$A = 3.5$$

Looking at tables, the annuity factor is closest to 41/2 years for a project with a 10% return. The results are summarized as follows:

Factor	Original estimate	Value for zero NPV	% difference
Original investment	£140,000	£151,640	8.3
Annual sales volume	10,000 units	9,232 units	7.7
Selling price per unit	£10	£9.69	3.1
Labour cost per unit	£3	£3.30	10.0
Material cost per unit	£3	£3.30	10.0
Cost of capital	10%	13%	30.0
Life of the project	5 years	$4\frac{1}{2}$ years	10.0

This highlights those factors which are the most sensitive and are most likely to undermine the profitability of the project, which in this case are selling price and sales volume.

The above example illustrates a simplistic view of sensitivity analysis but even this level of analysis enables the decision-maker to gain a grasp of the crucial factors in the project.

USE OF PROBABILITIES

The use of probabilities enables a whole range of possible outcomes for each factor to be considered, providing that it is possible to assess the probability of each outcome occurring. It is then possible to calculate a range of possible NPVs for the project. In practice, this can be difficult to achieve but as with sensitivity analysis the exercise offers the opportunity for the decision-maker to become familiar with the key factors in the project.

Using the above example, it will be assumed that all factors are known with certainty except sales volume and the material costs. In practice, all factors should be assigned probabilities as none can be determined with certainty. However, this would produce a large volume of calculations which, in practice, would need to be calculated with the aid of a computer. Let us say that extensive market research indicates that annual demand will either be:

(a)   11,000 covers (0.3 probable),
(b)   10,000 covers (0.5 probable), or
(c)   9,000 covers (0.2 probable)

The possible outcomes are:

NPV at 11,000 units	=	$-140,000 + 11,000 (10-6) 3.791$
	=	26,804

NPV at 10,000 units	=	$-140,000 + 10,000 (10-6) 3.791$
	=	11,640

NPV at 9,000 units	=	$-140,000 + 9,000 (10-6) 3.791$
	=	(3,524)

This could then be combined with possible outcomes for a second factor. Independent of sales volume, the cost of materials will either be:

(a)   £3 per cover (0.6 probable),
(b)   £4 per cover (0.3 probable), or
(c)   £2 per cover (0.1 probable)

The situation now becomes more complicated because there are a total of nine possible outcomes based on three alternatives for sales volume and three alternatives for material costs.

The possible outcomes are:

(a)   Material costs of £3 per cover

A NPV at 11,000 units	=	$-140,000 + 11,000 (10-6) 3.791$
	=	26,804

B NPV at 10,000 units	=	$-140,000 + 10,000 (10-6) 3.791$
	=	11,640

C NPV at 9,000 units	=	$-140,000 + 9,000 (10-6) 3.791$
	=	(3,524)

(b)   Material costs at £4 per cover

D NPV at 11,000 units	=	$-140,000 + 11,000 (10-7) 3.791$
	=	(14,897)

E   NPV at 10,000 units   = $-140{,}000 + 10{,}000\ (10-7)\ 3.791$
                                       =   (26,270)

F   NPV at 9,000 units   = $-140{,}000 + 9{,}000\ (10-7)\ 3.791$
                                       =   (37,643)

(c) Material costs at £2 per cover

G   NPV at 11,000 units   = $-140{,}000 + 11{,}000\ (10-5)\ 3.791$
                                       =   68,505

H   NPV at 10,000 units   = $-140{,}000 + 10{,}000\ (10-5)\ 3.791$
                                       =   49,550

I   NPV at 9,000 units   = $-140{,}000 + 9{,}000\ (10-5)\ 3.791$
                                       =   30,595

In order to assess the probabilities of two events occurring, the probabilities need to be combined and this is achieved by multiplying the two values together. The following list indicates the possible outcome and probability in order of size.

Possible outcome	NPV	Probability
A	166,804	0.18
B	151,640	0.30
C	36,476	0.12
D	25,103	0.09
E	13,730	0.15
F	2,357	0.06
G	108,505	0.03
H	89,550	0.05
I	70,595	0.02
		1.00

Using the above data, only one of the above options can occur. Only projects with a positive NPV should be accepted and, from the above data, it is possible to conclude that there is a 50 per cent chance of a positive NPV occurring.

CONCLUSION

This chapter investigates the important practical issues that have to be considered when evaluating capital investment projects. The general manager needs to be aware of the implications of inflation, taxation and risk on the capital investment decision and how to assess the effect of these factors in practice. Specific issues such as taxation will need the input of specialist advice to determine the current implications for a particular organization. However, a major requirement of general management is to be able to assess and manage risk to ensure that exposure is minimized. It is important to be able to identify risk within the project and there are a range of financial techniques available to assist in this. These include an analysis of key ratios and cashflows. The techniques described in this chapter can be effectively used and developed further with the use of computer software such as spreadsheets or more complex simulation packages.

FURTHER READING

McLaney, E. (1994) *Business Finance for Decision Makers*. London: Pitman Publishing.

REFERENCES

British Association of Hotel Accountants (1993) *Recommended Practice for the Valuation of Hotels*, London: BAHA.

Collier, P. and Gregory, A. (1994) Strategic management accounting: a UK hotel sector case study, *International Journal of Contemporary Hospitality Management*, 7(1): 18–23.

Collier, P. and Gregory, A. (1995) *Management Accounting in Hotel Groups*, London: Chartered Institute of Management Accountants.

Mills, R. and Stiles, J. (1994) *Finance for the General Manager*, London: McGraw Hill Book Company.

12

Managing the cost of capital

INTRODUCTION

The potential sources of funds available to an organization have already been described in detail in Chapter 9. These can basically be divided into two main groupings, those classified as equity sources and those which can be termed as borrowings. It has already been noted that equity sources can expect a varying level of return whereas borrowed funds normally require a fixed return in the form of interest. Generally, the providers of the finance expect a level of return which is directly linked to the perceived level of risk. The higher the risk, the greater the expected return.

The purpose of this chapter is to illustrate how the cost of capital can be calculated for each of the sources of funds and how an overall value can be determined, reflecting the capital structure of the business. Establishing the cost of capital is often quite difficult in practice and the financial theories available are quite complex. The aim of this chapter is to provide a simple overview of the key issues surrounding the cost of capital calculation in order to enable the manager to understand the principles involved.

COST OF CAPITAL

If a company is to survive in the long term it must achieve a return in excess of the cost of the funds invested in that company. The total cost is dependent on the cost of funds from equity sources and on those from borrowings. The return on equity is made up of the returns paid to shareholders in the form of dividends and also the funds that belong to shareholders which have been retained within the company for reinvestment. The simplest approach to finding the cost of capital requires estimating the cost for each source of funds and combining these to provide a single value using a weighted average. However, there are other approaches, which are considerably more complex, and these will only be described briefly in this text.

COST OF EQUITY

Equity comprises both the share capital and the retained profits. Retained profits are often, mistakenly, considered to be a free source of finance. However, this is not the case, there is an opportunity cost associated with using these funds. The calculation for the cost of equity should therefore reflect this fact. The cost of equity can be calculated in two ways. The first of these, the *dividend growth model*, provides the simplest way of determining the cost of equity. The second, the *capital asset pricing model*, is more complex and will only be considered briefly here. However, some of the issues surrounding the second approach are of importance and these merit further discussion.

The dividend growth model

This model calculates the cost of equity from the dividend payment and the current market price of the share, this being the dividend yield ratio.

$$\text{Dividend yield per cent} = \frac{\text{Dividend}}{\text{Market price}}$$

This simple ratio only represents the cost of capital when the dividend remains the same for each following year and of course this is not always the case. Additionally, the method is flawed in that it is unable to cope with a dividend payout of zero.

The dividend growth model is an attempt to overcome this shortfall by building into the equation an estimate for future increases in dividend levels. The most common version is known as the Gordon's growth model where:

$$\text{Cost of equity} = \frac{(d(1 + g) + g)}{M} \times 100$$

where
$$d = \text{the last dividend paid out}$$
$$g = \text{expected dividend growth rate in percentage terms where investors expect the dividend to grow at a constant rate into the future}$$
$$M = \text{the market price of the share}$$

This formula is demonstrated with the following example.

Where a company pays a current dividend of 12p per share and the current market price of the share is 96p, if the anticipated growth rate is 4% the cost of equity (Ke) will be:

$$Ke = \frac{(12(1 + 0.04)}{96} + 0.04) \times 100\%$$

$$= 17\%$$

The model provides a simple approach to finding the cost of capital but the relationship should be used with care. In practice, it is difficult to establish a value for g, the growth rate, with any certainty. The model also assumes that g will be less than the cost of capital. This is proven by rearranging the formula to show the market price of the share, M.

$$M = \frac{D(1 + g)}{Ke - g}$$

If the long-term growth rate is equal to the cost of capital, the formula shows the value of the company as infinite, which is clearly not practical.

The capital asset pricing model

This model of estimating the cost of equity is based on the returns expected by the investor for buying the share. It assumes the greater the risk, the greater the expected return. The level of risk is measured via a factor known as beta. This is combined with two other factors to determine the cost of equity. These are the risk free rate and the market risk premium. The *risk free rate of return* represents the most secure rate of return which could be achieved and is normally quoted as being the rate available from government stocks. The *market risk premium* represents the excess return above the risk free rate that investors expect in order to compensate them for holding riskier investments.

Beta is the measure of systematic risk, that is the riskiness implied by a business activity and the way in which it is financed. Risk measured by beta is that part of the total risk a business faces which cannot be diversified away because it is present in the general business environment and will affect all businesses in some form. The beta can be measured in a number of ways but the most usual method is to estimate it using standard regression techniques based upon historical share prices. This is the approach adopted by the London Business School's Risk Measurement Service which publishes beta values for industry use. The cost of equity is thus calculated with the following formula.

Cost of equity = risk-free rate of return + (beta × market risk premium)

To apply the formula in practice one must know the beta factor for a particular business. These are published for companies while estimates for the other two factors are freely available in the UK.

The capital asset pricing model (CAPM) is also useful for unquoted companies where there is no available market price for the shares. In this case a beta factor for a similar company might be used to enable a cost of equity value to be calculated. The CAPM has generally become an acceptable method of calculating the cost of capital. However, there are still some problems associated with it.

Evidence suggests that it is not always possible to summarize the market related risk with a single indicator such as beta. The approach also assumes that the past is an accurate indicator of the future. This is not necessarily true in a changing economic environment.

COST OF LOAN CAPITAL

A second element in the cost of capital calculation is the cost of the borrowings. Loans can be classified into two types:

- Irredeemable where only interest is required
- Redeemable where both interest and capital repayments are required.

The true cost of loans can be calculated quite simply where the debt is irredeemable. In this case the cost of debt is calculated using the following formula.

$$\text{Cost of debt} = \frac{\text{Interest}}{\text{Market value of the security}}$$

When the debt is redeemable or repayable in full, the cost of capital is found by discounting the cashflows. The discount rate which equates the present value of the future cashflows to the current market value of the debt is the cost of capital for those borrowings. The following example illustrates this.

Loan stock was originally issued at a part value of £100. The current market value is £93. The repayment of the original amount is due in five years' time and interest of 10% is due annually on the original amount. The cost of the loan stock is calculated by considering the cashflows over the next five years.

	Cashflow (£)	Discount factor	Present value (£)
Year 0	(93)	1.000	(93)
1	10	0.909	9.09
2	10	0.826	8.26
3	10	0.751	7.51
4	10	0.683	6.83
5	110	0.621	68.31

At 10% discount factor a positive present value of £7 is achieved. If a discount factor of 12% is used the resulting net present value is almost zero and this, therefore, equates to the cost of debt. The drop in the value of the loan stock has occurred because the return of £10 or 10% must be below the market rate of interest. As a result, the perceived value of the stock falls below the original value of £100.

A business may have more than one source of debt finance. The overall cost of the debt can be calculated by taking a weighted average of the individual components.

Loan capital and tax relief

The interest payable on borrowings attracts corporation tax relief so the true cost of loan capital should reflect the benefit derived from this. The true cost of the interest payment is calculated as follows:

$$Cost = i(1 - T)$$

where   T = the corporation tax rate
       i = the interest rate

WEIGHTED AVERAGE COST OF CAPITAL (WACC)

Having calculated a cost of capital for each element of the capital structure, the resulting cost of capital is calculated by combining these values as a weighted average, as shown in the following example.

At present, a company is funded by a combination of equity and debt capital. The equity shares were originally issued at 60p and have a current market price of £2.70. The current dividend is 10p per share and this has been growing at a rate of 5% per annum in recent years. The loan capital issued by the company is irredeemable and has a current market value of £95 against an original cost of £100. Interest is paid out at a rate of 12%. The company has 70% of its operations funded by equity with the remainder funded by borrowings.

The weighted average cost of capital is calculated from the cost of the two sources of funds. The cost of equity is found using the dividend growth model.

$$\text{Cost of equity} = \frac{10p \ (1 + 0.05)}{270p} + 5\%$$

$$= 8.9\%$$

The cost of the borrowings is found as follows:

$$\text{Cost of debt} = \frac{12}{95p}$$

$$= 12.6\%$$

The weighted average cost is found from

$$(70\% \times 8.9\%) + (30\% \times 12.6\%) = 10.01\%$$

EFFECT OF GEARING ON THE COST OF CAPITAL

A very large proportion of businesses have some level of gearing. It is important, therefore, to consider the relationship between gearing and the cost of capital. The more common approach is known as the traditional view and is based on the assumption that as gearing increases the perceived risk increases and equity investors and

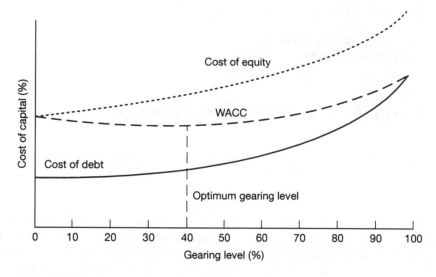

Figure 12.1   Weighted average cost of capital (WACC) – traditional view

lenders will require a higher return. It is suggested that at lower levels of gearing neither investor group requires greatly increased returns and, as loan sources tend to be cheaper than equity sources, the weighted average cost of capital will decrease.

At higher levels of gearing risk becomes more important to investors and the WACC starts to increase significantly. As a result, there is a point where the WACC is at a minimum and this is described as the optimum level of gearing. This effect is shown in Figure 12.1.

The approach was questioned in the 1950s by Miller and Modigliani (MM) (1958) who published what is now considered to be an extremely significant article questioning the basis of the traditionalists' view. MM argued that it is not possible for a business to borrow additional funds and, by so doing, reduce its weighted average cost of capital. Their view is that when additional cheap loan finance is introduced, the weighted

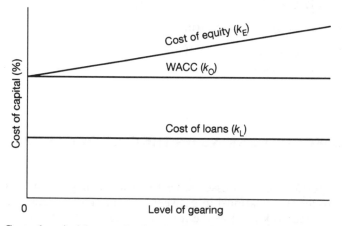

Figure 12.2   Cost of capital for varying levels of gearing – the MM (pre-tax) view

average cost of capital is not affected because there is a corresponding increase in the cost of equity. The effect is illustrated in Figure 12.2.

As a result, MM conclude that there is no optimum level of gearing. Since MM proposed their theories there has been much debate by academics on the issue of cost of capital and gearing. It has since been shown that some of the assumptions underlying the MM approach are incorrect, although there is some logic in the MM theory. As a consequence, a compromise position is recommended whereby WACC is likely to fall as gearing increases but that this trend will change when equity holders and lenders become increasingly conscious of risk.

CONCLUSION

The cost of capital is an important concept to be understood in all types of organization. All sources of funds have a cost of servicing associated with them, either in the form of variable or fixed charges. Accurate determination of the cost of capital is vital as this figure represents the discount rate used in capital investment decisions. If a figure is calculated which is higher than the actual level, this may result in profitable projects being rejected. Conversely, an estimate which is too low means that unprofitable projects will be accepted. There are different approaches to the calculation of the cost of capital value and each has its inherent difficulties. The level of gearing in a company is thought to affect the cost of capital of the component sources of finance based on the perception of risk. It is generally believed that increased gearing up to a certain level reduces WACC. However, Miller and Modigliani have proposed that gearing makes no difference to the cost of capital. The theories remain unproved and consequently the general consensus is that gearing does have some bearing on the resultant cost of capital.

FURTHER READING

McLaney, E. (1994) *Business Finance for Decision Makers*. London: Pitman Publishing.

PART 5
STRATEGIC IMPLEMENTATION AND EVALUATION

INTRODUCTION

The speed of change in the hospitality industry during the 1980s and 1990s has proven that it is essential for hospitality firms to monitor market trends continually and adapt internally to meet each new challenge. Structural changes in the industry have led to the emergence of new international hospitality firms as a consequence of merger and acquisition activity and the increasing influence of Pacific Rim developers. The traditional patterns of ownership have been replaced with a complex arrangement of franchising, management contracts, joint ventures and strategic alliances aimed at reducing the cost and risks associated with development.

Technological developments in systems, processing capability and connectivity will revolutionize marketing, management information systems and customer expectations. Pressures from the external environment will compel hospitality organizations to review their internal structures. Teare and Ingram (1993) forecast that structural changes are likely to include:

- Flatter organizational structures with fewer levels of management, improved responsiveness and information processing capability
- Managers who co-ordinate expert operatives rather than control subordinates
- More decentralized operations which promote involvement through responsibility, participation and commitment from a better-educated workforce.

Structural change in the hospitality industry has greatly affected the range of tasks which operational managers now undertake:

> with head office staff reduced in number to the minimum possible and growth no longer the overriding strategy of most firms, unit managers are now being asked to perform differently. They are being asked to compete effectively on the local level, where conditions are extremely competitive, to scan the environment for threats and opportunities, and to build a strategic plan for their units based on this type of analysis. This leaves the unit manager with the need to become a much more independent decision maker and one who is much more aware of the forces in the environment and how they effect the future of the unit. (Olsen, 1991: 23)

Chapter 13 reviews the problems associated with valuing a business and focuses in particular on problems associated with the hospitality industry. Chapter 14 looks at the implications of global expansion on accounting-based information systems and Chapter 15 examines some of the forecasts and predictions currently being proposed for the future of management accounting.

REFERENCES

Olsen, M.D. (1991) Structural changes: the international hospitality and firm, *International Journal of Hospitality Management*, 3(4): 23.

Teare, R. and Ingram, H. (1993) *Strategic Management: A Resource Based Approach for the Hospitality and Tourism Industries*. London: Cassell.

13

Measuring the value of a business

INTRODUCTION

The principal aim for measuring the value of a business is to provide a monetary measure which accurately reflects the true worth of that business. The issue of business valuations and the choice of appropriate methodology is somewhat controversial in accounting circles and the UK hospitality industry has been particularly troubled in this area, especially in the hotel sector. This has been clearly illustrated by events in the early 1990s, particularly between 1990 and 1991, when it was reported that the value of London hotels fell by up to 22 per cent for three star operations, 19 per cent for four star ratings and 13 per cent for five star properties. One company to be devastated by the impact of revaluation was Queens Moat House plc.

Queens Moat House plc
The Queens Moat House group of hotels was founded in 1968 when John Bairstow, formerly the founder of the company Bairstow Eve, which he later sold to Hambros Bank for £77 million, bought a Moat House in Essex and opened it as a hotel. There followed over the next 20 years a programme of rapid expansion both in the UK and abroad, financed by high levels of debt and several rights issues.

In 1982 26 hotels were purchased from GrandMet and by 1983 the group was confirmed as being UK's largest provincial hotel chain. By 1987, following four rights issues in as many years, the group had purchased 24 hotels in Europe plus the Dutch Bilderberg Hotels. In 1991 a further 15 hotels were purchased following the eighth rights issue.

The group continued to appear to be trading as a healthy concern right up to January of 1993, when distinguished brokers such as Robert Fleming Securities were still urging investors to buy shares in the company with the encouragement that 'the rating on the (Queens Moat) shares is still absurdly low'.

By 31 March 1993 shares were suspended from trading at a price of 47.5p. This followed the announcement of the 1992 year end trading results with a pre-tax loss of £1.04 billion, the second largest loss in UK corporate history.

Much of this loss is attributed to the write down of property values and considerable controversy has surrounded the size and background to this write down. In December 1991 (QMH year end) the valuers Wetherall, Green and Smith (WGS) valued the assets at £2 billion. A year later the assets were revalued at £1.35 billion, while a second valuer, Jones, Lang Wootten (JLW) valued the same assets in December 1992 as being worth £861 million. Both valuations were prepared on an open market, willing seller basis following guidelines laid down by the Royal Institution of Chartered Surveyors (RICS). QMH directors chose to accept the lower valuation, hence the write down of almost £1.2 billion on the group's hotel portfolio.

There are many valuation techniques available and often the most appropriate method will depend on the subsequent use of the valuation. These potential uses include providing a balance sheet figure for accounts preparation as well as setting a value for acquisition purposes, insurance assessment, investment monitoring, such as return on capital employed measures, and also possibly to provide a figure to banks as the basis of collateral valuations when raising a loan. The most appropriate method depends not only on the end purpose of the value but also on the size and type of business. This chapter will consider the application of a variety of approaches to business valuation, namely

- Dividend yield basis
- Price/earnings basis
- Net assets basis
- Comparable transactions
- Earnings multiple
- Net present value using discounted cashflows.

Finally the issue of hotel valuations will be considered in light of the recommendations offered by the British Association of Hotel Accountants.

MEASURING SECURITY VALUE

The larger-sized business, which has shares trading on an apparently efficient stock market, can be evaluated by simply multiplying the shares in issue by the current share price. This provides an estimate for the value of the entire company and the figure is known as market capitalization. However, in many cases such an approach is not possible because the company does not have public shares trading and hence no current market price per share is available. In other cases it is not the total value of the company which is sought but instead a value required for a particular asset or group of similar assets. In these cases other approaches are required.

DIVIDEND YIELD BASIS

This method of valuation is based on the principle of estimating the value of the total equity within a business. It assumes that the ordinary shares of two different businesses should have a similar dividend yield ratio provided that they are similar in size, activity, capital gearing and proportion of profit paid in dividend. If the shares of one of these businesses are quoted, then this will enable the price to be set for the unquoted business. The value of the business in question can then be found by applying the following ratio.

$$\text{Gross dividend yield} = \frac{\text{Dividend paid (gross)}}{\text{Current market price per share}}$$

where

$$\text{Current market price} = \frac{\text{Dividend paid (gross)}}{\text{Gross dividend yield}}$$

The following example demonstrates the method in practice.

Z Ltd is a small business which at the end of the last financial year paid out a dividend of £12,000 gross. The dividend yield value for a similar listed business is 8% gross. Using this a market price for the business can be estimated.

$$\text{Estimated market price} = \frac{12,000}{8\%}$$
$$= £150,000$$

There are a number of inherent difficulties in using this method in practice. It may well be difficult, if not impossible, to find a similar business for comparison purposes. And even if this were possible, the approach assumes that the dividend paid always reflects the level of the market price for the share which may not be valid.

PRICE/EARNINGS BASIS

This approach is based on the ratio between current market share price and the earnings of the business. The ratio is as follows.

$$\text{P/E} = \frac{\text{Current market price per share}}{\text{Post-tax earnings per share}}$$

where

Current market price = P/E × earnings per share

The method assumes that the P/E ratio will be the same for similar firms and therefore can be applied to calculate a share price which can be used to estimate a value for market capitalization. The following example demonstrates the method in practice.

A Plc and B Ltd are two businesses of similar size, activity and capital structure. A is quoted on the Stock Exchange whereas B is not. The P/E ratio for A is 10 and the annual earnings after tax for B have been a static 40p per share. B has 1 million shares in issue. Using the formula then.

$$10 = \frac{\text{Current market price per share}}{40p}$$

The market capitalization of the business is estimated to be £4 million.

The choice of P/E ratio to be used is often dependent on one or more of the following factors:

- Economic conditions
- Type of industry
- Size of operation
- Marketability of shares
- Reliability of forecasted profits
- Levels of gearing.

As a result, it can be quite difficult to establish an appropriate value to use and it is not uncommon for a specific sector to have a wide range of values.

NET ASSETS BASIS

This method is based on the book value of the assets, as stated in the balance sheet, and the valuation is based on the net assets less outstanding long-term loans.

The approaches described so far are fairly theoretical and do not provide the solution to finding the value to specific assets. The following section will now consider this particular problem.

PRACTICE OF VALUING ASSETS

The Companies Act allows UK companies to adopt accounting policies other than purely historical cost accounting when preparing their financial statements. As a result, tangible fixed assets, such as property, may be stated at either market value on the date they were last valued or at current cost. Where market values are used the valuations should be kept up to date but the difficulty occurs in establishing what this market value should actually be. An accounting policy peculiar to the UK is that properties such as hotels need not be depreciated on an annual basis as it is assumed that with sufficient ongoing maintenance expenditure they will at least hold their value. However, it is estimated that approximately 10 per cent of total revenues should be spent on maintenance activities for this assumption to hold true.

Establishing a true value for the assets of a business is required for a variety of purposes. Generally, the shareholders and investors expect to see the assets stated at current value so that profit performance can be assessed in relation to the capital investment via the return on capital employed ratio. The shareholder will also want to make comparisons with the performance of other companies in the hotel industry and also with companies in other industries, and it is therefore, essential that the bases used for valuation are realistic and adequately disclosed.

The responsibility for ensuring that the valuation of assets has been correctly stated is solely that of directors of the company, specifically the finance director, and this is monitored by the auditors of the company, whose job it is to ensure that the prepared financial statements give a true and fair view. In the past, UK hotel companies tended to revalue a third of their properties each year, ensuring that all assets were revalued at least every three years. However, following the dramatic changes in property values in the last few years, several leading companies now revalue on a more regular basis.

The Ladbroke Case
In 1993 Ladbroke, owner of Hilton International, undertook to reduce the book value of its assets by £195.6 million. The loss was deducted from the revaluation reserve in the balance sheet, creating a £146.7 million loss in the profit and loss account.

In the UK, guidelines for revaluation are provided by the Royal Institution of Chartered Surveyors (RICS). The British Association of Hotel Accountants (BAHA) has also produced guidelines for a recommended practice for the valuation of hotels (published in 1993) and recommends working with RICS to establish a common approach.

The following methods offer a more practical solution to the problem with the final approach, that of discounted cashflows, being the method that is recommended by the BAHA guidelines.

COMPARABLE TRANSACTIONS

This approach is based on the market value for the business if it is sold for its existing use. An existing hotel operation might typically include the land and buildings, items such as fixtures, furniture, equipment, computers, goodwill and stock. All of these assets are classified as being tangible, excluding goodwill which is an intangible asset, and can be identified as being derived from the location, the operational strengths of the site and finally the personal flair of the existing management team. An estimate for all of these should be included in the valuation although in practice this can be quite difficult to achieve. The total value of the site can be set by simply considering similar and comparable transactions where competitive operations have already been sold for what is considered to be a fair value using a measure such as the price per room achieved. It may be necessary to increase or decrease the measure used depending on how the strengths of the operation compare to the competitive operation.

This approach is often more practical for the smaller operation where there may be many similar businesses on which to make a comparison. However, for the larger, possibly more individual operation in a unique position it may simply not be possible to determine the value by considering similar transactions. In this case it may be necessary to use an alternative approach.

EARNINGS MULTIPLE

This approach is based on simply applying a multiple to maintainable earnings, which are defined as the adjusted net cashflows in present value terms which can be sustained over an extended time period. The resultant estimate of stabilized earnings will be capitalized at the appropriate multiplier, reflecting all appropriate considerations. While the maintainable earnings can be estimated fairly easily, the determination of the multiplier must reflect the perceived risk or security associated with the investment.

NET PRESENT VALUE USING DISCOUNTED CASHFLOW

The value of an asset or a business in total can be estimated by predicting the future cashflows and then discounting these with an appropriate cost of capital. The particular elements which need to be considered in the valuation process are

- Sales growth rate and operating profit margins
- The timings associated with the projected earnings
- The working capital requirements
- The hotel's residual capital value
- The magnitude of recurring levels of maintenance, capital expenditure and any additional investment required
- The cost of capital.

Theoretically, this approach is the soundest in that it takes into account the timing and value of future earnings. However, it is dependent on an accurate forecast for the future cashflows and the correct estimation of the appropriate discount rate. The following is an example to demonstrate the methods in practice:

A colleague of yours is considering purchasing a chain of 21 public houses, the summarized accounts of which appear below.

Balance Sheet at 31 December

	1994 £m	1994 £m	1995 £m	1995 £m
Fixed assets (net of depreciation)		8.0		8.5
Current assets:				
Stocks	3.3		5.6	
Debtors	0.5		0.8	
Bank balances	0.3		0.1	
		4.1	6.5	
		12.1		15.0
Current liabilities (amounts falling due within one year)				
Creditors	3.8		3.3	
Bank overdraft	0.3		1.5	
Dividends	0.7		0.9	
Taxation	0.7		1.0	
		5.5		6.7
Total assets less current liabilities		6.6		8.3
Long-term liabilities (amounts falling due after more than one year)				
Long-term loan @ 10% pa		1.4		1.4
		5.2		6.9
Financed by:				
Called-up share capital				
4 million ordinary shares @ £1		4.0		4.0
Share premium		0.2		0.2
Reserves		1.0		2.7
		5.2		6.9

The financial record for the business for the last two years is summarized below:

Profit and Loss Account Year Ended 31 December

	1994 £m	1995 £m
Revenue	15.40	17.50
Profit before interest	2.34	3.74
Profit before taxation	2.20	3.60
Taxation on profit	0.70	1.00
Profit after taxation	1.50	2.60
Dividends (net)	0.70	0.90
Retained profit	0.80	1.70

Industry analysts advise that quoted companies in similar industries have an average P/E ratio of 5, a gross dividend yield of 15% and a cost of capital of 12%.

You estimate the net cashflows to be achieved following the purchase to be:

Year 1–5   £800,000 per year
Year 6   £1,200,000 per year

Advanced Corporation Tax is 3/7 of the net dividend. A value for the business can be calculated using a range of approaches.

The dividend yield valuation can be worked out, providing that the dividend is converted to a gross value as follows:

$(0.9 \times 3/7) + 0.9 = 1.29$

$$\text{Market price} = \frac{1.29}{15\%}$$

$= £8.6$ million

The price earning valuation is as follows:

$2.6 \times 5 = £13$ million

The net assets as quoted at book value amount to

£8.3 million $-$ £1.4 million $=$ £6.9 million

allowing for repayment of the long-term loan. The calculation for net present value is as follows:

Year	Cashflows (000s)	Discount factor	Net present value (000s)
1	800	0.893	714.4
2	800	0.797	637.6
3	800	0.712	569.6
4	800	0.636	508.8
5	800	0.567	453.6
6	1,200	0.507	608.4
			3,492.4

The purchase price is a maximum of £3.4 million.

CONCLUSION

Considerable difficulties face the hospitality industry in setting asset values. This is particularly true in an economic environment where asset values are more likely to go down than go up. Case histories indicate that the current methods are far from satisfactory and, in response to this, the British Association of Hotel Accountants has gone as far as to offer guidance as to the most satisfactory approach based on discounted cashflows. Academically, this approach is superior because it is based on forecasted cashflows and a discount rate which should be calculated using the cost of capital, anticipated risk and predicted inflation.

REFERENCES

Recommended Practice for the Valuation of Hotels (1993), British Association of Hotel Accountants, London.
McLaney, E. (1994) *Business Finance for Decision Makers*, London: Pitman Publishing.

14

The globalization of hospitality organizations

INTRODUCTION

A feature of the late 1980s and early 1990s was the rapid acceleration in overseas expansion demonstrated by hospitality firms on a worldwide basis. Early examples in the growth of multinationals, that is firms operating in more than one country, were initially confined to US-based companies which expanded their operations into Europe through acquisition and non-acquisition approaches such as franchising. However, global expansion strategies now appear to dominate the growth patterns for more and more companies from around the world. This has been clearly demonstrated by the continued growth of US firms in Europe, while of late more and more Asian and European companies have established hotel subsidiaries internationally and have even successfully penetrated the highly competitive US markets. Leading analysts project that the hospitality and tourism industries will continue to be a key sector for developing international expansion. The purpose of this chapter is to consider some of the issues facing the hospitality organizations that have chosen to pursue strategies of expansion overseas. These include:

- The nature of international involvement
- Forms of international development
- Accounting issues facing multinational enterprises.

NATURE OF INTERNATIONAL INVOLVEMENT

Generally, a business wishes to expand overseas in order to increase sales by penetrating new markets. For manufacturing companies, expansion may also mean gaining access to raw materials and other factors of production which may not be available in the home country or are available overseas for considerably less cost. This pursuit of resources may also extend to gaining access to up-to-date knowledge and new technology. The prime reason for the growth of hospitality firms overseas seems to be a response to the extent of the local competition, although additional incentives exist when the demand from overseas markets allow a larger unit profit margin to be made, while at the same time increasing the worldwide presence of the group. This is true for McDonald's, the world's largest restaurant chain, which has witnessed its American trade declining while international operations have continued to thrive and expand, with profitability in Europe being quoted as being higher than in comparable operations in the USA. In those locations of the world where operations are very much at the growth stage of the product life cycle, a premium selling price can ensure that profitability is maintained despite local resource servicing issues.

The United Nations Centre on Transnational Corporations (UNCTC) has produced a general study to investigate the trends in foreign investment that occurred in the 1980s in comparison to those of the 1970s. A significant increase in foreign direct investment was identified as having taken place in the mid-1980s and in the following period. The reasons for this surge in growth were identified in the study as being:

- The strong economic growth rates in developed and developing countries
- The improved economic performance of several developing countries
- The emergence of several newly industrializing economies
- The growth in cross-border mergers and acquisitions (particularly in the EC)
- The increasing importance of the service sector.

In general, the five major investor companies during the 1980s were identified as being France, Germany, Japan, the USA and the UK, with the host countries including Europe, the USA, Japan and a range of developing countries in South America, Asia and the Pacific Rim.

FORMS OF INTERNATIONAL INVOLVEMENT

The expansion of hospitality operations overseas requires a greater commitment than say for manufacturing businesses where the approach to international involvement is often characterized by the simple importing and exporting of goods and services. For hospitality firms a tangible presence is required in the importing country. This may take the form of a management contract where the exporting hospitality operation receives a fee in return for managing a facility owned by local investors. Alternatively, a concept or a production process may be licensed to an overseas location and the owner receives a royalty in return for the use of this intangible asset. This agreement may be formalized by a franchise contract where the franchisor allows the franchisee to use the name and expertise of the franchisor to sell a certain product. The agreement may extend to bulk purchasing and central administration arrangements. Finally, a firm may get involved in direct investment in an overseas operation which may take the form of an acquisition of existing operations, a joint investment with an overseas partner or the development of new 'greenfield' investment.

The trend in recent years has been to build and operate larger properties which require larger investments. As a result, ownership and management are often separated, and while owners continue to provide the investment, the management of the operation may be approached in a variety of ways. Hotel companies such as Four Seasons, Hyatt Corporation, Ladbroke, Marriott Hotels and Resorts and Saison rely primarily on management contracts for their expansion, whereas others, such as Accor and Holiday Corporation, rely on franchising. Alternatively, a combination of approaches may be appropriate, as demonstrated by The Sheraton Corporation which has a mixed portfolio of both management contracts and franchise-operated properties. Expansion through a non-investment approach offers a range of advantages to the operator including:

- economies of scale
- international image and presence
- the utilization of common marketing programmes
- common staff training contracts
- bulk purchasing contracts.

Direct investment in the form of complete ownership or equity participation tends to be limited to developed economies where the risk is perceived to be less than for the developing countries. Service-driven operations, such as those typified by the hospitality industry, face certain issues when pursuing a strategy of global development. These include decisions about the product itself, whether to offer a highly internationally standardized product or recognize local differentiation, as well as management and control issues. International operations may well require a differing organizational structure in order to co-ordinate operations globally with reliable networks and systems. One of the key issues in managing international operations is deciding what types of decision should be made at the corporate level and what responsibility should be retained at the local level.

ACCOUNTING ISSUES FACING MULTINATIONAL ENTERPRISES

A range of issues need to be considered when a firm decides to pursue a strategy of expansion through investment overseas. These include:

- Financing of overseas subsidiaries
- Foreign financial statement analysis
- National differences in accounting principles
- Management of foreign currency translation
- Management control of global operations
- Performance evaluation systems
- International taxation issues.

Each of these aspects will now be considered in more detail.

Financing overseas subsidiaries

The decision to finance a subsidiary involves considering the nature and size of the initial investment, as well as decisions regarding the policies for the reinvestment of retained profits and the local management of debt and working capital. The method of financing the subsidiary will be reliant on the size of the investment. A sizeable equity investment or long-term loan would indicate a long-term commitment on the behalf of the parent company, whereas funding from debt capital and short-term credit would indicate a short-term policy.

A multinational company has the same sources of finance available as the 'domestic' company as described in Chapter 9. However, it is also possible to make use of sources of finance derived from foreign sources. Eurocurrency loans are short- or medium-term loans raised in a foreign currency. The term 'eurocurrency markets' refers to the financial centres such as London where the funds are available. 'Eurobonds' are short-term or long-term loans raised from domestic and foreign investors and are similar in nature to debentures. The advantages of borrowing in a foreign currency to finance overseas operations in the same currency are that the assets and liabilities in the same currency can be matched, thereby avoiding exchange losses on conversion in the group's annual accounts, and the revenues in the foreign currency can be used to repay borrowings in the same currency, thus eliminating the problem of losses due to variable foreign exchange rates. There is a range of factors to consider when appraising overseas investments, which include:

- The method and ease for obtaining the return from the overseas operation. A combination of methods such as dividends, interest and management fees may be preferable in case restrictions are placed on dividend payments.
- The level of political interference in overseas operations in the form of employee legislation, local taxes, etc. may serve to reduce the profitability of the investment and should be anticipated in the forecasting process.

Taxation and accounting differences may also significantly affect the resulting profit, and these should also be considered to ensure that local accounting requirements are met and that these do not serve to undermine the measurement of operational performance.

Foreign financial statement analysis

The ability to analyse international statements is the key to successful investment overseas for investors wishing to purchase the whole or a share in existing companies. In order to undertake such an analysis potential investors need to have access to data but the extent and the availability of data varies from country to country. The timelags between the year end and the regulatory publication of the auditors' report vary considerably, as Table 14.1 illustrates, and it may be even longer before the information is translated for foreign audiences.

Information barriers that are commonly associated with foreign financial statement analysis include language and terminology, although many countries now offer English-language translations of all or a portion of the accounts as a norm. However, it is possible to use published accounting lexicons to translate titles and key headings. Differences in statement format can also prove to be awkward when attempting to interpret foreign statements but, although different layouts may be used for, say, the balance sheet, the double-entry book-keeping system is the same, ensuring that the underlying structure of statements is quite similar. The extent of disclosure varies

Table 14.1 Period of days between year end and the publication of reports

Number of days	Countries
31–60	Brazil
	Canada
	USA
61–90	Australia
	Denmark
	Finland
	Netherlands
	Norway
	Sweden
91–120	Belgium
	France
	West Germany
	India
	Malaysia
	South Africa
	Switzerland
	UK
121 and over	Austria
	Italy

considerably with companies in countries such as the USA and the UK being required to produce far greater detail than is required in many other countries. Differences in accounting principles exist from country to country despite attempts to harmonize accounting practice. Fortunately, there are many published information sources which provide insights into a country's accounting practices.

Experience and research has indicated that business is conducted differently from one country to another and these differences arise from economic, educational, sociocultural, legal and political factors. The environmental influences on accounting practice in particular, arise from a variety of factors. These include:

● The nature of enterprise ownership
● The enterprise business activities
● The sources of finance and nature of capital markets
● The taxation system
● The sophistication of the accounting bodies and professions
● The nature of the political systems and social climate
● The rate of inflation
● The legal system and the nature of accounting regulation.

National differences in accounting principles

Accounting principles can differ considerably from country to country and can seriously impact on the reported earnings and financial position of a company. For example, research has indicated that UK earnings, calculated in accordance with UK accounting principles, could be up to 25 per cent higher than earnings calculated under US accounting principles. While US accounting policies are significantly more conservative than the UK, they are still significantly less conservative than those in other areas in Europe and in Japan. The cultural norms within a country will also influence how the financial performance is actually evaluated, with the UK and USA focusing on stock market measures such as earnings per share and dividend yield whereas Europe and Japan focus on the reduction of taxation payments and meeting the needs of creditors and loan finance providers rather than maximizing returns to the shareholders. The principal differences in the increased flexibility of the UK accounting system in comparison with the more conservative US approach are summarized in Table 14.2.

Simmonds and Azieres (1989) have carried out a simulation exercise using the simplified accounts of a multinational company to establish the effect of the differences in accounting policy on stated earnings by making a comparative analysis of the impact of accounting measurement differences on a range of European countries (Table 14.3).

The overall results indicate that the highest profit and return on assets occurs in the case of the UK, whereas Spain comes out as the lowest.

The Japanese experience

Cultural differences in Japan ensure that, despite an increasing internationalization of accounting practice, the interpretation of performance as well as the accounting procedure in preparing the statements differs from other key areas in the world such as the UK, Europe and the USA. In Japan, for example, higher levels of gearing and short-term creditors are acceptable because of long-term and improved relationships with banks and suppliers. A long-term view of profitability is taken and emphasis is placed instead on sales growth and market share. Japanese accounts often demonstrate low interest coverage ratios, low current ratios, longer debt collection periods and examples of short-term debt to finance long-term investments.

Table 14.2 Differences in the UK and US accounting systems

	US – more conservative	UK – more conservative
Asset valuations	x	
Business combinations	x	
Consolidated financial statements	x	
Accounting for goodwill	x	
Foreign currency translation	x	
Inventory valuation	x	
Investment properties	x	
Capitalization of interest costs		x
Research and development expenditure	x	
Intangible assets including brands	x	
Taxation accounting	x	

Table 14.3 Comparative analysis of the impact of different accounting measurements

Millions of European currency units	Net profit	Net assets	Return (%)
Belgium	135	726	18.6
Germany	133	649	20.5
Spain	131	722	18.2
France	149	710	21.0
Italy	174	751	23.2
Netherlands	140	704	19.9
UK	192	712	27.0

Source: A. Simmonds and O. Azieres *Accounting for Europe: Success by 2000 AD?*, 1989, p. 42.

Management of foreign currency translation

A multinational company with overseas operations, each maintaining its own accounts in the local currency, will need to convert the accounts to the holding company's currency in order to allow for the group accounts to be consolidated at the end of each accounting year. The effect of translating the assets and liabilities into the holding company's local currency may give rise to a gain or a loss. The risk of heavy losses being incurred from this process can be minimized by matching foreign currency assets with foreign currency liabilities. The *Financial Times* provides information about the exchange rates for sterling against other currencies, the exchange rate being defined as the amount of one currency that must be given to acquire one unit of another currency. The rates quoted are the 'spread', that is the highest and lowest rates from the previous day and the closing value at the end of the previous days trading. The 'spot rate' is the rate quoted for current currency transactions up to two days later and represents the current exchange rate.

Translation of foreign currency statements

The translation of foreign statements involves two key issues: the exchange rate to be used for the actual conversion and the treatment of the subsequent gains and losses arising from the translation. In the process of translation, all foreign currency balance sheet and trading statements need to be restated in terms of the reporting currency by multiplying the foreign currency amount by an appropriate exchange rate factor. There are essentially two recognized techniques for setting the exchange rate, although variations on these methods do exist around the world. The first is the closing rate (or current rate) method where the amounts in the balance sheet and the profit and loss account are translated into the reporting currency of the investing company using the rate of exchange ruling at the balance sheet date. The advantages of this method are that the business does not need to refer back to historical rates and perhaps more significantly, the relationships between the values, such as return on net assets, remain the same as in the original accounts.

Alternatively, the temporal method dictates that each transaction should be translated into the company's local currency using the exchange rate in operation on the date that the transaction occurred, although if the rates do not fluctuate significantly an average rate may be used. Current assets and liabilities may be translated at the current rate while fixed assets can be translated at the rate at the time when it was purchased. The temporal method is more suited to the operation whose affairs are very closely linked to the investing company and whose trading environment is heavily dependent on that of the investing company. Details regarding these methods are contained in SSAP 20, 'Foreign Currency Translation'. The arising gains and losses accrued as a result of translation should be shown in the profit and loss account and in the reserves.

Management control of global operations

The challenge facing an expanding organization is how to control and manage that operation effectively as the parts become more and more widely dispersed. It may be appropriate to pursue a 'multidomestic' strategy where the individual parts of the organization operate relatively independently of each other. Alternatively, it may be more suitable to pursue a global strategy where there is a significantly greater degree of co-ordination. The process of control will depend on the extent of both formal and informal mechanisms present in the organization. Formal structural mechanisms include

- The nature of the groupings of the activities of the organization
- The extent of centralization or decentralization of activities
- The formalization of procedures and standards
- The extent of strategic planning and operational budgeting.

Informal and subtle methods include the extent of meetings and communications that are encouraged across the formal boundaries and the nature of the organizational culture. The nature of the management information system will obviously change as the organization expands, and the successful development of a good information system will ensure that strategic decisions are made based on high-quality information. The information needs of a multinational organization are similar to those of a domestic operation in that data need to be assembled and presented as information to a variety of users. The additional burden is that the multinational organization needs to analyse the financial position of each operation in terms of its geographical position as there may be different internal and external factors influencing the nature of trading. Generally speaking, however, the finance and accounting functions in a multinational organization tend to be more centralized than other functions, such as personnel or marketing, in order to achieve a means of comparability on a worldwide basis. This is often supported by a system of internal audit whereby procedures are monitored to ensure that company policies are being followed correctly and the assets of the organization are being safeguarded.

Budgeting

The strategic planning process provides the organization with a set of financial plans that reflect the key strategic moves to be made in the long-term future of the organization. Previous chapters explain that these then need to be translated into detailed operational plans for the immediate future in the form of the budget. The key advantages of the budgeting process are centred on the benefits to be derived from communicating the plans for the organization downwards to operational managers and by encouraging those managers to then plan for the effective use of resources. These benefits apply equally to the multinational organization. However, certain additional issues need to be considered. At a practical level it is necessary to establish in which currency the budget should be prepared and how the foreign currency element should be dealt with when translating the budget from one currency to another. This will have implications for subsequent monitoring performance. On a wider scale, the budgeting process is affected by cultural differences, national differences in budget perceptions and the attitude towards performance evaluation. Research based on US and Japanese managers indicates that there can be significant differences in the way the budgeting process is used. Finally, the budgeting process for a multinational organization will be significantly more affected by unstable economic environments which create difficulties in achieving effective forecasts. The crucial factors in making sales and profit forecasts are normally competition, size, market share, facilities and service levels. However, other factors, such as inflation and erratic exchange rates, will also need to be considered and this can mean that accurate sales forecasts are impossible to complete.

Performance evaluation systems

Many of the problems relating to performance evaluation apply to multinational operations as they do to domestic operations. With any system it is difficult to establish a single measure which is appropriate to all types of operation and yet there are further difficulties associated with assessing performance with a multiple set of criteria. Research has indicated that the most commonly used measures of financial performance in foreign subsidiaries are similar to those used in domestic subsidiaries, that is return on investment. This is most commonly used in the form of profit before interest and tax or profit after interest but before tax. However, due to the inherent problems in using this measure, as described in Chapter 8, supplementary measures are nearly always used and this is often in comparison to budget.

The most commonly used budgets are capital budgets, operating budgets, cashflows and balance sheets. Other important ratios include return on sales, return on assets, return on equity and return on investment. In addition to these, the measurement of cashflows has become increasingly important, focusing on long-term cashflows that are discounted in the same way as capital budgeting. The usage of these performance criteria varies from culture to culture. Shields *et al.* (1991) undertook an extensive survey of the performance evaluation practices used by a variety of general US and Japanese multinational organizations. The results indicate the performance criteria that are considered to be the most important when evaluating divisional managers (Table 14.4).

Finally, it is important to separate manager performance evaluation from that of the operation because a profitable unit can exist independently of good management and a good manager can work in a difficult and unprofitable environment.

International taxation issues

Systems for implementing taxation vary from country to country but it is commonly accepted that each country has the right to tax profits earned within its borders. This

Table 14.4   Most important criteria in evaluation of divisional managers

	Japan (%)	USA (%)
Sales	69	19
Sales growth	28	28
Market share	12	19
Asset turnover	7	13
Return on sales	30	26
ROI	7	75
Controllable profit	28	49
Residual income	20	13
Profit minus corporate costs	44	38
Manufacturing costs	28	13
Other	8	17

implies that foreign source profit should be taxed where it is earned and not mixed with domestic profit, and that earnings from foreign subsidiaries are not taxed in the parent company until remitted as a dividend to shareholders.

The complexity regarding taxation means that a multinational organization must consider a range of factors based on the type and location of the operation. The nature of the operation, whether it is based on export, licensing, branches or subsidiaries, will affect the assessment for taxation and the location of the operation may mean that benefits can be derived from local tax incentives, tax rates and tax treaties. As an example tax laws in some countries encourage investment through capital allowances and 'tax holidays' whereby tax payments are cancelled for a given period. Consequently, international tax-planning forms an essential part of the management of multinational operations.

CONCLUSION

Global expansion represents the way forward for the majority of large hospitality operators and such development brings with it the specific requirement to design accounting systems which meet the needs of an effective control system. The service sector differs from the manufacturing sector where overseas expansion may mean the export of products to an overseas market. In order to pursue a similar strategy the hospitality organization must make a considerable investment in what is possibly an unknown market. This chapter attempts to highlight where difficulties commonly arise, particularly in the areas of target-setting and performance measurement.

FURTHER READING

Go, F., Sung Soo, P., Uysal, M. and Mihalik, B. (1990) Decision criteria for transnational hotel expansion, *Tourism Management.* December. Butterworth Heinemann.

Mathe, H. and Perras, C. (1994) Successful global strategies for service companies, *Long Range Planning*, 27(1): 36–49.

Radebaugh, L. and Gray, S. (1993) *International Accounting and Multinational Enterprises*, 3rd edn, New York: Wiley.

REFERENCES

Shields, M., Chow, C., Kato, Y. and Nakagawa, Y. (1991) Management accounting practices in the US and Japan: comparative survey findings and research implications, *Journal of International Financial Management and Accounting*, 3(1): 68.

Simmonds, A. and Azieres, O. (1989) Accounting for Europe: success by 2000 AD?, In Touche Ross, *Europe*, 1989, p. 42.

15

The way forward

INTRODUCTION

It is widely reported that during the eighties and nineties the international hospitality industry witnessed a period of tremendous change which in turn had implications for all of the functional activities within the business including the finance function. The growth in multinational operations with diversified interests increased the need for accurate and timely information for performance measurement and control. Research undertaken by Burgess (1995) focusing on the changing role of the hotel financial controller, confirms this. The research shows that the modern controller is increasingly faced with the challenge of harnessing the tremendous potential deriving from the continuing application of information technology to the systems for measurement and control, and ensure that optimum benefit is being provided.

The purpose of this book has been to highlight criticisms and weaknesses in the traditional approaches to management accounting in the hospitality industry. It is widely recognized that in many industry sectors management accounting has failed to keep up with advances in other aspects of business practice and strategy.

There are a number of specific issues currently affecting the hospitality industry which will have a far-reaching effect on the future nature of hospitality finance systems. These include developments arising from the:

- integration of the finance and management function
- increased use of information technology
- Uniform System for Accounts for Hotels
- changing patterns of ownership within the industry
- brands versus products.

CHANGING ROLES

Traditionally the role of accounting has been heavily biased towards the comparison of costs with revenues while focusing on the internal operations of the business. Accounts are by definition historical and inward looking and accounting practice is informed by prudence. In many hospitality operations the accountant is still traditionally viewed as the 'bean counter' focusing on historical results. Obviously there is still some relevance in this role. However, in most modern organizations it has become essential to produce accounting information with a strategic perspective. In practice this means not only reviewing internal operations but also the external environment and the role of the competition. The results of an extensive study by Collier and Gregory (1994) focusing on the practice of strategic management in hotel groups concludes that strategic management accounting is being increasingly used for planning, evaluating market conditions and for competitor analysis. The research identifies two main strategic management accounting areas. First, the provision of information which assists in the development of strategic plans and, second, the monitoring of the market, competitors' price structures and competitors' costs. The development of strategic plans includes the preparation of long range plans for up to five years including profit & loss account, balance sheet and cashflow using spreadsheet technology for modelling. The monitoring of the market is made easier due to the open nature of the industry and the availability of some revenue and cost data and as a result the research indicates that regular monitoring of the competition is often included in the remit of the accounting function. Consequently, increasingly the hotel accountant is viewed as a member of the management team bringing specific expertise to the decision-making process.

The role of the manager has also dramatically changed in response to the increasingly competitive environment where decisions need to be made frequently and quickly. Failure to make the right business decision can lead to loss of profitability or even business demise. As a result, in order to make quick and correct decisions the available supporting information needs to be timely and of the necessary quality.

ROLE OF INFORMATION TECHNOLOGY

The tremendous advances in technology provide the potential for developing information systems which can meet the needs of the current business environment. Information can be processed more quickly with a wider range of applications providing vast quantities of detail. In order to harness the benefits to be derived from this, it is essential that the information system is linked to the critical success factors or the key drivers of the business. This includes not just looking backwards at historical performance but also forecasting in to the future to anticipate competitor strategy.

Management accounting in the hospitality industry is governed by the operational features of an industry which is characterized by fixed supply of certain resources such as rooms and covers, perishability and seasonality of the product and high fixed costs in particular, labour and maintenance. Research published by the management consultants Pannell Kerr Forster (PKF, 1995) seeks to determine the key critical success factors for the hotel industry by identifying those factors which have significant effects on hotel profitability. In Chapter 1 these were identified as:

- company philosophy and culture towards staffing and payroll costs
- operating cost controls
- competitor analysis
- long-term planning.

While assuming that the fundamental criteria for location, market and quality have already been met.

Payroll is the largest single controllable cost in most hotel operations and savings in this area will have a dramatic effect on profitability. Effective cost control throughout the business requires applying well-known techniques such as process engineering consistently and thoroughly in every aspect of the operation. Competitor analysis provides the opportunity to monitor not just 'how did we do' but also to track the performance of the competition in terms of revenues and market share. Historically, medium and long-term planning is often an activity in the hospitality industry which fails to have enough time and resources directed towards it and as a result a traditional incremental approach is often adopted. Finally, PKF believe that company philosophy and culture are by far the most important factors for creating an environment in which all employees feel that they are actively involved in the control of costs. We can conclude at this stage that there is still tremendous scope for improving financial practice in these areas.

Information technology is also set to influence the way in which the hospitality operation of the future is likely to function. The most exciting development for the very near future must be the marketing opportunities offered by the Internet. Its facilities include the Travelweb which provides a marketing tool which has no printing cost, no distribution cost and allows for the flexibility of frequent updates and changes. A significant portion of the world's population already have access to the Internet and this figure is rapidly increasing, providing access to markets in a way which has never been witnessed before.

The process of price-setting is being revolutionized by the growing use of computerized Yield Management systems currently known as Revenue Maximization Systems. This import from the airline industry is tailored to carry out maximization of both revenue and occupancy. Computerized systems replace intuition and allow for more complex computations of room rate and the effects on demand. To date UK hotel groups have been slow to implement this tool falling behind their US counterparts. However, as hotel groups grow accustomed to this management system it is likely that published tariffs will disappear and there will be a whole range of specific prices which will vary daily and will carry with them not only the class of room but also check-in and check-out restrictions as well as restrictions on access to service and facilities.

Electronic data interchange (EDI) is the process of electronically exchanging business data between organizations. Although again slow to be implemented in the UK hospitality industry EDI has been used in other industries for several years. EDI is most commonly applied to the purchasing cycle, leading to, for example high potential savings in labour costs and to a lower cost of sales. The implementation of EDI systems is still fairly expensive and as yet not a viable option for hotel groups without large buying power. However, as the nature of ownership changes with more UK hotels being owned, managed or represented by larger groups or consortia, the introduction of EDI seems near.

UNIFORM SYSTEM OF ACCOUNTS FOR HOTELS

The UK version of the Uniform Accounting System was developed by the Hotel and Catering Economic Development Council in 1969. However, it is the US system, the

Uniform System for Accounts in Hotels, which is more widely used. The aim of the system is to create a standardized approach to performance measurement and control. This system was first published by the Hotel Association of New York City in 1926. The Uniform System may be defined as a manual of instructions for preparing standard financial statements and schedules for the various operating and productive units which make up a hotel. The purpose of this manual is to provide a simple formula for the classification of accounts which could then be adopted by any hotel regardless of size or type. In practice most of the major hospitality companies do use the system or an abridged version. New developments to this system are likely to include recommendations for the improved use of computer technology and specific guidelines for the accounting treatment of issues such as maintenance and depreciation expenses.

CHANGING PATTERNS OF OWNERSHIP

Traditionally ownership in the hospitality industry has been very dispersed resulting in an industry which is dominated by independent owners and operators. The first international hotel companies were formed in the late 1940s with the growth of American companies such as Hilton International, Inter-Continental and Sheraton. Large multinational companies have continued to grow and to expand throughout the world posing a constant threat to the independent operator who cannot compete in the key functional areas of marketing, information technology, purchasing power and financing. Organizational growth is achieved through the traditional path of acquisitions but also through other means such as franchising, management contracts and joint-ventures. In the US it is estimated that 70 per cent of hotels are associated with a major brand name while in Europe it is only 30 per cent. But this figure is likely to increase rapidly, particularly as recent trends indicate that hotel ownership is risky. Recession in the early nineties was accompanied by a property market which was weaker than in the recession of the early 1970s. Asset values of hotels fell often to values below the loans secured upon them resulting in many properties falling into receivership. This in turn resulted in the growth of the hotel management contract where the property is owned by the bank and is managed for a fee and possibly a share of the profits. Several of the major hotel operators now include managed hotels in their portfolio of properties. The nature of these arrangements mean that the emphasis in the accounting information is focused on revenue and operating profit maximization as these are normally the two figures on which the management fee figure is calculated. Traditional figures such as return on capital employed are obviously of less importance to the company managing the operation.

The introduction of FRS 5, 'Reporting the substance of transactions' has meant that this form of arrangement can give rise to a variety of accounting issues including whether the hotel is in effect the asset of the management company, with the owner effectively providing a source of off-balance sheet finance.

The deciding factor is the nature of the arrangement and whether the agreement (substantially) passes all risk and rewards associated with ownership of the hotel to the management company.

Franchising is another approach to expansion enabling the franchiser to grow rapidly at a relatively low risk. This is done by charging the franchisees for the use of a brand name and by providing resources such as marketing and purchasing in return for a fee (normally between 1 per cent and 10 per cent of the franchisee's room revenue).The accounting of the franchise tends to vary in practice as there are no clear UK guidelines.

BRANDS VERSUS PRODUCTS

The multinational hospitality industry is increasingly driven by the use of brand names. Such a business strategy emphasises the brand over the product and as a result management accounting systems need to be adapted to this approach. It has already been stated that management accounting systems have tended to be historical and inward looking. The use of the brand approach demands that the systems should be externally focused on the market environment in which these products are sold. Financial information needs to be tailored to this strategic emphasis on brands rather than on the other more tangible assets employed in the business. To be really useful, financial information should be organized so that the basic sales and cost data are recorded by brand wherever possible.

The traditional product life-cycle was reviewed in detail earlier in the text and each product is assumed to go through a cycle of growth, maturity and decline. Does this apply to a brand?

Brand names can be transferred from one product to another and as a result a brand may be transferred to a product in the early growth stage of the cycle.

CONCLUSIONS

Hospitality education is obliged to provide a graduate entering the industry with a competence enabling him or her to understand the developments currently affecting the long-term future of the industry and to harness these changes to drive the industry forward. This is certainly true in the teaching of the finance function where the education provided should be relevant and specific to the individual needs of the industry providing the graduate general manager of the future with the skills required to manage the business effectively. This is particularly relevant in the light of research which has indicated (Burgess, 1995) that approximately a third of graduates specialize in finance as their careers progress. Effective education needs to be supported by research and yet historically research in the field of hospitality finance has been lacking. It is therefore exciting to note the emergence of new projects focusing on specific issues relating to the world of hospitality accounting and information systems. There is clear evidence that effective performance measurement systems are of paramount importance for the future, with a range of specific areas which still merit further investigation including property valuations, non-depreciation of assets and the financial implications of strategic alliances such as management contracts and franchising. These aspects will hopefully be researched in the not too distant future.

REFERENCES

Burgess, C. (1996) Five years on: survey of hotel financial controllers, *Financial Management Beyond 2000 Conference*, Malta.

Collier, P. and Gregory, A. (1994) Strategic management accounting: a UK hotel sector case study, *International Journal of Contemporary Hospitality Management*: 18–23, 71.

Croston, F. (PKF 1995) Hotel profitability: critical success factors. *Accounting and Finance for the International Hospitality Industry*. P. Harris (ed.). Oxford: Butterworth Heinemann.

APPENDIX 1
PRESENT VALUE TABLE

Present value of £1 in n years at discount rate r.

Discount rate (r)

Periods (n)	1%	2%	3%	4%	5%	6%	7%	8%	9%	10%	
1	0.990	0.980	0.971	0.962	0.952	0.943	0.935	0.926	0.917	0.909	1
2	0.980	0.961	0.943	0.925	0.907	0.890	0.873	0.857	0.842	0.826	2
3	0.971	0.942	0.915	0.889	0.864	0.840	0.816	0.794	0.772	0.751	3
4	0.961	0.924	0.888	0.855	0.823	0.792	0.763	0.735	0.708	0.683	4
5	0.951	0.906	0.863	0.822	0.784	0.747	0.713	0.681	0.650	0.621	5
6	0.942	0.888	0.837	0.790	0.746	0.705	0.666	0.630	0.596	0.564	6
7	0.933	0.871	0.813	0.760	0.711	0.665	0.623	0.583	0.547	0.513	7
8	0.923	0.853	0.789	0.731	0.677	0.627	0.582	0.540	0.502	0.467	8
9	0.914	0.837	0.766	0.703	0.645	0.592	0.544	0.500	0.460	0.424	9
10	0.905	0.820	0.744	0.676	0.614	0.558	0.508	0.463	0.422	0.386	10
11	0.896	0.804	0.722	0.650	0.585	0.527	0.475	0.429	0.388	0.350	11
12	0.887	0.788	0.701	0.625	0.557	0.497	0.444	0.397	0.356	0.319	12
13	0.879	0.773	0.681	0.601	0.530	0.469	0.415	0.368	0.326	0.290	13
14	0.870	0.758	0.661	0.577	0.505	0.442	0.388	0.340	0.299	0.263	14
15	0.861	0.743	0.642	0.555	0.481	0.417	0.362	0.315	0.275	0.239	15

	11%	12%	13%	14%	15%	16%	17%	18%	19%	20%	
1	0.901	0.893	0.885	0.877	0.870	0.862	0.855	0.847	0.840	0.833	1
2	0.812	0.797	0.783	0.769	0.756	0.743	0.731	0.718	0.706	0.694	2
3	0.731	0.712	0.693	0.675	0.658	0.641	0.624	0.609	0.593	0.579	3
4	0.659	0.636	0.613	0.592	0.572	0.552	0.534	0.516	0.499	0.482	4
5	0.593	0.567	0.543	0.519	0.497	0.476	0.456	0.437	0.419	0.402	5
6	0.535	0.507	0.480	0.456	0.432	0.410	0.390	0.370	0.352	0.335	6
7	0.482	0.452	0.425	0.400	0.376	0.354	0.333	0.314	0.296	0.279	7
8	0.434	0.404	0.376	0.351	0.327	0.305	0.285	0.266	0.249	0.233	8
9	0.391	0.361	0.333	0.308	0.284	0.263	0.243	0.225	0.209	0.194	9
10	0.352	0.322	0.295	0.270	0.247	0.227	0.208	0.191	0.176	0.162	10
11	0.317	0.287	0.261	0.237	0.215	0.195	0.178	0.162	0.148	0.135	11
12	0.286	0.257	0.231	0.208	0.187	0.168	0.152	0.137	0.124	0.112	12
13	0.258	0.229	0.204	0.182	0.163	0.145	0.130	0.116	0.104	0.093	13
14	0.232	0.205	0.181	0.160	0.141	0.125	0.111	0.099	0.088	0.078	14
15	0.209	0.183	0.160	0.140	0.123	0.108	0.095	0.084	0.074	0.065	15

APPENDIX 2
ANNUITY TABLE

Present value of £1 receivable at the end of each year for *n* years at discount rate r.

Discount rate (r)

Years (n)	1%	2%	3%	4%	5%	6%	7%	8%	9%	10%	
1	0.990	0.980	0.971	0.962	0.952	0.943	0.935	0.926	0.917	0.909	1
2	1.970	1.942	1.913	1.886	1.859	1.833	1.808	1.783	1.759	1.736	2
3	2.941	2.884	2.829	2.775	2.723	2.673	2.624	2.577	2.531	2.487	3
4	3.902	3.808	3.717	3.630	3.546	3.465	3.387	3.312	3.240	3.170	4
5	4.853	4.713	4.580	4.452	4.329	4.212	4.100	3.993	3.890	3.791	5
6	5.795	5.601	5.417	5.242	5.076	4.917	4.767	4.623	4.486	4.355	6
7	6.728	6.472	6.230	6.002	5.786	5.582	5.389	5.206	5.033	4.868	7
8	7.652	7.325	7.020	6.733	6.463	6.210	5.971	5.747	5.535	5.335	8
9	8.566	8.162	7.786	7.435	7.108	6.802	6.515	6.247	5.995	5.759	9
10	9.471	8.983	8.530	8.111	7.722	7.360	7.024	6.710	6.418	6.145	10
11	10.37	9.787	9.253	8.760	8.306	7.887	7.499	7.139	6.805	6.495	11
12	11.26	10.58	9.954	9.385	8.863	8.384	7.943	7.536	7.161	6.814	12
13	12.13	11.35	10.63	9.986	9.394	8.853	8.358	7.904	7.487	7.103	13
14	13.00	12.11	11.30	10.56	9.899	9.295	8.745	8.244	7.786	7.367	14
15	13.87	12.85	11.94	11.12	10.38	9.712	9.108	8.559	8.061	7.606	15

Years (n)	11%	12%	13%	14%	15%	16%	17%	18%	19%	20%	
1	0.901	0.893	0.885	0.887	0.870	0.862	0.855	0.847	0.840	0.833	1
2	1.713	1.690	1.668	1.647	1.626	1.605	1.585	1.566	1.547	1.528	2
3	2.444	2.402	2.361	2.322	2.283	2.246	2.210	2.174	2.140	2.106	3
4	3.102	3.037	2.974	2.914	2.855	2.798	2.743	2.690	2.639	2.589	4
5	3.696	3.605	3.517	3.433	3.352	3.274	3.199	3.127	3.058	2.991	5
6	4.231	4.111	3.998	3.889	3.784	3.685	3.589	3.498	3.410	3.326	6
7	4.712	4.564	4.423	4.288	4.160	4.039	3.922	3.812	3.706	3.605	7
8	5.146	4.968	4.799	4.639	4.487	4.344	4.207	4.078	3.954	3.837	8
9	5.537	5.328	5.132	4.946	4.772	4.607	4.451	4.303	4.163	4.031	9
10	5.889	5.650	5.426	5.216	5.019	4.833	4.659	4.494	4.339	4.192	10
11	6.207	5.938	5.687	5.453	5.234	5.029	4.836	4.656	4.486	4.327	11
12	6.492	6.194	5.918	5.660	5.421	5.197	4.988	4.793	4.611	4.439	12
13	6.750	6.424	6.122	5.842	5.583	5.342	5.118	4.910	4.715	4.533	13
14	6.982	6.628	6.302	6.002	5.724	5.468	5.229	5.008	4.802	4.611	14
15	7.191	6.811	6.462	6.142	5.847	5.575	5.324	5.092	4.876	4.675	15

Index

PERTH COLLEGE
LIBRARY